A Sense of the Whole

Gary Snyder's library on his Kitkitdizze homestead in the Sierra Nevada foothills

A SENSE *of the* WHOLE

Reading Gary Snyder's
Mountains and Rivers Without End

Edited by **MARK GONNERMAN**

72352
A SENSE OF
THE WHOLE
READING GARY
SNYDER'S
MOUNTAINS AND RIVERS
WITHOUT END
Mark Gonnerman, ed.
Counterpoint. 28.00 **5.98**
Pulitzer Prize and National
Book Award winner Gary
Snyder compared his epic
poem *Mountains and Rivers
Without End* to an excur-
sion on Class V rapids—"if you're going to make it to
take-out, you're going to need a guide"—and this collec-
tion of commentaries and background readings is that
guide. The result of a yearlong research workshop that
invited writers, teachers, and scholars to speak on vari-
ous aspects of Snyder's great work, this book captures
the excitement of these gatherings, inviting us to enter
the poem through essays and talks by poets like Wendell
Berry, Nanao Sakaki, and Robert Hass. Here too are
interviews with Snyder and some of his own notes on
the poem.   (352/2015)

COUNTERPOINT
BERKELEY

LIBRARY OF CONGRESS CATALOGUING-IN-PUBLICATION DATA

A sense of the whole : reading Gary Snyder's Mountains and rivers without end / edited by Mark Gonnerman.

   pages   cm

ISBN 978-1-61902-456-4 (hardback)

1. Snyder, Gary, 1930– Mountains and rivers without end. I. Gonnerman, Mark, editor.

PS3569.N88M6237 2015

811'.54—dc 3

2014036209

Interior design by VJB/Scribe

COUNTERPOINT

2560 Ninth Street, Suite 318, Berkeley, CA 94710

www.counterpointpress.com

Distributed by Publishers Group West

Printed in the United States of America

10 9 8 7 6 5 4 3 2 1

For Christopher

and

Whole Earth Inhabitants — Past, Present, and Future

CONTENTS

Introduction
Cultivating a Sense of the Whole: Gary Snyder's *Mountains
and Rivers Without End*

Hearing Native Voices

Making Pacific Rim Connections

Appendices

KEY TO ABBREVIATIONS FOR IN-TEXT CITATIONS
FROM GARY SNYDER'S WRITINGS

APIS   *A Place in Space* (1995)

EHH   *Earth House Hold* (1969)

GSJ   Gary Snyder Journals (1947–1995)

M&R   *Mountains and Rivers Without End* (1996)

M&T   *Myths & Texts* (1960)

PW   *The Practice of the Wild* (1990)

RCMP   *Riprap and Cold Mountain Poems* (1959)

SSPO   *Six Sections from* Mountains and Rivers Without End, *Plus One* (1970)

TI   *Turtle Island* (1974)

TRW   *The Real Work* (1980)

~

Art takes nothing from the world; it is a gift and an exchange. It leaves the world nourished. The arts, learning grandmotherly wisdom, and practicing a heart of compassion, will confound markets, rattle empires, and open us up to the actually existing human and nonhuman world.

—- Gary Snyder, "Ecology, Literature, and the New World Disorder" (2003)

INTRODUCTION

~

To know the spirit of a place is to realize that you are a part of a part and that the whole is made up of parts, each of which is whole. You start with the part you are whole in.

— Gary Snyder, *The Practice of the Wild* (1990)

Cultivating a Sense of the Whole

Gary Snyder's *Mountains and Rivers Without End*

MARK GONNERMAN

> Cultivating a sense of the whole functions to place each individual
> part in greater and more coherent perspective, and thus to trans-
> form one's experience of what is present and at hand.
>
> — Dale Wright, *Philosophical Meditations on Zen Buddhism*
> (1998)

In the academic year 1997–98, I formed a yearlong research workshop at the Stanford Humanities Center to explore Gary Snyder's long poem, *Mountains and Rivers Without End.*[1] Together we read, reread, and reflected on this work while enjoying its expansive, compelling vision. Our literary adventures concluded with a daylong symposium, "Ethics & Aesthetics at the Turn of the Fiftieth Millennium."[2] This companion volume to the poem contains critical essays, discussions, interviews, and other fruits of what came to be known among students, faculty, and diverse community members as the Mountains & Rivers Workshop.[3]

I have gathered these materials here with two main objectives in mind. First, this book serves as an introduction to a complex, engaging, and, I presume, enduring work of art. Like many of Snyder's readers, I long anticipated the completion of *Mountains and Rivers,* a work first imagined when the poet joined painter Saburo Hasegawa for tea and conversation at his San Francisco apartment on Shakyamuni Buddha's birthday, 8 April 1956 (M&R 155).[4] The poem was published in the spring of 1996, and, in December of that year, I heard Snyder read from it at Kepler's, an independent bookstore just down the road from Stanford.[5] Snyder began this reading with reference to whitewater rapids ratings, saying most of his work is like a Class III run where you can probably get through on your own, but that *Mountains and Rivers* is more like Class V: If you're going to make it safely to take-out you will need a guide. As a collection of commentaries and other relevant readings, this book is one such guide.[6]

Second, this book aims to inspire others to organize learning communities around poetic and allied arts. Our Mountains & Rivers Workshop began in an effort to turn the contemporary research multi-versity into a university once again, if only for a moment. One of the most pressing problems in American education and society at large is a breakdown of community owing to specialization, a trend that has infected even undergraduate life. As biologist David Orr of Oberlin College writes, "We have fragmented the world into bits and pieces called disciplines and subdisciplines, hermetically sealed from other such disciplines. As a result, after 12 or 16 or 20 years of education, most students graduate without any broad, integrated sense of the unity of things. The consequences for their personhood and for the planet are large."[7] If one does not cultivate a sense of the ways various parts of the whole are connected to each other in spite of bureaucratic, disciplinary demarcations, one will not likely understand one's own place within, connections to, and responsibility toward that whole. Such understanding is an exercise of imagination, and promotion of this exercise is an intention in Snyder's work.

I. EATING PAINTED RICE CAKES

> The imagination is not only holy, it is precise
> it is not only fierce, it is practical
> men die everyday for the lack of it,
> it is vast & elegant.
>   — Diane di Prima, "Rant" (1985)

Mountains and Rivers Without End evades simple classificatory schemes. Is it an "American epic poem" (M&R dust jacket)? A multimedia poem cycle? A contribution to American mythology?[8] A collection of poems depicting major ecosystem types?[9] Is it a spiritual autobiography — a pilgrim's progress — aimed at effecting some kind of religious conversion? Is this "a sort of sūtra — an extended poetic, philosophic, and mythic narrative of the female Buddha Tārā" (M&R 158)? Or is this book a score for the kind of live performance the poet has envisioned and experimented with since 1957?[10] Is the work a thought experiment — a creative, critical Buddhist commentary — on the place of art in human religious life? Though I will concentrate on the last of these possibilities here, the attentive reader will discover that Snyder's creative effort entails all of the above and more.

Mountains and Rivers is richly "intermedial," and readers will find — or lose — themselves amidst various types, levels, and layers of representation. Reproductions of two visual artworks are part and parcel of this complex work. First, the book's cover is graced by *Evening Glow at Yosemite Falls*, a woodcut by Chiura Obata completed in 1930, the same year Snyder was born in San Francisco.[11] Chosen by Snyder for the cover after the writing was done, Obata's print both honors a teacher and introduces the reader to four key images: mountains, waters, pines, and skies. Second, this book's endpapers present a Sung period landscape painting, *Ch'i Shan Wu Chin*, described in the opening eponymous, ekphrastic poem, "Endless Streams and Mountains."[12] *Ekphrasis* — a term from Greek rhetoric meaning "to tell in full" — is "the verbal representation of a visual representation," and the genre has received much critical attention in recent years.[13] An ekphrastic poem takes its inspiration from one of the visual arts, usually painting. In his note on "Endless Streams and Mountains," Snyder mentions that "East Asian landscape paintings invite commentary. In a way the painting is not fully realized until several centuries of poems have been added" (M&R 159). *Ch'i Shan Wu Chin* has been enjoyed this way for centuries, and *Mountains and Rivers* is yet another commentary that again brings this painting — its words and images — to life.

That *Mountains and Rivers* is in large part commentary on the place of art in the cultivation of humane sensibilities is indicated by the work's second epigraph from the "Painting of a Rice Cake" fascicle of Zen Master Dōgen's *Shōbōgenzō* (*The Treasury of the Eye of the True Dharma*). Here Snyder presents an elliptical summation of a translation of statements from this 1243 lecture on the saying of "an ancient Buddha": "A painted rice cake does not satisfy hunger." Typically, this was taken to mean that the study of texts — sūtras, commentaries, and other secondhand offerings — has little or no relation to the work of becoming truly human. In characteristic fashion, Dōgen reverses the common meaning and says so-called secondhand offerings are themselves a necessary kind of firsthand experience and are to be appreciated as such: "Since this is so, there is no remedy for satisfying hunger other than a painted rice cake. Without painted hunger you never become a true person."[14] To think otherwise is to remain in the grip of the dualistic thinking Dōgen's work aims to correct. Dōgen thus makes real the products of imagination, and so does Snyder:

> At a moment of climax,
> > The Mountain Spirit whispers back:
> "All art and song
> is sacred to the real.
> As such."   (M&R 146)

The "real as such" exists in multiple modalities, and Snyder puts it this way: "I don't invent things out of my head unless it is an actual experience — like seeing a bear in a dream, this is a true mode of seeing a bear" (TRW 20). At the same time, not everything is delivered in a dream: there is a fundamental world of matter sensed "as such."[15] Here we begin to discern the ends of a continuum that meet in the work of art. On the one hand, there are worlds of matter; on the other hand, there are worlds of mind, dream, and imagination. Emphasis on one end of the spectrum at the expense of the other presents an imbalance. As a way of integrating matter and mind, art — "interweaving physical life and inward realms" (M&R 154) — affirms a Middle Way.

Mountains and Rivers, then, is literally and figuratively framed by a meditative approach to a painting that in its own production was an artist's "meditative exercise" (M&R 154). Snyder reports that Saburo Hasegawa thought "the landscape paintings were for Zen as instructively deeply Buddhist as the tankas and mandalas are for Tibetan Buddhism" (M&R 154). I take this to mean they were instructive because they realized and engaged the realm of imagination. If, as Diane di Prima shouts in "Rant," "THE ONLY WAR THAT MATTERS IS THE WAR AGAINST THE IMAGINATION / ALL OTHER WARS ARE SUBSUMED IN IT," we cannot avoid knowing that the work of art is intensely political: "the war of the worlds hangs right here, right now, in the balance / it is a war for this world, to keep it / a vale of soul-making."[16]

II. ARTICULATING AN AVATAṂSAKA VISION

> So, Zen being founded on *Avataṃsaka,* and the net-network of things; and Tantra being the application of the "interaction with no obstacles" vision on a personal-human level — the "other" becomes the lover, through whom the various links in the net can be perceived. As Zen goes to anything direct — rocks or bushes or people — the Zen Master's presence is to help one keep attention undivided, to always look one step farther along, to simplify the mind: like a blade which sharpens to nothing.
>
> — Gary Snyder, "Japan First Time Around" (1956)

The teachings of the Hua-yen (Flower Garland) school of Buddhism are gathered in the *Avataṃsaka-sūtra.* The version of this sūtra in eighty scrolls, first translated into Chinese between 695 and 699, breaks into thirty-nine sections that form, in Luis Gómez's words, "an unwieldy compilation of disparate texts held together by a thin narrative thread."[17] The final section of this long discourse, extant in Sanskrit as the *Gaṇḍavyūha-sūtra* (Entering the Realm of Enlightenment Sūtra), tells the story of Kumara Sudhana, the son of a merchant who stands at the beginning of the Buddhist Path and seeks to understand that Path in relation to his day-to-day concerns. His helpers as he proceeds — all regarded as advanced bodhisattvas — include laymen, laywomen, Brahmins, and female night-spirits. Sudhana begins his quest at the behest of Manjushri, the bodhisattva of wisdom, and ends it in the realm of Samantabhadra, a bodhisattva of boundless goodwill, thus showing that the pilgrim has come to realize both wisdom and compassion in his everyday life.[18]

The *Avataṃsaka-sūtra* is said to represent Shakyamuni Buddha's state of mind in the long meditation that followed immediately upon his great awakening at the base of the bodhi tree at Bodh Gaya before he was persuaded by Indra to share his hard-won insights with others. The sūtra is thus regarded as a direct expression of Truth without concession to the limitations of ordinary human understanding.[19] This text offers, then, an imagined expression of the flowing, interpenetrating, unified world as comprehended by a fully enlightened being.

In his explication of the Buddha's *Avataṃsaka* vision, Tu Shun

(557–640), the first ancestor of the Hua-yen School, introduces the bejeweled "net-network" of Indra. Here the universe is imagined as a vast net with a jewel at each node: "This jewel can show the reflections of all the jewels at once — and just as this is so of this jewel, so it is of every other jewel: the reflection is multiplied and remultiplied over and over endlessly."[20] In this realm, things arise out of ongoing, dynamic interactions where everything is distinct without being separate. This vision, which is now often employed to link Buddhism and ecological thinking, has numerous theoretical and practical implications, all of which discourage dogmatic attachment to any one point of view. From this perspective, each viewpoint reveals just one facet of a whole available in its totality only to a Buddha.

As Zen Buddhism developed in China alongside the Hua-yen School, teachers borrowed from *Avataṃsaka* imagery to articulate their insights. As D. T. Suzuki put it, "When it [Zen] had to have recourse to intellection, it was a good friend of the Hua-yen philosophy."[21] That philosophy enabled comprehension of a worldview where direct experience "of rocks or bushes or people" could intimate awareness of the Whole — one node in the "net-network" was said to contain universes. In "Old Woodrat's Stinky House" (M&R 119–21), for example, the whole universe appears in a grain of scat.

In *Mountains and Rivers*, the *Avataṃsaka-sūtra* is quoted but once, though Hua-yen images and ideas are woven throughout. At the start of "With This Flesh" we read:

> *"Why should we cherish all sentient beings?*
> *Because sentient beings*
>   *are the roots of the tree-of-awakening.*
> *The Bodhisattvas and the Buddhas are the flowers and fruits.*
> *Compassion is the water for the roots."*   (M&R 75)[22]

These words — appearing just before Señor Francisco de Ulloa arrives to conquer "new Spain ... cutting trees with his sword,/ uprooting grass,/ removing rocks from one place to another" (M&R 75) — are spoken by Samantabhadra to Sudhana at the end of his aforementioned spiritual quest. Samantabhadra's statement reminds the reader of the first epigraph in *Mountains and Rivers*, words from Tibet's Saint Milarepa (1025–1135), another re-mover of rocks (see M&R 107–08, 128): "The notion of Emptiness engenders Compassion" (M&R n.p., 149).[23]

The vision of both the *Avataṃsaka-sūtra* and *Mountains and Rivers* is predicated on this very "notion of Emptiness" (*śūnyatā*), the keynote of all Buddhist understanding.[24] In public readings, Snyder has recited the *Heart Sūtra* in Sino-Japanese before reading and chanting through "The Circumambulation of Mt. Tamalpais" (M&R 85–89, 161). The *Heart Sūtra* — "the one-page condensation of the whole philosophy of transcendent wisdom" (M&R 160–61 [see Appendix 1]) — reiterates the teaching that no thing has its own being but exists in an interdependent, interconnected constellation that causes phenomena to appear as they appear from moment to moment. Recurrent and various images of "water" in *Mountains and Rivers* offer one good example of this, for water's form depends on the surrounding elements and conditions: Mist, clouds, rain, snow, glaciers, and flowing H_2O all express the "nature" of "water."

From the standpoint of Emptiness, everything flows: "Streams and mountains never stay the same" (M&R *passim*). Wood shifts shape: "& make of sand a tree / of tree a board, of board (ideas!) / somebody's rocking chair" (M&R 36), just as in "The Flowing" where "a cedar log . . . hopes / to . . . be / a great canoe" (M&R 70). As Snyder writes in *The Practice of the Wild*:

> Even a "place" has a kind of fluidity: it passes through space and
> time — "ceremonial time" in John Hanson Mitchell's phrase. A
> place will have been conifers, then beech and elm. It will have
> been half riverbed, it will have been scratched and plowed by ice.
> And then it will be cultivated, paved, sprayed, dammed, graded,
> built up. But each is only for a while, and that will be just another
> set of lines on the palimpsest.   (PW 27)

Much of *Mountains and Rivers* is a hymn to Sarasvati, "The Flowing One," Indian goddess of music, poetry, and intellectual pursuits.[25]

Other images of Emptiness appear in references to dancing and coupling, especially in "Cross-Legg'd" (M&R 128–29), an echo of Snyder's recognition of Tantra in the epigraph for this section as "the application of the 'interaction with no obstacles' vision on a personal-human level." With "the double mirrors" in "Bubbs Creek Haircut" (M&R 33), the equivalence of items in "The Market" (M&R 47–51), and an homage to the sun in "The Boat of a Million Years" (M&R 39), *Mountains and Rivers* articulates a Hua-yen Buddhist's vision. As Wilfred Cantwell Smith has observed, "In order to understand Buddhists, one must look not at something called Buddhism, but at the universe, so far as possible through Buddhist eyes."[26] *Mountains and Rivers* invites us to do just that!

It is not surprising that Hua-yen images and ideas run throughout Snyder's work, especially when one remembers that his formal Buddhist education took place in a Rinzai Zen seminary in Kyoto and that the founder of that order, Rinzai (Lin-chi [d. 867]), was indebted to this school.[27] Consider also that the *Avataṃsaka-sūtra* is a meditation on the Buddha Vairocana (Great Sun Buddha), who represents a cosmic source of light and life.[28] Vairocana and the universe are one:

> Clearly know that all *dharmas*
> Are without any self-essence at all;
> To understand the nature of *dharmas* in this way
> Is to see Vairocana.[29]

Consider, further, that Tārā is Vairocana's consort, and that Snyder is a devotee of Fudō-myōō, a tough manifestation of the Vairocana Buddha incarnate in North America as Smokey the Bear.[30] Unlike Fudō, Vairocana holds no sword, for, as D. T. Suzuki notes, "he is the sword itself, sitting alone with all the worlds within himself."[31] As a manifestation of Mind, Vairocana is that "blade which sharpens to nothing."[32]

III. FRAMING PARTS AND WHOLES

> I will not repeat myself now, except to remind you that my theory involves the entire abandonment of the notion that simple location is the primary way in which things are involved in space-time. In a certain sense, everything is everywhere at all times. For every location involves an aspect of itself in every other location. Thus every spatio-temporal standpoint mirrors the world.
>
> — Alfred North Whitehead, *Science and the Modern World* (1925)

In *Beat Zen, Square Zen, and Zen,* Alan Watts explores the art of life as he plays with the idea of "framing": "Every framework sets up a restricted field of relationships. . . . A frame outlines a universe, a microcosm, and if the contents of the frame are to rank as art they must have the same quality of relationship to the whole and to each other as events in the great universe, the macrocosm of nature."[33] To make "art," then, is to recognize and represent a certain "quality of relationship" between and within described parts and wholes. Watts considers the maker of photographs:

> Now a skilled photographer can point his camera at almost any scene or object and create a marvelous composition by the way in which he frames and lights it. An unskilled photographer attempting the same thing creates only messes, for he does not know how to place the frame, the border of the picture, where it will be in relation to the contents. How eloquently this demonstrates that as soon as we introduce a frame anything does *not* go.[34]

Art is an expression of that judgment or skill — intuition born of discipline, craft — which freezes the flow of ongoing activity and exposes an order that lingers in chaos.

Each of the thirty-nine poems in *Mountains and Rivers* presents a snapshot or set of snapshots, slices of the real from a particular point of view. Each poem arrests a pattern suggested by a title that enjoins a theme. Consider, for example, "Macaques in the Sky":

> Then — *wha!* — she leaps out in the air
> the baby dangling from her belly,
> they float there,
> — she fetches up along another limb —
> and settles in.   (M&R 114)[35]

The poem — which poet Michael McClure thinks "perfect" (see his contribution to this volume) — goes on to make the analogy that we, like the dangling baby, "hang on beneath" the "Milky Way, / mother of the heavens,/ crossing realm to realm / full of stars" (M&R 115).

"Macaques in the Sky" is one of many reminders that *Mountains and Rivers*— all poetry and language itself, in fact — is an exercise of an analogical imagination that proceeds by way of metaphors. In *Philosophy in a New Key*, a book Snyder read carefully at Reed College while completing his 1951 bachelor's thesis on a Haida myth, Susanne Langer, building on Philip Wegener's observation that common-sense language is a "repository of 'faded metaphors,'" states: "If ritual is the cradle of language, metaphor is the law of its life. It is the force that makes it essentially *relational*, intellectual, forever showing up new, abstractable forms in reality, forever laying down a deposit of old, abstracted concepts in an increasing treasure of general words."[36] Langer's thesis coincides nicely with the notion of Emptiness, for a word's meaning will depend on its place in a changing, interdependent lexical network. Analogously, the meaning of any one part of *Mountains and Rivers* (including the visual art, epigraphs, end matter, and margins) will depend on its place in the interdependent network of the bounded whole.

In the "net-network" of this poem cycle, no one "snapshot" is necessarily more or less important than any other, though everything may be said to revolve around "The Circumambulation of Mt. Tamalpais" (M&R 85–89), with Mt. Tam an analog of Mt. Meru at the center of Buddhist cosmology. As various parts of the book are encountered and compared over time (as one reads and rereads), their meaning and significance change. To juxtapose "Old Bones" (M&R 10) and "Old Woodrat's Stinky House" (M&R 119–21), for example, enables insights that do not surface when "Old Bones" is set beside, say, "Under the Hills Near the Morava River" (M&R 96). The interplay of framed parts (and parts of parts) in view of the whole is endlessly illuminating.

IV. EXPLORING THIS VOLUME

> Thus the movement of understanding is constantly from the whole to the part and back to the whole. Our task is to expand the unity of the understood meaning centrifugally. The harmony of all the details with the whole is the criterion of correct understanding. The failure to achieve this harmony means that understanding has failed.
>
> — H. G. Gadamer, *Truth and Method* (1960)

The transcribed talks, discussions, and essays that follow present a variety of ways to enter into *Mountains and Rivers Without End*. They are intended to inspire each reader's own engagement, critical reflection, commentary on, and conversation with and about Snyder's work. Some authors represented here were present throughout the course of our Mountains & Rivers Workshop meetings, some appeared once at the Stanford Humanities Center and made a presentation, and some traveled to campus from afar for the May 1998 "Ethics & Aesthetics" symposium and related events. Two of the contributors to this volume, Wendell Berry and Julia Martin, did not join us on campus.

Our book proper begins in the next chapter with a transcript of the 8 October 1997 public conversation with Gary Snyder, writer Carole Koda, and Jack Shoemaker, Snyder's editor, publisher, and longtime friend. Carole Koda (1947–2006), Snyder's wife (see "Cross-Legg'd" [M&R 128–29]), spoke briefly about the process of assembling her family history, published in a limited edition as *Homegrown: Thirteen Brothers and Sisters, a Century in America*.[37] Koda's remarks were not recorded, but I hope her model presentation of one Japanese-American family story might become more readily available and widely read. With Snyder and Shoemaker's discussion of the production of *Mountains and Rivers*, along with their responses to questions from those who assembled at East House that evening, our workshop was underway!

As a pioneer in the field of ethnopoetics, Snyder knows poetry lives through the spoken word.[38] With this in mind, the poet performed a major portion of *Mountains and Rivers* before a full house in Kresge Auditorium on the Stanford campus the following night. In his introduction to this 9 October reading he remarked: "The one complaint one hears from students most about poetry is, 'I don't understand it.' Well, who ever said you have to understand it? Only the high school teachers say that. [Audience laughter.] What a mistake in teaching poetry. You don't have to understand it, you just have to listen to it, let it sink in, come back to it, come back to it again — forget it if it doesn't do anything for you — but taste the flavors." This reading (the program notes for which are available as Appendix 2 of this volume) was, then, for many, a first taste of what would become an ongoing painted-rice-cake feast.

On Saturday, 11 October, everyone was invited to join a ritual circumambulation of Mt. Tamalpais, a practice encouraged by the poem and its refrain: "Walking on walking,/ under foot earth turns./ Streams and mountains never stay the same" (M&R *passim*). While following the route around the mountain and reciting chants found in the poem at the very center of *Mountains and Rivers* (M&R 85–89), workshoppers began to get acquainted. While walking, members set a foundation for exploring interconnections between bodily senses, poetics, and place.[39]

Then, over the course of three academic quarters, we convened for fifteen workshop presentations and discussions with scholars from a variety of fields, including Japanese Nō drama, Chinese poetics, Buddhist studies, art history, hydrology, and American literature. We also met regularly to read and discuss parts of the poem line by line. This simple exercise yielded startling insights as our colleagues illuminated obscure passages with reference to their own knowledge and experience, often surprising even themselves! In May 1998, the Department of Art hosted a fine-art photography exhibition in the Nathan Cummings Art Gallery by David Robertson, *Mattering Without End: For Gary Snyder and the Community on the San Juan Ridg*e. Nanao Sakaki arrived from Japan for a Friday poetry reading with Gary at the Stanford Bookstore, and the "Ethics & Aesthetics" symposium convened on Saturday, 16 May. The workshop concluded with another circumTam (as it is often called) with about eighty people on the trail, including Gary Snyder. We enjoyed steady participation throughout the year with members of the local community and students and faculty from Stanford, UC Berkeley, UC Santa Cruz, and UC Davis in attendance. In addition, we offered a five-week course on *Mountains and Rivers* through Stanford Continuing Studies.

In the first section of what follows, "Hearing Native Voices," three essays touch upon the theme of the vocation of the poet as someone who works with and represents the range of voices that resonate upon the land. As a residential faculty fellow at the Stanford Humanities Center for the duration of our Mountains & Rivers Workshop, Tim Dean (chapter 2) composed an essay showing "how the poem's creation of an impersonal voice enables the work of art to engage ethical questions concerning nonhuman nature and our relation with it." With reference to "shamanism as a model for understanding impersonalist poetics," Professor Dean makes a distinction between *speaking on behalf of* and *speaking through* and investigates implications of his observation that "more than one third of the poems in *Mountains and Rivers Without End* close with somebody else's [not the poet's] voice."

Jim Dodge (chapter 3) draws on Carl Jung's scheme of modes of perception to appreciate how Snyder's poem is a "long meditation on the manifold possibilities of communion with the natural world and offers a 'model of mind' for such imaginative explorations." Dodge also touches upon Snyder's ability to get past his self and evoke a shared identity with the landscape and other beings through the agency of poetic imagination. He also celebrates the ways Snyder's encyclopedic mind informs "a poem of complex philosophical and mythic intelligence." As for his "Dharma shoot-out at the OK Dairy" reference, each reader will have to determine for him- or herself what Dodge is really getting at here.

David Abram's contribution (chapter 4) approaches the work as a "long cycle of journey poems . . . primarily a bundle of . . . songlines, of dreaming tracks" such as those of the central Australian aboriginal peoples who are in touch with the Dreamtime where "*the land itself dreams, continually.*" In this record of his spoken presentation, Abram claims that "for all of the rich scholarship and the density of literary allusions in *Mountains and Rivers*, one of the things this poem cycle is doing is renewing oral culture." Abram recommends that we learn from the page in order to leave it behind and inhabit more responsibly an unmediated, more-than-human world.

In the next section, "Making Pacific Rim Connections," we learn from Katsunori Yamazato (chapter 5), the doyen of Snyder studies in Japan, and Nanao Sakaki (chapter 6), whose poetry has, as Snyder observes, "the flavor of oral literature with its riddles, sayings, fables, and formulaic devices; little ways of unfolding narrative that go back millennia."[40] In a beautifully crafted paper, Professor Yamazato presents his research on ways Snyder's study of Japanese Nō theater informs both *Mountains and Rivers* and "his search on a planetary scale for myths and wisdom traditions that will bring about a new humanistic vision." Nanao's contribution frames his reading of three poignant and playful poems with parts of his life story relevant to the theme of "*Mountains and Rivers* and Japan." This chapter concludes with comments by Snyder on how his experience in Japan and with Nanao has inspired and enriched the quest for a new humanity that, as Yamazato points out, is a keynote of his life and art.

In the third section, "Exploring Poetic Roots," we are treated to presentations by three eminent American scholar-poets: Wendell Berry, Robert Hass, and Michael McClure. Here we publish Mr. Berry's "interim thoughts" on *Mountains and Rivers*, written soon after he received it from the poet late in 1996.[41] Berry (chapter 7) is especially interested in ways the poem puts *everything* in motion: "Travel, in fact and metaphor, is its formal principle." He compares Snyder's perspective with John Milton's, whose world was created "at the beginning, once and for all": "In Mr. Snyder's version, we are living in a world that is still and always being made; human history is not being made 'on' or 'in' the world, but is involved by intricate patterns of influence and causation in the continuous making of the world. This is an extremely important difference — morally, practically, and prosodically."

On 2 February 1998, Professor Robert Hass (chapter 8) drove from Berkeley to Stanford amidst a raging storm. When the former U.S. Poet Laureate's talk began at 4:15, lights in the Humanities Center Annex were strangely dim. With blinds wide open, we proceeded until it became too dark to read. Following Hass's capsule history of the American long poem, we walked in the downpour to Mariposa House where, in a well-lit setting, he explicated passages from *Mountains and Rivers,* illuminating aspects of Snyder's creative process and demonstrating how to read and "proceed by clues." Hass shared that as a graduate student at Stanford he arranged his own "counter-university" course on Snyder's *Myths & Texts*, an occasion for Snyder's first visit to Stanford in 1965. The storm continued during dinner with Hass that evening as Palo Alto streets turned into roily rivers. The license plate on the car ahead of me as I slowly headed home read: KP WLKNG. What a fitting way to end a most memorable day that produced an engaging and essential contribution to this volume!

When Michael McClure (chapter 9) came to visit on 9 February 1998, he related his reading and rereading of Snyder's work to the many associations it conjures from the poet's own life as a littérateur and student of Dharma.

Here McClure suggests we approach *Mountains and Rivers* as "a medicine bundle in the guise of autobiography, with the whole thing being a wisdom book like the *Tao Te Ching*."

In our final section, "Engaging Buddhist Perspectives," Carl Bielefeldt (chapter 10) presents a nuanced consideration of Buddhist influences ("whatever that means," he says) on Snyder's art. As a historian of religions, he reminds us that "we need to think not just about Buddhism in the abstract but about the history of Gary's encounter with the religion, the various kinds of Buddhist environments in which he's actually lived and how they figure in the work" and makes the interesting observation that "Gary's poem grew up with the growth of American Buddhism." Here Bielefeldt pays particular attention to the place of Dōgen's *Mountains and Waters Sūtra* in the evolution of Snyder's thought. What he does not mention — though Gary comments on this in the opening conversation at East House (see chapter 1) — is that it was *his* 1972 MA thesis translation of the *Mountains and Waters Sūtra* that caused Gary to slow down his work on *Mountains and Rivers* by going more deliberately and deeply into Dōgen. Professor Bielefeldt's chapter provides an excellent starting point for many readers.

Stephanie Kaza (chapter 11) begins her exposition with a passage from the *Mountains and Waters Sūtra* and approaches this and Snyder's text as a Zen student seeking, in Dōgen's words, "actualization of the ancient Buddha way." As a practitioner and professor of environmental studies, she turns to Snyder's work as a source of instruction on how one might live at a time when "we not only fear loss of irreplaceable species, but the collapse of whole systems through global warming, ocean death, soil and groundwater poisoning." Her basic premise is that *Mountains and Rivers Without End* helps us understand where we are in the Big Time and Place Story and that such knowledge helps create the conditions for more ethical behavior. Professor Kaza then offers her American Buddhist reading of this American Buddhist poem.

Our book concludes with a never-before-published May 1998 interview with Gary Snyder and three appendices. The interview, conducted by Eric Todd Smith, who was at the time a graduate student in the literature of place in Snyder's department at UC Davis, reflects on the Stanford symposium and further probes issues and ideas out of *Mountains and Rivers Without End*. The appendices provide additional material for further study of the poem and Snyder's work in general.

The reader will also find throughout the book brief excerpts from invited workshop presenters (Anthony Hunt, Julia Martin, Richard Vinograd) and short, relevant excerpts from Snyder and others pertaining to themes in *Mountains and Rivers*. Of course these brief synopses of the considered contributions to this volume do not capture the richness that will emerge as readers work through this book and relate what they find to the poem and larger wholes.

V. READING (AND REREADING) WELL

> All processes in nature are inter-related; and thus there could be no complete sentence (according to this definition) save one which it would take all time to pronounce.
>
> — Ernest Fenollosa, "The Chinese Written Character as a Medium for Poetry" (c. 1902)

If *Mountains and Rivers* has an overriding purpose apart from the aesthetic pleasures it provides, it is to engender a conversion in the heart-mind of the reader (see M&R 161). The desired shift in this case is from identification with outmoded nation-state systems to participation in local community life, from centralized hierarchy to decentralized collaboration, from the stresses of competition to the satisfactions of mutual regard and cooperation, from modern monocultural monotheism to promiscuous postmodern poly-theism, from consumerism to conservation, from fragmentation to a sense of the whole.[42] This shift may begin in the very activity of reading. *How* one reads affects *what* one learns and, for many, reading has become just another consumer activity. The Mountains & Rivers Workshop was organized in large part as an effort to curtail (if only for a moment) consumerist habits of reading that are now widely taught and reinforced in ways that eclipse the importance if not the existence of other reading modes.

It is an oversimplification, perhaps, but there are two basic approaches to reading: reading to take in information and reading as meditation, an approach that expands awareness and deepens insight.[43] Consumerist reading is a less reflective, more linear activity of moving straight through a text without slowing down, a one-shot deal that may serve necessary and useful purposes. This kind of reading is nothing new. Jean-Jacques Rousseau, for one, exposed this approach in 1761 when he observed that the typical reader of his time "reads much; but . . . reads only new books, or rather hurries through them, for his purpose is not to read them but only to say he has read them; [whereas] the Genevan reader reads only good books; he reads them; and he digests them; he doesn't judge them, but knows them."[44] While there is certainly a need to hunt and gather information, mere information should not be confused with *knowledge*, for knowledge is information verified and set within a context of larger wholes. Knowledge is cultivated through the effort of rereading, rethinking, and — to use a favorite Snyder image — going forward by looping back.

The more meditative approach — reading for insight and edification — is an age-old practice among literate religious people, including Zen Buddhists.[45] In traditions that invest authority in books, this practice becomes one of returning again and again to familiar texts, often rereading in relation to a liturgical calendar. Over time, it may become unclear whether the reader is reading the text or the text the reader, as both are transformed in the light of ongoing life experience. If one rereads a familiar, classic text (one that has endured the test of time) in the state of what John Ruskin calls "awed attention" it will likely reveal secrets yet undetected over and over again.[46] Such texts prove inexhaustible; they can bear whatever critical weight we put upon them. I offer this volume with a belief rooted in knowledge from my own experience that *Mountains and Rivers Without End* is one such text.

When writer Kurt Vonnegut visited Stanford some years ago, he spoke of the threat of aliteracy, defined as "a disinclination to read fiction on the part of people who can read quite well." He went on to report that he had recently taken up a meditation practice and then realized he had already been meditating for years: "We in the Occident were already meditators, only we did it with books."[47] Vonnegut's observation is meant to encourage contemplative, intensive, insightful reading and rereading, what Benedictine monks call *ruminatio*: reading as a slow process of chewing and digestion typical of cattle and other ruminants.[48]

In "Reading," the third chapter of *Walden*, Thoreau writes: "To read well, that is, to read true books in a true spirit, is a noble exercise, and one that will task the reader more than any exercise which the customs of the day esteem. It requires a training such as the athletes underwent, the steady intention almost of the whole life to this object. Books must be read as deliberately and reservedly as they were written."[49] Consider that *Mountains and Rivers* was crafted over a span of forty years. How deliberate must we be?

If reading well demands a kind of mental athleticism, I recommend approaching it as a team sport where both individual effort and collaboration make possible a good outcome for all. Our workshop was envisioned as such a collaborative exercise where people from various directions would meet to play on the common field of Snyder's original book. While the lectures and papers that follow represent key aspects of how and what we learned, some of our finest moments came as we sat around a table reading and discussing sections of the poem line by line. In this simple process, we discovered over and over again that everyone is student and teacher and that all participants are capable of bringing knowledge and experience to the text in ways that are instructive to others.

VI. MOVING FORWARD WITH TĀRĀ IN MIND

> Metaphor -- indeed, Tārā --
>   To ferry across (*pherein*)
>   "she who saves"
>   — Gary Snyder (6 October 1987 GSJ)

> Mind is fluid, nature is porous, and both biologically
> and culturally we are always fully part of the whole.
>   — Gary Snyder, "A Village Council of All Beings" (1992)

Before bringing this introduction to a close, I want briefly to examine Snyder's cryptic comment that *Mountains and Rivers* is "a sort of sūtra — an extended poetic, philosophic, and mythic narrative of the female Buddha Tārā" (M&R 158). Sūtra means "thread" in Sanskrit, so the chanting and contemplation of sūtras is a way of weaving Buddhist teachings into everyday life. Sūtras are typically venerated as sermons of the Buddha, but critical scholarship and common sense indicate that the almost countless sūtras convey the Dharma as heard in particular places and times by various students. This is not at all unusual in the history of religions, for a great, ongoing challenge in religious life is knowing how to interpret a tradition's teachings in relation to the circumstances of their production and immediate reception. In fact, ambiguities and debates over interpretation are the engine that keeps texts, teachings, and traditions in flight (see "The Dance," M&R 133–36).

As "a sort of sūtra," *Mountains and Rivers* interprets Buddhist teachings on behalf of Mother Earth who — in spite of human failings — is "Green enough to go on living / Old enough to give you dreams" (M&R 148). Snyder's intention, it seems, is to help us hear the voice of this old Buddha, knowing, as in Su Tung-p'o's metaphor, "The stream with its sounds is a long broad tongue / The looming mountain is a wide awake body" (M&R 138). Or as Dōgen puts it in the first sentence of his *Mountains and Waters Sūtra*: "These mountains and waters of the present are the actualization of the word of the old Buddhas" (Bielefeldt translation). One is reminded of Ki no Tsurayuki's preface to the *Kokinshū* (c. 905) where he connects the genesis of poetry with the fact that all living beings respond to the natural world in the form of song: "When we hear the warbling of the mountain thrush in the blossoms or the voice of the frog in the water, we know every living thing has its song."[50] Or, as Makoto Ueda translates this same line, "On hearing a warbler chirp in plum blossoms or a kajika frog sing on the water, what living thing is not moved to sing out a poem?"[51] It is time we humans join the other critters and sing out on behalf of the Wild. As Nanao bellowed during our symposium dinner, "Why not sing a song?"

But why a song of Tārā? The rereader will find that *Mountains and Rivers* is populated by goddesses at every turn. We meet rivers and rains ("Into the pools of the channelized river / the Goddess in tall rain dress / tosses a handful of meal" [M&R 63]), rabbits, mice, cows, and many birds. We greet Parvati, Anahita, Sarasvatī, Europa, Artemisia, Amaterasu, Yamamba, and the Mountain Spirit. We find Mā, Maya, Prajñāpāramitā, the Bear Mother, Izanami, and the Milky Way. And throughout we encounter Tārā, hearing slightly different invocations of her name: "Joy of Starlight" (M&R 80), "lady of the stars" (M&R 112), "the embodiment of compassion" (M&R 155), and "'She Who Brings Across,' . . . a female Buddha of both Compassion and Wisdom" (M&R 162). As Tibetan mythology has it, while there are twenty-one Tārā forms (both peaceful and wrathful), the so-called White and Green Tārās are most common. She is said to have been born from a tear wept by Avalokiteśvara, the Bodhisattva of Compassion, "Perceiver of the Cries of the World."[52] She has vowed to serve humankind in the body of a woman *until this world is emptied out* (M&R 108–09) — until, that is, everyone has made it safely to take-out and is at home on the Other Shore.

On page 112 of *Mountains and Rivers*, there is a small line drawing of Green Tārā, recognizable as such because her right leg moves off her meditation cushion as if about to spring into action with her clear and attentive blade-mind. To remember Tārā is to remember the welfare of all beings and *work actively in the world* on their behalf.[53] Sincere recitation of her vow ("may I . . . serve the needs of beings / with my body") is the true offering (*puja*) for Tārā extolled in the long poem of that same name (M&R 106–112). This "Offering for Tārā," a devotional high point of *Mountains and Rivers* — a celebration of Himalayan rock, water, community, art, and song — was born out of Snyder's September 1992 journey to speak at the Ecology Center of the Upper Indus Watershed, western Tibetan plateau, town of Leh, nation of Ladakh, province of Jammu and Kashmir, state of India.

Snyder's talk at the Leh conference, "A Village Council of All Beings: Community, Place, and the Awakening of Compassion," serves as an excellent prose preface to *Mountains and Rivers,* for it also aims at promoting a sense of the whole: "Although ecosystems can be described hierarchically in terms of energy flow, from the standpoint of the whole all of its members are equal" (APIS 76).[54] This insight from ecological science "suggests a leap into a larger sense of self and family . . . that goes beyond intrahuman obligations and includes nonhuman nature" (APIS 77). How might one make this magnificent leap? Where or how does one imbibe that "spiritual education that helps children appreciate the full interconnectedness of life and encourages a biologically informed ethic of nonharming?" (APIS 80).[55] Our workshop suggests that one way toward such awareness is through deep hanging out with fellow travelers and challenging works of art.

Snyder is quick to point out that "the Mind of Compassion is a universally known human experience and is not created by 'Buddhism' or any other particular tradition" (APIS 78). Awareness of interdependence is — or should be — an unsentimental common sense that has been obscured by "the last two hundred years of scientific and social materialism [which] have declared our universe to be without soul and without value except as given value by human activities" (APIS 77). Snyder proposes we remedy this disastrous misunderstanding by paying attention to what is immediately at hand and becoming involved in the local, place-specific politics of our own households, neighborhoods, and bioregions. In other words, we might read, ruminate, rise off our cushions and, with Tārā in mind, conjoin wisdom and compassion by walking, meeting our neighbors, cleaning up creeks, and following the poet's example of singing out with and for the Wild.

NOTES

1. Gary Snyder, *Mountains and Rivers Without End* (Washington, DC: Counterpoint Press, 1996). Hereafter, this will be cited M&R in the text.

2. See Gary Snyder, "Entering the Fiftieth Millennium" in *The Gary Snyder Reader* (Washington, DC: Counterpoint Press, 1999), 390–94.

3. For a list of Mountains & Rivers Workshop sponsors and contributors, see my Note of Appreciation at the end of this volume.

4. Snyder's plan for *Mountains and Rivers* first became public via Jack Kerouac's *The Dharma Bums* (New York: Penguin Books, 1958), 200. In this roman à clef, Japhy Ryder is Kerouac's (Ray Smith's) impression of Gary Snyder when they saw a lot of each other and Allen Ginsberg (Alvah Goldbook) in San Francisco and environs in the spring of 1956.

5. "Finally finished 'Mountains and Rivers' texts at 8:30 pm on this (25:I) day" (25 January 1996 GSJ).

6. See also a number of contributions in Patrick Murphy, "Gary Snyder: An International Perspective," *Studies in the Humanities* [Special Issue] 26/1–2 (1999): 1–136; Eric Todd Smith, *Reading Gary Snyder's* Mountains and Rivers Without End (Boise, ID: Boise State University, 2000); and Anthony Hunt, *Genesis Structure and Meaning in Gary Snyder's* Mountains and Rivers Without End (Reno: University of Nevada Press, 2004).

7. David W. Orr, *Earth in Mind: On Education, Environment, and the Human Prospect* (Washington, DC: Island Press, 1994), 11. Compare Kenneth Boulding, writing in

1956: "The universe of discourse is crumbling into a multiverse, and in one's more depressed moments one looks forward to a time when the progress of science will grind to a standstill in a morass of mutual incomprehensibility. Out of our intellectual pride, we may be building a new Tower of Babel" (*The Image* [Ann Arbor: University of Michigan Press, 1961 (1956)], 139).

8. On the flyleaf of his copy of James E. Miller, Jr., *The American Quest for a Supreme Fiction: Whitman's Legacy in the Personal Epic* (Chicago: University of Chicago Press, 1979), Snyder has written (in pencil, no date): "M&R: a contribution to American mythology."

9. In his end-of-1990–91 Academic Year Review for the University of California at Davis where he is a distinguished professor of English, Snyder writes: "I have now entered the last phase on a major book of poems on which I first began work in 1959. It is called *Mountains and Rivers Without End*. A set of the sections completed up to 1965 was published under the title *Six Sections from Mountains and Rivers Without End*. Sections written since then have been published, some quite recently. Several sections are finished but not yet published. A number are still in progress. It is a series of poems evoking and exploring several major wild ecosystem types of the planet, particularly in North American and eastern Asia, toward a rhetoric of ecological and mythological relationships. Last year I was working on Manhattan and Los Angeles. Right now I am working with the north Pacific rim (from Alaska to Japan), the Basin and Range province, and the Colorado Plateau."

10. "I mean, on my return, to spend time studying Noh music & recitation with an angle of perfecting a poetry-reading technique for my stuff with chorus and percussive accompaniment, part of a big project & idea I have about masks, dance, drums, flutes, & oral rendering of literature" (Snyder to Lew Welch from USNS *Sappa Creek*, Bay of Bengal, 14 September 1957, in Lew Welch, *I Remain: The Letters of Lew Welch & The Correspondence of His Friends, Volume I: 1949–1960* [Bolinas, CA: Grey Fox Press, 1980], 114). On 11 August 2000, Snyder performed the entirety of *Mountains and Rivers* in a six-hour-long musical collaboration with Ludi Hinrichs, Daniel Flanigan, and Sean Kerigan, with dancing by Azriel Getz, at the North Columbia Schoolhouse Cultural Center on the San Juan Ridge, Nevada City, California. A version of this at the Sogetsu Hall in Tokyo on 5 July 2002 is available on CD as *Gary Snyder:* Mountains and Rivers Without End *in a Musical Collaboration* (Yamakei Publishers, 2003).

11. Chiura Obata, *Evening Glow at Yosemite Falls*, 1930, from the *World Landscape Series: America*, color woodcut, 15¾ × 11 in., printed by Tadeo Takamizawa, Takamizawa Print Works, Tokyo, Fine Arts Museums of San Francisco, Achenbach Foundation for Graphic Arts, 1963.30.3.3126.23. On Obata see Janice T. Dreisbach and Susan Landauer, ed., *Obata's Yosemite: The Art and Life of Chiura Obata from his Trip to the High Sierra of 1937* (Yosemite National Park, California: Yosemite

Association, 1993). Also see Kimi Kodani Hill, Timothy Anglin Burgard and Ruth Asawa, ed., *Topaz Moon: Chiura Obata's Art of Internment* (Berkeley: Heyday Books, 2000). Snyder first mentions Obata in the 1 October 1953 GSJ: "Obata sensei is a rare & wonderful being: observance of nature — drawing pines — he starts with the cone & ends with the beauty of the dead tree. 'PAINT FROM A CLEAR MEMORY' . . . sez Obata." Obata taught Snyder how to "grind the ink, wet the brush, unroll the / broad white space" (M&R 9) while the poet was a student of Asian languages at the University of California, Berkeley in 1953–56 (M&R 153). Obata's granddaughter, Kimi Kodani Hill, spoke to the Mountains & Rivers Workshop on "The Life and Work of Chiura Obata" on 12 January 1998.

12. See Anthony Hunt, "Singing the Dyads: The Chinese Landscape Scroll and Gary Snyder's *Mountains and Rivers Without End*," *Journal of Modern Literature* XXIII/1 (1999): 7–34. Tony Hunt, Professor of English (now retired) at the University of Puerto Rico, Mayagüez, presented our first workshop lecture — a grand overview of *Mountains and Rivers* — the afternoon before Snyder's 9 October 1997 reading at Kresge Auditorium. Tony was also one of the presenters at our concluding symposium in May 1998. In the summer leading up to the workshop, Tony shared with me his then unpublished book-length commentary on the poem (see note 6 above). I owe much to Tony's contagious enthusiasm, insight, and generous participation in this project.

13. This definition is from James Heffernan, *Museum of Words: The Poetics of Ekphrasis from Homer to Ashbery* (Chicago: University of Chicago Press, 1993), 3, italics removed. In addition to "Endless Streams and Mountains" (M&R 5–9), ekphrastic sections of *Mountains and Rivers* appear in "The Arroyo," Part III of "With This Flesh" (M&R 77–78), and Part III of "An Offering for Tārā" (M&R 111).

14. Snyder follows the translation of Dōgen's "Painting of a Rice-cake" by Dan Welch and Kazuaki Tanahashi in *Moon in a Dewdrop: Writings of Zen Master Dōgen*, ed. Kazuaki Tanahashi (San Francisco: North Point Press, 1985), 134–39.

15. See Gary Snyder, "Is Nature Real?" (1996) in *The Gary Snyder Reader: Prose, Poetry and Translations, 1952–1998* (Washington, DC: Counterpoint Press, 1999), 387–89.

16. Diane di Prima, "from Rant," in Jeremy Rothenberg and Pierre Joris, ed., *Poems for the Millennium*, vol. II: From Postwar to Millennium (Berkeley: University of California Press, 1995), 449–50.

17. Luis Gómez, "*The Avataṃsaka-Sūtra*," in *Buddhist Spirituality I: Indian, Southeast Asian, Tibetan, and Early Chinese*, ed. Takeuchi Yoshinori (New York: Crossroad, 1993), 160. At first glance, the same might be said of *Mountains and Rivers*, which is also in thirty-nine sections.

18. See Thomas Cleary, trans., *Entry into the Realm of Reality, the Text: The Gandhavyuha, the final book of the Avataṃsaka Sutra* (Boston: Shambhala, 1989); *Entry*

into the Realm of Reality, the Guide: A Commentary on the Gandavyuha by Li Tong-xuan (Boston: Shambhala, 1989); *The Flower Ornament Scripture: A Translation of the Avataṃsaka Sutra*, 3 vols. (Boston: Shambhala, 1983–86).

19. On this point see Peter Gregory, "What Happened to the 'Perfect Teaching'? Another Look at Hua-yen Buddhist Hermeneutics," in *Buddhist Hermeneutics*, ed. Donald S. Lopez, Jr. (Honolulu: University of Hawaii Press, 1988), 207–30.

20. Tu Shun, "Cessation and Contemplation in the Five Teachings of the Hua-yen," trans. Thomas Cleary in *Entry Into the Inconceivable: An Introduction to Hua-yen Buddhism* (Honolulu: University of Hawaii Press, 1983), 43–68, at 66. The "Jewel Net of Indra" section of Tu Shun's discourse is also available in Stephanie Kaza and Kenneth Kraft, ed., *Dharma Rain: Sources of Buddhist Environmentalism* (Boston: Shambhala, 2000), 58–61.

21. D. T. Suzuki, *Zen and Japanese Culture* (Princeton: Princeton University Press, 1959 [1938]), 50. Note that Suzuki writes extensively on the *Avataṃsaka-Sūtra*, especially the *Gaṇḍavyūha* portion, in his *Essays in Zen Buddhism* (Third Series) (London: Rider and Company, 1953 [1934]).

22. As translated in Garma C. C. Chang, *The Buddhist Teaching of Totality: The Philosophy of Hua Yen Buddhism* (University Park: Pennsylvania State University Press, 1971), 194–95.

23. Snyder first read "The notion of emptiness (absence of real self) engenders Compassion" from "The Song of Milarepa" in Marco Pallis, *Peaks and Lamas* (New York: Alfred A. Knopf, 1949 [1939]), 144, having purchased this book in June 1951. The photograph of an unnamed Tibetan location on pp. 330–31 has the caption, "The Notion of Emptiness Engenders Compassion" and depicts an "emptiness" similar to what Snyder experienced on his hitchhiking trip through the Great Basin on his way to Indiana for graduate school in the fall of 1951 (see Gary Snyder, "On the Road with D. T. Suzuki," in *A Zen Life: D. T. Suzuki Remembered*, ed. Masao Abe [New York: Weatherhill, 1986], 207–09). Note that the Great Basin is also the location of the final scene in the final poem of *Mountains and Rivers*, "Finding the Space in the Heart."

24. For a discussion of Emptiness in relation to compassion by a philosopher of religion, see Keiji Nishitani, *Religion and Nothingness*, trans. Jan Van Bragt (Berkeley: University of California Press, 1982 [1961]). The first four essays that make up this book, plus part of the final essay, were first published in 1954–55. Nishitani (1900–1990) writes (where "nothingness" means "Emptiness," "shunyata"): "The standpoint on which one sees oneself in others and loves one's neighbor as oneself means that the self is at the home-ground of every other in the 'nothingness' of the self, and that every other is at the home-ground of the self in that same nothingness. Only when these two are one — in a relationship of circuminsessional interpenetration — does

this standpoint come about. If this is what loving one's fellow man as oneself is, it follows that the field where that love obtains is in fact not simply a field of the love of fellow men, a love between *men*; but must be a field of Love toward all living beings, and even toward all things" (279–80).

25. "The activity of thinking is essentially an expression of flowing movement. Only when thinking dwells on a particular content, a particular form, does it order itself accordingly and create an idea. Every idea — like every organic form — arises in a process of flow, until the movement congeals into a form" (Theodor Schwenk, *Sensitive Chaos: The Creation of Flowing Forms in Water and Air* [New York: Schocken Books, 1976 (1965)]). A photograph from this book's many illustrations of "flow" in nature adorns the cover of Snyder's *Regarding Wave* (New York: New Directions, 1970).

26. Wilfred Cantwell Smith, "Objectivity and the Humane Sciences: A New Proposal" (1975) in *Religious Diversity*, ed. Willard G. Oxtby (New York: Crossroad, 1982), 171.

27. Heinrich Dumoulin, *Zen Enlightenment: Origins and Meaning*, trans. John C. Maraldo (New York: Weatherhill, 1979 [1976]), 63.

28. On Vairocana see Francis H. Cook, *Hua-yen Buddhism: The Jewel Net of Indra* (University Park: Pennsylvania State University Press, 1977), chapter 7.

29. Cook, *Hua-yen Buddhism*, 107–08. This verse of the *Avataṃsaka-sūtra* is from a chapter called "Peak of Sumeru."

30. Snyder is the once-anonymous author of the "Smokey the Bear Sutra" (widely reproduced and in *The Gary Snyder Reader*, 241–44). See Snyder's "Regarding 'Smokey the Bear Sutra'" in *Back on the Fire* (Emeryville, CA: Shoemaker & Hoard, 2007), 123–27.

31. D. T. Suzuki, *Zen and Japanese Culture* (Princeton: Princeton University Press, 1959 [1938]), 90.

32. From Henry David Thoreau: "If you stand right fronting and face to face to a fact, you will see the sun glimmer on both its surfaces, as if it were a cimeter, and feel its sweet edge dividing you through the heart and marrow, and so you will happily conclude your mortal career. Be it life or death, we crave only reality" (*Walden* [Princeton: Princeton University Press, 1971 (1854)], 98).

33. Alan Watts, *Beat Zen, Square Zen, and Zen* (San Francisco: City Lights Books, 1959), 10, 15.

34. Watts, *Beat Zen, Square Zen, and Zen*, 11.

35. Watts writes (in explaining "Zen" as a Middle Way between Beat and Square extremes): "But the quarrel between the extremes is of great philosophical interest, being a contemporary form of the ancient dispute between salvation by works and salvation by faith, or between what the Hindus called the way of the monkey and the cat. The cat — appropriately enough — follows the effortless way, since the mother

cat carries her kittens. The monkey follows the hard way, since the baby monkey has to hang on to its mother's hair" (*Beat Zen, Square Zen, and Zen*, 22).

36. Susanne K. Langer, *Philosophy in a New Key: A Study in the Symbolism of Reason, Rite, and Art* (Cambridge, MA: Harvard University Press, 1957 [1942]), 141. Langer dedicates this book to her teacher, Alfred North Whitehead, who argued throughout his corpus for "a provisional realism in which nature is conceived as a complex of prehensive unifications. Space and time exhibit the general scheme of interlocked relations of these prehensions. You cannot tear any one of them out of its context. Yet each one of them within its context has all the reality that attaches to the whole complex. . . . Thus nature is a structure of evolving processes. The reality is the process. It is nonsense to ask if the colour red is real. The colour red is an ingredient in the process of realisation. The realities of nature are the prehensions in nature, that is to say, the events in nature" (*Science and the Modern World* [New York: The Macmillan Company, 1939 (1925)], 105–06).

37. Carole Koda, *Homegrown: Thirteen Brothers and Sisters, a Century in America* (Santa Barbara, CA: Companion Press, 1996). See Snyder's foreword to this volume, "Grown in America," in *Back on the Fire*, 159–60.

38. Sherman Paul defines "ethnopoetics" as that "'other' tradition" that "would restore the outcast poet-trickster-shaman and the full range of communal uses that oral poetry had in pre-literate cultures. (Incidentally, . . . this would include its epic didactic task and thus account for some of the long poems of our time.) In reoralizing poetry it would also restore the performative, 'event'-ful aspect of poetry, take poetry off the page and bring it to life. . . . The extent to which it represents an other tradition — the tradition of the other — is easily seen. Its politics — its connection with ecological awareness and the destruction of diversity, human and otherwise — is clear enough ("Ethnopoetics: An 'Other' Tradition," *North Dakota Quarterly* 53/2 [1985]: 44). See also Gary Snyder, "The Politics of Ethnopoetics" (1975) in *The Old Ways* (San Francisco: City Lights, 1977), 15–43; and "Poetry and the Primitive: Notes on Poetry as an Ecological Survival Technique" in *Earth House Hold* (New York: New Directions, 1969), 117–30.

39. On this ritual and the provenance of this poem, see David Robertson, *Real Matter* (Salt Lake City: University of Utah Press, 1997), chapters 4–5. Robertson addressed the Mountains & Rivers Workshop on 17 November 1997 with a talk on "Gary Snyder: Riprapping in Yosemite, Circumambulating Mt. Tamalpais, Practicing on the San Juan Ridge." Also see Matt Davis and Michael Farrell Scott, *Opening the Mountain: Circumambulating Mount Tamalpais: A Ritual Walk* (Emeryville, CA: Shoemaker & Hoard, 2006).

40. Gary Snyder, "Foreword" in Nanao Sakaki, *How to Live on the Planet Earth: Collected Poems* (Nobleboro, ME: Blackberry Books, 2013), 16.

41. See Chad Wigglesworth, ed., *Distant Neighbors: The Selected Letters of Wendell Berry and Gary Snyder* (Berkeley: Counterpoint, 2014), 189–93.

42. For an essay that clarifies what is at stake in this shift, see David Loy, "The Religion of the Market," *Journal of the American Academy of Religion* 65/2 (1997): 275–90.

43. See Paul Griffiths, *Religious Reading: The Place of Reading in the Practice of Religion* (New York: Oxford University Press, 1999). Griffiths writes (pp. ix–x): "Most academic readers are consumerist in their reading habits, and this is because they, like me, have been taught to be so and rewarded for being so. . . . It's also possible to read religiously, as a lover reads, with a tensile attentiveness that wishes to linger, to prolong, to savor, and has no interest at all in the quick orgasm of consumption. . . . I argue that religious reading is a good and that consumerist reading is not only indifferent to religion, but actively hostile to it. I would like (though I do not expect) our educational institutions to pay attention to the argument and to reconsider the pedagogical dominance of consumerist reading. I would like also (though I expect this even less) those who have made the study of religion their intellectual avocation to show a proper humility before a mode of engagement with the world and with texts that their training has not equipped them to understand."

44. Rousseau in Matei Calinescu, *Rereading* (New Haven: Yale University Press, 1993), 88.

45. "Although there is a great deal of rhetoric about Zen understanding being beyond books and texts, right from their first year Zen monks are studying a text called the *Zenrin kushū* (Zen phrase collection) as part of their *kōan* practice. In the advanced stages of *kōan* practice (which most monks do not experience because they leave at less advanced stages), monks spend a great deal of time researching Zen and other texts in order to compose essays in Japanese and poetry in classical Chinese which they write in brush and submit for approval to the *rōshi* (G. Victor Sōgen Hori, "Teaching and Learning in the Rinzai Zen Monastery," *Journal of Japanese Studies* 20/1 [1994]: 11). On the *Zenrin kushū* see Snyder's foreword to *A Zen Forest: Sayings of the Masters*, trans. Sōiku Shigematsu (New York: Weatherhill, 1981), vii–xii. For further discussion of Zen and reading, see Dale Wright, *Philosophical Meditations on Zen Buddhism* (Cambridge: Cambridge University Press, 1998), especially chapter 2, "Reading: The Practice of Insight." Note that Manjushri, bodhisattva of wisdom and patron of Zen meditation halls, holds a sword in one hand and a sūtra book in the other.

46. Ruskin in Calinescu, *Rereading*, 79.

47. As reported by Jane Bahk, "Vonnegut Bemoans 'Creeping Illiteracy,'" *Campus Report,* Stanford University (19 May 1993): n.p.

48. See Jean Leclercq, *The Love of Learning and the Desire for God: A Study of Monastic Culture,* trans. Catharine Misrahi (New York: Fordham University Press, 1982

[1961]), 73. On Zen Buddhist images of reading as digestion and "wise eating" (Huang Po), see Wright, *Philosophical Meditations on Zen Buddhism*, 36–38.

49. Thoreau, *Walden*, 100–01. When I teach this text I begin with the third chapter, for it offers good advice on how to proceed with the rest of this or any other book.

50. Ki no Tsurayuki, "Kanajo: The Japanese Preface," in *Kokinshū: A Collection of Poems Ancient and Modern*, trans. L. R. Rodd and M. Henkenius (Princeton: Princeton University Press, 1984), 35.

51. Makoto Ueda, *Literary and Art Theories of Japan* (Cleveland: The Press of Western Reserve University, 1967), 3.

52. "If you translate the Bodhisattva Avalokitesvara or Kuan Yin's name literally, it means 'Regarding the Sound Waves.'. . . So there's a thread that runs all the way through the Far Eastern Culture that has to do with enlightenment and the sense of hearing. . . . The title of the poem ["Regarding Wave"] is an instruction" Snyder in Katherine McNeil, *Gary Snyder: A Bibliography* (New York: The Phoenix Bookshop, 1983), 36–37.

53. "Though there are Taras in other colors as well, the Green Tara is the most popular. In Tantric symbolism, green is the color of the Action Family, of those Buddhas and Bodhisattvas who specialize in the Wisdom of All — Accomplishing Action. This color is consonant with Tara's constant activity to help and save beings. Thus, it is often explained at a Green Tara initiation that her *sadhana* [visualization and practice exercise] is especially recommended for active people who have major projects under way" (Rita Gross, *Buddhism After Patriarchy: A Feminist History, Analysis, and Reconstruction of Buddhism* [Albany: State University of New York Press, 1993], 111). Also see Stephen Beyer, *The Cult of Tārā: Magic and Ritual in Tibet* (Berkeley: University of California Press, 1973).

54. See also Snyder's essay, "Ladakh," in *The Gary Snyder Reader: Prose, Poetry and Translations, 1952-1998* (Washington, DC: Counterpoint Press, 1999), 353–59.

55. One simple effort toward such education is recitation of the following meal grace: We venerate the Three Treasures*/ And are thankful for this meal / The work of many people / And the sharing of other forms of life.

　　*From 5 July 1973 GSJ:

　　Three treasures: power, knowledge, love

Buddha	Dharma	Sangha
Power	Knowledge	Love
Teachers	The Wild	Friends

See *The Practice of the Wild*, chapter 9, "Survival and Sacrament," for further discussion of this teaching.

~

What I find is that every poem I do in *Mountains and Rivers* takes a different form and has a different strategy, and I have to let the strategy work itself out. When I get enough distance from it at some point I'll be able to understand more clearly what I've done. But every poem has a different strategy and they come in various ways from various quarries, many-faceted.

— Gary Snyder to Ekbert Faas in *Towards a New American Poetics: Essays & Interviews* (1978)

Opening Conversation

GARY SNYDER & JACK SHOEMAKER

East House at Stanford University
8 October 1997

GARY SNYDER: Good evening. I can't tell you how surprised, delighted, and amazed I was to begin to get communications from Mark Gonnerman describing his plans for the Mountains & Rivers Workshop. It is very gratifying and challenging that so many people are going to come to *Mountains and Rivers* from their various disciplines and interests and see what they can do with it.

What really intrigues me is the collaborative nature of a project like this. I have written many poems that are clearly more or less my poems. This is to say, whatever Muse brings me poems brought them to me personally, and I got to write them down. But, *Mountains and Rivers* has been a co-emergent, co-production of my mind and many other minds from the time I was twenty-three or twenty-four years old. If you are out tracking and are on the track of one thing, it is possible to follow it. It's not too difficult. You get the sign, and you follow the sign, and you get the patterns of what the sign leaves. But with this long poem I found myself tracking about twenty-five things at the same time. That meant I had to spread out over a lot of territory, going back and forth, you know, trying to pick up different traces as I went, staying on their trail. So that is why it took so long.

This poem owes so much to my teachers at Berkeley, especially Ch'en Shih-hsiang, in Chinese, and Ed Schafer, in Chinese history and Chinese literature, who published the marvelous book, *The Golden Peaches of Samarkand*.[1] Also the painter Saburo Hasegawa; my teacher in sumi-brush, Chiura

Obata-sensei; and countless other people in Japan, and in America and other places, with whom I was constantly resonating and working, and hanging out, as you, Mark, say. (I love Mark's way of looking at this workshop as hanging out with art.) I was hanging out with Nō drama, with Chinese and East Asian painting and calligraphy, with oral performance, with storytelling, with varieties of singing and song, over the years.

All of this was somehow working into my sense of *Mountains and Rivers* as I hung out with geologists and hydrologists, geomorphologists, and biologists while shamelessly trying to get their best information. As I said somewhere in an essay, artists strive very hard to be at the top of the information chain.[2] Like fast, mobile raptors that come over the treetops, they grab a bit of physicist stuff, and a bit of geology stuff, and bit of some other kind of scholarship, and then make off with it. The next thing you know it is in a poem somewhere. We get accused of appropriating, not to mention, stealing. But as somebody said, "Mediocre artists borrow, great artists steal." That is what I tell my Native American friends sometimes, and they don't always get the joke.

Part of that collaborative emergence of *Mountains and Rivers* I owe to Carl Bielefeldt, who was translating Dōgen's *Mountains and Waters Sūtra* early on. I don't think I ever read any of it until I saw it in Carl's MA thesis at Berkeley. I could read a little classical Chinese, I could read a little modern Japanese, but nobody ever showed me how to read Dōgen. So I was really grateful to stumble onto Carl's work. Dōgen's *Mountains and Waters Sūtra* slowed me down ten years on this project because I had to think about it. It was such a wonderful exercise to try and absorb that and take it back to my meditation and my scholarship and play with it some more. And part of the collaborative work has been publishing the poems over the forty years — about one poem a year. A volume of six of them came out in 1965 from Donald Allen's old Grey Fox Press in San Francisco.[3] These poems have been part of the intellectual and aesthetic ambiance of the marginal radical West Coast culture since that time.

Jack Shoemaker and I were friends for many years, and then I began working with North Point Press in 1980 or '81. Jack's reading of my work, and his astute way of guiding me into the institutional literary world, has been invaluable.

All of these collaborations have made it possible for me to have finished and put out in the world something called *Mountains and Rivers Without End*. Frankly, I am not entirely able to describe it to myself, even. But I love learning how to perform it, by practicing reading it, as I have done now maybe twenty-five or thirty times. Performance of poetry is where the poem is most alive for me, and how I learn the most from it. I'm still learning from things I wrote twenty-five, thirty years ago. Suddenly I get what it was that I was doing or what was being given to me. It is a lesson that goes on.

MARK GONNERMAN: What are you working on now?

SNYDER: Well, I've been telling everyone I'm not working on anything. While I wrote *Mountains and Rivers* I published fourteen other books and — let's see — cut 115 cords of wood, raised about 100 chickens, went through four trucks and three chainsaws. I've been telling everybody that what I'm doing is cleaning up the workshop. I'm getting the chips off the floor. And in a sense, that is what I'm still doing.

But, I had a flash just the other day about where I'm going next! It involves some stuff I started on some seven or eight years ago. Wildlife: the wildlife of Botswana and Zimbabwe, Africa, where I traveled with both my sons.[4] There is the panorama of the procession of elephants and gazelles on the horizon at dawn and the panorama of elephants and gazelles walking on the Paleolithic caves of Southwestern France between ten and thirty-five thousand years ago, which I visited the summer before last.[5] Plus the panorama three years ago of yaks winding around toward the base camp at Mount Everest in the Khumbu district of Nepal. That is part of what I'm trying to put together, and it has something to do with meat, and bones, and hyenas, and the nature of the body and the body's impermanence, the flaying and opening of the body as in the *Chöd* meditations in Tibetan Buddhism.

So what came to me was the idea that there is the *Garbhadhatu* mandala, the Womb-realm mandala, and there is the *Vajradhatu* mandala, the Consciousness-realm mandala.[6] *Mountains and Rivers Without End* completes my work with the *Garbhadhatu*, the Womb-realm, the realm of the environment. But this other stuff I want to work on now is the *Vajradhatu*, it's the realm of the body and the mind. So, I'm off on a new track!

JACK SHOEMAKER: Let me say something about editing poetry. When you are editing occasional lyrics you try to put together the strongest of a set of lyrics written over a period of time, generally organized chronologically not thematically. This is because poets want to have a book every now and then to see what they have written. Gary and I have worked on books like that over the years, where we look at a whole body of work of his, and try to make some sense of it as a book of occasional lyric poetry. Keats did the same thing.

When you are working with a long poem, however, the process is remarkably different. If you had asked Gary — and certainly if you had asked me in 1969 what *Mountains and Rivers Without End* was going to become — I would have said a road poem, a biographical road poem. That was all the evidence we had. What happens with a long poem is a matter of accretion, so that as new poems get added to the mix, they change the earlier poems. First you have a road poem, "Night Highway 99," very much in the mode of Kerouac. But then Snyder came up with "The Blue Sky," and you think: how does that fit in this? That is not a hitchhiking poem, that's something else. Something else is going on. And it changes the entire reading of both "Night Highway 99" and "The Blue Sky."

I have a letter from Gary in 1972 that says, "I'll be finished next year." But the poem came in and out of focus, and as material got added to it, it changed organizationally, from Gary's own understanding. It was a privilege and a matter of extreme excitement to see how this thing unfolded as the individual poems would come in. They would be published first in magazines like *Origin* and *Caterpillar*. Some of the new poems didn't make it into the final book. That was always kind of interesting, too. Things that you thought were *Mountains and Rivers* turn out to not be *Mountains and Rivers*.

I think what happened is the poem changed into a geologic spiritual poem. It has a lot to do with *The Cantos*. And it has a lot to do with the organic way Whitman's work unfolded over a long period of time. If Whitman is the grand American poet of extravagance, then this is a poem of a certain extravagant bent. Gary described twenty-five different things he was trying to follow during the course of his aesthetic and spiritual life. All those are referenced there. You will have a chance to see everything — from American blues to ancient Chinese — in this poem. And as he said, he worked on lots of things in the interim, and those things, each individually, informed going back to *Mountains and Rivers*. At least, for me, when we would finish something like *Axe Handles* and get back to *Mountains and Rivers*, just reading "Bubbs Creek Haircut" would be changed. That will happen to you all as you read. Reading a long poem is not like reading a lyric poem because it changes as you change — you spend time together, you grow and change together.

SNYDER: Jack, it was my experience in writing this poem that I grew and changed, but so did the culture around me. When I started writing *Mountains and River Without End*, there were no Americans who could talk about it, the way that it will be talked about here. Consciousness and scholarship have evolved with the poem! They have co-evolved, so that now there is a sophisticated enough knowledge of Japanese Buddhism, for example, that people can come forward and talk about it. I don't think you could have found that even ten years ago. Some of the scholars here at Stanford who will read the poem this year are just about the same age as the poem. So maybe *Mountains and Rivers* is not just a manifestation of some aspect of West Coast semi-marginal culture. More than that, it is culturally a manifestation of something happening in American society, too, on a larger scale.

GONNERMAN: You must have a sense of your own role in changing this culture, in helping people pay attention to new things. For example, Rick Vinograd, the chair of Stanford's art department, told me the other day that if it hadn't been for your poetry he would never have paid attention to Chinese landscape painting. And now it's his scholarly focus!

SNYDER: Well, as Paul Ehrlich says, it's co-evolutionary!

QUESTION: Is *Mountains and Rivers* being translated into other languages? Are you performing it overseas? If so, where is it resonating?

SNYDER: It is being translated into Japanese right now, and also into Korean. A French version just got underway, and Jack tells me that we have interest from Germany, Spain, and Portugal.[7]

SHOEMAKER: This is an interesting time in publishing American poetry, because unlike the 1970s and early '80s there is almost no interest in Europe in American poetry. For a while American poetry was the driving literary influence in Europe, and everybody was available there. Now the driving American influence in Europe, and Eastern Europe especially, is American fiction. So Richard Ford is well translated, but there is very little translation going on of what we think of as the New American poets.

QUESTION: Are you being read in the United Kingdom, for example? Ireland?

SNYDER: To some extent. England is not well inclined toward American poetry. Ireland, much more so, or the Continent. And for years I've had a very strong, interested readership in the People's Republic, in Taiwan, and in Japan, where I am widely translated and read, in terms of sheer numbers. And in the Czech Republic, too. Eastern Europe shows a lot of interest in American poetry, actually. Czesław Miłosz pointed out that there are more copies of Robinson Jeffers in print in Polish than there are in English.

QUESTION: Gary, I would be interested in hearing about what pieces of land have been the most compelling for you? What geography has been the best teacher, in your experience?

SNYDER: I'll answer that, but first I want to challenge the priority we give to charismatic landscapes. I've had my share of experience with charismatic landscapes, but it is important to develop the kind of sensibility that can learn from very plain landscapes, too. My initial excitement with landscapes was with the North Cascades of Washington State, the snow peaks of the Northwest, and much of the time in the context of work: seasonal work for the U.S. Forest Service, lookout work, trail crew work, fire fighting work, and a certain amount of just recreational backpacking and mountaineering. I got to spend long summers in the Cascades, and then later, in the Sierras, by being a seasonal worker for the Park Service or the Forest Service. Or in the case of one season, logging.

And then I began to branch out more: the mountains of Japan and the low country of Japan. The story of my relationship with landscapes is a story of increasing diversification and appreciation for variety, including empty spaces, barren spaces, and even the urban and the suburban. You know, we've got to get away from discrimination.

What high mountains teach you, prior to airplanes, is how to see large spaces. What I learned from being on a lookout was how big a space one can see. And that carried my imagination to the question of how do you represent huge space. Seeing East Asian landscape paintings was one insight into the representation of large space: "Aha!" Those guys took on the question of large space. And that was very instructive and very exciting. So I went to the Seattle Art Museum to study Chinese landscape painting, but the question of representing space would not have arisen if I had not been a mountaineer, and a lookout, and spent a lot of time at very high elevations looking out over vast spaces.

My question, "How would you represent this?" is an artist's question, right? Not everybody asks that question. I was already thinking as a poet, and so my question was, "How would I represent this in poetry? Would it be possible?" So, in a sense, that became the challenge for me: to see that the East Asian landscape painting had taken on big space. And then ask myself, "Could I do it in poetry?"

But then I moved out into other spaces. I spent nine months working on tankers, as a seaman, crossing the Pacific five or six times, where you see nothing but the Pacific every day for six weeks. And where you get to see all the stars, from horizon to horizon. So that is when I learned my stars, too.

Or the Great Basin, over the passes into the east, which is another marvelous space to look at. But then, Chinese, East Asian — I keep trying to make sure and say East Asian landscape painting, because it's not just Chinese — evolved from mountains and rivers to rocks and trees, to little tiny streams, to catfish and gourds and bugs. By the time of the Ch'ing Dynasty they are doing those wonderful close-ups of nature. So don't overlook the close-ups. They didn't get into the poem, *Mountains and Rivers*, but it did get into one of my essays in the book, *A Place in Space*, where I was examining the local watershed on the micro-scale, on my hands and knees, crawling under the manzanita bush.[8] What you discover on your hands and knees is that everything is fractal, especially watersheds. So, you find exactly the same water and erosion patterns in a little channel between rocks and in the Grand Canyon! Mountains and rivers are fractal. The whole planet is one watershed, or you can get on your hands and knees and be in a watershed.

What's most important to remember is that landscapes themselves are not the teachers, it is what we do in the landscapes that teaches us — walking in them, or spending time in them.

QUESTION: What is the Yuba Watershed Institute currently doing?

SNYDER: That's our local watershed group. Community members involved with issues in the Yuba system of rivers, the South, Middle, and North Yuba River, in Nevada County, Yuba County, and Sierra County, California. At the moment we are most concerned about proposed logging and road-building on the upper San Juan Ridge, on part of the Nevada City Ranger District of the Tahoe National Forest. That is the kind of thing we are always concerned about. That is our latest brush fire.

And I just put in an order for the draft Environmental Impact Report, for which the feedback is supposed to be due by October 20th. They always give you deadlines that are too short. So, we are going to ask for an extension. That's about it. You guys who do that kind of thing know what I'm talking about. We are always doing something like that: "Eternal vigilance is the price of liberty."

QUESTION: Jumping back to *Mountains and Rivers Without End*, how did you know over the years that some poems belonged in *Mountains and Rivers* and others didn't?

SNYDER: Well, I felt it. When I'm writing I can immediately discriminate between poetry — "Oh, yeah, that's a poetry idea. That's a poetry line." — and prose, not meaning less valuable, or less important, or less demanding, but different. And then, within the poetry category, I could always tell if something belonged to *Mountains and Rivers*. It was always clear, instantly. "Ah, that's a *Mountains and Rivers* thing." The idea came as a cluster of language or cluster of imagery with different colors around it, so to speak. Maybe not colors . . . an aura, a buzz.

SHOEMAKER: It always interested me, for example, that little poem, "The Rabbit," which you published in *Poetry*, as part of *Eight Songs of Clouds and Water*. I think you held "The Rabbit" out for *Mountains and Rivers* later on.

SNYDER: Right. And I've made a few mistakes. Like I published "The Canyon Wren" in the *Axe Handles* collection. And then, almost instantly, realized that isn't where it really belonged. So I pulled it out and also got permission to also put it in *Mountains and Rivers* because I felt it belonged there.

COMMENT: It really feels good there.

SNYDER: Yeah. But there was very little confusion between the two categories of poems. And I have to confess, it was completely intuitive, a working intuitive sense of things. I could be more specific about what I think it is. It's different rhythms, actually. And it is a different cluster of image types. And it is a different class of information. All of those things are part of that distinction.

SHOEMAKER: You also said some things were missing, and you would want something in the larger scheme of things, like "The Dance."

SNYDER: Aha! Partly in ending the project, I began to see where the gaps were. And I applied myself to filling in the gaps, if you can do that. Apply yourself to being available. That's an old trick!

NOTES

1. Edward H. Schafer, *The Golden Peaches of Samarkand: A Study of T'ang Exotics* (Berkeley: University of California Press, 1963).

2. See Gary Snyder, "The Forest in the Library" (1990) in *A Place in Space: Ethics, Aesthetics, and Watersheds* (Washington, DC: Counterpoint, 1995), 199–204.

3. See Gary Snyder, *Six Sections from Mountains and Rivers Without End* (San Francisco: Four Seasons Foundation, 1965). This volume contains "Bubbs Creek Haircut"; "The Elwha River"; "Night Highway Ninety-Nine"; "Hymn to the Goddess San Francisco in Paradise"; "The Market"; and "Journeys."

4. Excerpts from Snyder's journals from the 1994 Africa trip are published as "Botswana and Zimbabwe" (1994) in *The Gary Snyder Reader: Prose, Poetry and Translations, 1952–1998* (Washington, DC: Counterpoint Press, 1999), 360–68.

5. See "Entering the Fiftieth Millennium" (1996) in *The Gary Snyder Reader*, 390–94.

6. "A great part of the Shingon teaching is encoded into two large mandala-paintings. One is the 'Vajra-realm' (Kongō-kai) and the other the 'Garbha-realm' (Taizō-kai). They are each marvelously detailed. In Sanskrit 'Vajra' means diamond (as drill tip, or cutter), and 'Garbha' means womb. These terms are descriptive of two complementary but not exactly dichotomous ways of seeing the world, and representative of such pairs as: mind / enviroment, evolutionary drama / ecological stage, mountains / waters, compassion / wisdom, the Buddha as enlightened being / the world as enlightened habitat, etc." (Gary Snyder, "Walking the Great Ridge Omine on the Womb-Diamond Trail," in *The Gary Snyder Reader*, 374).

7. See *Montagnes et rivières sans fin*, trans. Olivier Delbard (Monaco: Rocher, 2002);

Owari naki sanka, trans. Katsunori Yamazato and Shigeyoshi Hara (Tokyo: Shi-chōsha, 2002); *Hory a řeky bez konce,* trans. Lubos Snizek (Prague: Mata, 2007); *Luputtomat vuoret ja joet,* trans. Jyrki Ihalainen (Tempere, Finland: Palladium Kir-jat, 2010).

8. See "Crawling" (1992) in *A Place in Space,* 192–95.

HEARING NATIVE VOICES

~

There are tens of millions of people in North America who were physically born here but who are not actually living here intellectually, imaginatively, or morally. Native Americans to be sure have a prior claim to the term native. But as they love this land they will welcome the conversion of the millions of immigrant psyches into fellow "Native Americans." For the non-Native American to become at home on this continent, he or she must be *born again* in this hemisphere, on this continent, properly called Turtle Island.

— Gary Snyder, *The Practice of the Wild* (1990)

2.

The Other's Voice

Cultural Imperialism and Poetic Impersonality in Gary Snyder's *Mountains and Rivers Without End*

TIM DEAN

> [H]ow do we encourage and develop an ethic that goes beyond
> intrahuman obligations and includes nonhuman nature?
> — Gary Snyder, "A Village Council of all Beings" (1992)

In 1996, Gary Snyder published a long poem cycle that he had been work-ing on for forty years. Comprising thirty-nine interlinked poems, *Moun-tains and Rivers Without End* is hugely ambitious; far more than a national epic, the book is conceived on a planetary scale. Among other things, it weaves together geology, ecological concerns, East Asian landscape paint-ing and Nō drama, Native Amerian mythology, and ethical reflection. Yet any such summary cannot do this book justice. It represents the culmina-tion of Snyder's career.[1]

In my account of *Mountains and Rivers Without End* I want to argue that since it harmonizes a vast range of disparate utterances into a collec-tive voice, the poem's voice should be understood as impersonal — that is, as something other than Snyder's individual voice or the expression of his personal sentiments. My sense of poetic impersonality derives from mod-ernist theories of this kind of voicing found in Yeats, Joyce, Pound, Eliot, and others; but my account of impersonality extends beyond their theories to accommodate Snyder's practice in a way that I hope will become clear as this essay progresses. Snyder himself has remarked that the individual poems in this book always held a different status: "Poems for *Mountains and Rivers* kept showing up at the rate of about one a year. I was writing other poems at the same time, but in a different and more lyrical mode" (M&R 156). These poems are less lyrical, less personal, even when they appear autobiographical and intimate.

Although in the wake of its publication Gary Snyder has given many stirring performances of his poem, I propose that a more thorough understanding of *Mountains and Rivers Without End* may be achieved if we bear in mind that it is not composed or spoken in his voice. In this paper I want to show how the poem's creation of an impersonal voice enables the work of art to engage ethical questions concerning nonhuman nature and our relations with it. I shall argue that only through a fully impersonal voice can art apprehend the otherness of nonhuman nature without transforming nature into something that merely serves human ends. Snyder's ethical commitment to beneficently engaging the natural world draws on the resources that poetry offers for generating or accessing impersonal voice; thus by means of impersonal modes of communication we can develop relationships with nature that aren't strictly human. There are resources within poetic traditions of both the East and the West that provide techniques for this kind of impersonal voicing — and hence relating. To that reservoir of poetic resources we can add now *Mountains and Rivers Without End.*

∼

Working on Snyder's poem in the Stanford University workshop was a very different experience from working on his poetry alone, as I did a decade ago when writing a book on Snyder. *Mountains and Rivers Without End* demands a collective response, and I'm not sure I could have written about it by myself. The poem and the workshop have refined my thinking about Snyder's poetry in a way that teaches me something substantial about the poem itself. I first wrote about Snyder's work in terms of a cultural unconscious, a transindividual dynamic that conditions what it means to be a United States subject — to be American and say "I." In *Gary Snyder and the American Unconscious* I wanted to show how Snyder fit into — or, rather, departed from — a long tradition of figuring the North American landscape and its native inhabitants in distinctly insidious ways. I argued that becoming a U.S. subject entails disavowing the history of the landscape and its expropriation from the Indians: to be American involves a commitment to ignorance concerning one's relationship with the land. It isn't simply a matter of not knowing about the landscape, but of actively wishing not to know. Psychoanalysis calls this wishing-not-to-know *the unconscious* — a negative motivation that, in terms of U.S. history and culture, renders voices from the land marginal to mainstream consciousness. In this way, the voice of the landscape becomes "other."

Poetry has always involved gaining access to other voices — or, perhaps, to a realm of otherness that we tend to humanize in terms of voice. In his essay on "The Other Voice," Mexican poet Octavio Paz describes this strange phenomenon:

> All poets in the moments, long or short, of poetry, if they are really poets, hear the *other* voice. It is their own, someone else's, no one else's, no one's, and everyone's. Nothing distinguishes a poet from other men and women but those moments — rare yet frequent — in which, being themselves, they are other.[2]

This access to the other voice, which for Paz defines the experience of poetry, can be understood psychoanalytically in terms of the unconscious ("the unconscious is the discourse of the Other") or philosophically in terms of impersonality.[3] The voice that is "no one's and everyone's" is an impersonal voice, a transindividual voice, in much the same way that the cultural unconscious names a transindividual dynamic.

The other voice to which Snyder's work provides access is that of the landscape: his poetry voices a different relation to the land, one silenced and obscured by the cultural engines of Americanization. In this respect, Snyder's impersonalist poetic ambition accords with that of Yeats, who, in a different postcolonial context, "tried to speak out of a people to a people."[4] Like Snyder, Yeats believed that the key to this collective poetic utterance lay in reimagining the landscape and its aboriginal myths. *Mountains and Rivers Without End* shows that the process of reimagining the landscape involves listening to the voices of nonhuman nature; it therefore entails a more expansive conception of "the people," as well as perhaps an extended conception of what counts as voice.

This effort to reimagine the landscape — or, more accurately, to reimagine our relationship to it — also leads Snyder to draw on cultural traditions of the East, as well as of the West. Hence his enlarged conception of "the people" necessarily entails a more expansive understanding of cultural tradition too. For instance, the title *Mountains and Rivers Without End* alludes to lines from the Chinese poet Tu Fu: "The country is ruined: yet / mountains and rivers remain" (quoted in Snyder, APIS 103).[5] These lines are so well known in China, according to Snyder, that they've reached proverbial status: words that belong to no one and thus to everyone. While I will have more to say later about Snyder's allusions to and borrowings from other cultural traditions, I would like to register here that words belonging to everyone can hardly be appropriated or stolen from their rightful owner. Having entered a transnational tradition of poetic utterance, such words and images exist as part of the resource for poetry. They form part of that "other voice" of poetry.

Though the nation is lost, the mountains and rivers remain: the continuity of mountains and rivers in the face of socio-political changes represents a deep theme informing all of Snyder's work. His poetic intention isn't simply to demonstrate the presence of the landscape as the ground of the nation (a ground conventionally repressed in the North American context), but rather to actively articulate a new set of relationships to the land in order to create a different mode of social organization. We see this process at work in, for example, "The Hump-backed Flute Player," a poem that appears at the very center of *Mountains and Rivers Without End* and takes as its subject the transformative power of poetry itself. The flute player, known as Kokop'ele, is a figure for the wandering poet, the music-maker who traverses the landscape.[6] In this poem's fourth section the poet summons ghosts of native animals for the purpose of transforming human relations with the landscape and, in so doing, transforming national identity:

> Ghost bison, ghost bears, ghost bighorns, ghost lynx, ghost
> pronghorns, ghost panthers, ghost marmots, ghost owls: swirling
> and gathering, sweeping down,
>
> Then the white man will be gone.
> butterflies on slopes of grass and aspen —

thunderheads the deep blue of Krishna
rise on rainbows
and falling shining rain
each drop —
tiny people gliding slanting down:
          a little buddha seated in each pearl —
and join the million waving grass-seed-buddhas
on the ground.   (M&R 80–81)

In an impersonal, shamanistic mode, the speaker calls on the spirits of the
dead, analogously to how more conventional Western poets call upon the
muse. I describe this mode as impersonal because the speaker implicitly
summons the power of "voices" other than his own to effect the desired
transformation.

The incantatory tone generated by alliteration in this passage — "Ghost
bison, ghost bears, ghost bighorns" — suggests that transformation involves
an ongoing process, a sense that is reinforced by the preponderance of
gerunds ("swirling," "gathering," "sweeping," "falling," "shining," "gliding,"
"slanting," "waving"). Given these present-tense participial constructions,
it seems significant that the end result of this process is figured in the future
tense — "Then the white man will be gone." In his note on the poem, Sny-
der offers the following comment: "'White man' here is not a racial designa-
tion, but a name for a certain set of mind. When we all become born-again
natives of Turtle Island, then the 'white man' will be gone" (M&R 161). This
note supports my previous argument that our relation to the landscape is
a function of consciousness or, more specifically, of the unconscious — "a
certain set of mind." Hence "white man" designates the U.S. subject whose
peculiar relationship to the landscape and its history is maintained through
disavowal. It's this relationship, stemming from a distinctive mental state,
that Snyder's work aspires to transform.

The transformation of consciousness evoked in "The Hump-backed
Flute Player" is framed in characteristically spiritual, even religious terms.
However, there is some tension between the Buddhist imagery in the poem
("a little buddha seated in each pearl") and the Fundamentalist rhetoric of
being "born again" in the note ("When we all become born-again natives of

Turtle Island"). Given that it was Christian missionary zeal that propelled the colonization of North America in the first place, another conversion narrative for the continent's population seems rather misguided, in that it risks simply replicating the original problem. Yet "The Hump-backed Flute Player" implies an alternative religious framework for understanding Snyder's project, one that is neither Buddhist nor Christian. As both a religious and a poetic practice, shamanism offers a particularly useful model for grasping the relationship between Snyder's spiritual and aesthetic commitments. From my perspective, shamanism also provides an excellent framework for appreciating the idea of poetic impersonality.[7]

≈

In the cultures in which he appears, the shaman works to heal both individuals and the community through ritualized song. Indeed, in some instances an individual becomes a shaman by first healing himself through song. In the classic account of shamanism as a religious practice, Mircea Eliade reports the following:

> Often when the shaman's or medicine man's vocation is revealed through an illness or an epileptoid attack, the initiation of the candidate is equivalent to a cure. The famous Yakut shaman Tüspüt (that is, "fallen from the sky") had been ill at the age of twenty; *he began to sing, and felt better.*[8]

Eliade adds that this shaman's good health remained contingent upon his continuing to sing: "if he went for a long time without doing so, he did not feel well."[9] Shamanic initiation involves a primordial encounter with the effectiveness of song—what in contemporary parlance we might call the performative power of ritualized utterances. A performative utterance is one whose words don't merely describe an existing state of affairs, but actually usher it into being. Speech act theorist J. L. Austin's classic example of a performative is the phrase "I do," spoken in the marriage ceremony to bring a new symbolic relationship into existence.[10] Performative utterances gain their power from the context in which they are enunciated: they draw on and manifest a social relationship between the speaker and his community. It is for this reason that performatives always require witnesses, community representatives who play a symbolic role by standing in for the world in which the performative achieves its intelligibility. Hence witnesses fulfill essentially the same role at a marriage ceremony as they do at a shamanic one. And since it is the context that confers upon performatives their power, this context must be created on successive occasions through ritual. Poetry can function as both a ritualistic element in the creation of context and a performative outcome of this creation.

Contemporary literary theory has devoted considerable attention to performative utterances, though much more has been said about how words can do harm — for example, in hate speech — than about how words can do good or can heal.[11] Our most sophisticated accounts of the performative concern injury; by contrast Snyder's poetry, like shamanism, draws on words' restorative potential, their rarer power to make whole. Indeed, Snyder always has treated poetry as performative and shamanic in this way. For example, in "The Blue Sky" he elaborates a series of etymological and mythological connections among the color blue, medicine, and song. These connections between poetry and healing crystallize in the set-off line "Medicine, measure, 'Maya' — " (M&R 43), in which Maya refers to, among other things, the power of a Hindu god to transform an idea into an element of the sensible world. "Maya" designates performative power, a capacity to actualize in the material realm something nonmaterial or spiritual.

These three words — "Medicine, measure, 'Maya'" — are connected not only alliteratively but also metonymically, as substitutable, and therefore they're linked conceptually too. An earlier version of the poem, published in *Six Sections from* Mountains and Rivers Without End*, Plus One* (1970), suggests that these terms also are linked etymologically, that they are related within the history of language itself. The three-word line we find in the poem's 1996 version has been condensed from the following passage:

Medicine.	medēri	Indo European	me —
	"to measure"		
"MAYA"	Goddess	illusion-wisdom	fishing net
			(SSPO 42)

Here we see that *measure* has been derived from *medicine* via its Indo-European root, and that *Maya* is the name of a goddess, part of whose role involves measurement, fitting, or enclosure, as the poem's subsequent imagery makes clear. In the poem's later version these connotations have been subordinated such that *measure* is one in a series of nouns, rather than standing as a verb. This shift in emphasis subtly elevates the poetic meaning of *measure*, in which the term functions as a synonym for meter, the pattern of accented or alliterated words and syllables in poetry. Since meter may be considered what primarily distinguishes poetry from other verbal forms, *measure* represents a synecdoche for poetry as such. Hence the line "Medicine, measure, 'Maya'" constitutes a metonymic chain paraphrasable as *healing — poetry — performative realization*. And, in this regard we might note that although Snyder's poetry is unmetered — he tends to avoid closed poetic forms in favor of *vers libre* — it is not unmeasured. His work has always focused on patterns of relationship, proportion, interpenetration, and balance — features that, in formal terms, concern measure and, in terms of content, concern ecology, social justice, and environmental ethics.

Both poetry and shamanism involve restoring balance in this broad sense, and it is noteworthy that Kokop'ele, the wandering poet figure, punctuates Snyder's earlier version of "The Blue Sky" eight times. His previous appearance in "The Blue Sky," which now ends the first section of *Mountains and Rivers Without End*, connects this poem with "The Hump-Backed Flute Player," which ends the book's second section. This connection reinforces the link between poetic and shamanic vocation, since for Snyder both are associated with the healing power of song. Indeed, the shaman's vocational scene — which, as I have said, entails encountering the performative power of song — closely resembles that of poetic vocation. In his helpful meditation on the four-part structure of vocation, poet Allen Grossman notes that "[t]he story about vocation is one part of a whole master-story: the story of the maintenance of the intelligibility of the human world by symbols."[12] By this Grossman means simply that our world makes sense to us because it is mediated by representation, and that the quadripartite narrative of vocation is bound up with this sense-making function of representation. Grossman continues:

In the story, the symbols that effect the maintenance of intelligibility obtain their stability in history because they are grounded in an axiomatically nonhuman "first" reality. The master story about vocation says that nonhuman reality continually calls certain persons, alienating them to its purposes, burdening the world with the recognition (poetic knowledge) that identity requires memory of transcendental relationship.[13]

I will return to Grossman's description shortly; but for now I want to note simply that it indicates how poetic vocation corresponds to the structure and significance of shamanic vocation. We may grasp his claim that "nonhuman reality continually calls certain persons, alienating them to its purposes" in terms of how the would-be shaman is lifted from the human realm into that of the sacred, so that in time he may become a conduit between the social community and the nonhuman world.

Eliade argues that this summoning of "certain persons" actually constitutes the sacred, since at its most basic level the sacred comes into being by way of singularization — that is, by the simple demarcation and separating out of a person, place, or object:

[S]ingularization as such depends upon the very dialectic of the sacred. The most elementary hierophanies, that is, are nothing but a radical ontological separation of some object from the surrounding cosmic zone; some tree, some stone, some place, by the mere fact that *it reveals that it is sacred*, that it has been, as it were, "chosen" as the receptacle for a manifestation of the sacred, is thereby ontologically separated from all other stones, trees, places, and occupies a different, a supernatural plane . . . . What it is important to note now is the parallel between the singularization of objects, beings, and sacred signs, and the singularization by "election," by "choice," of those who experience the sacred with greater intensity than the rest of the community — those who, as it were, incarnate the sacred, because they live it abundantly, or rather "are lived" by the religious "form" that has chosen them (gods, spirits, ancestors, etc.).[14]

Singularization and sacralization thus can be seen as two sides of the same coin, in that the very fact of singularization creates a heterogeneous domain of existence — what, in the passage above, Grossman refers to as the transcendental.

It may be possible, however, to describe this phenomenon in less metaphysical terms once we recognize that the singularization of poetic and shamanic vocation entails a depersonalization — even a dehumanization — of the person who is called. Not only does the initiatory call of vocation hail from a point that cannot be identified with any individual person, but the response to this call likewise entails some forfeiture of personhood by the respondent. Eliade characterizes this double-bind thus: "the desire to enter into contact with the sacred is counteracted by the fear of being obliged to renounce the simple human condition and become a more or less pliant instrument for some manifestation of the sacred (gods, spirits, ancestors, etc.)."[15] This is a more extreme situation than initially may be apparent, since the individual selected for a shamanic vocation is *lived by* the religious form (gods, spirits, ancestors) that has chosen him. Just as sacralization requires a radical ontological separation of the object or place deemed sacred, so shamanism entails a radical ontological transformation of the person concerned. It is almost as if the shaman is reduced to a mere host of the virtually parasitical force of otherness. The would-be shaman must give up his own personal life in favor of the life that comes to possess him. And, indeed, the metaphor of possession is far from idle in this context; it indicates the extremity of self-loss entailed in any authentic response to this vocational call.[16]

Eliade's characterization of the would-be shaman's dilemma is uncannily similar to T. S. Eliot's characterization of the modern poet, who must surrender his individual personality in favor of ancestral voices, words from the dead — must, in other words, become a more or less pliant instrument for "the other voice." In "Tradition and the Individual Talent," his critique of poetic originality, Eliot famously observes that "we shall often find that not only the best, but the most individual parts of [the poet's] work may be those in which the dead poets, his ancestors, assert their immortality most vigorously."[17] Poetry for Eliot thus involves forms of *speaking through* or *being spoken by* one's ancestors, rather than more conventional forms of self-expression. The way in which Eliot's model of the impersonalist poet conforms to a shamanistic paradigm complicates received wisdom concerning his religious orthodoxy. Eliot's proto-shamanism also illuminates his conception of the poet's cultural role, since the modern poet, like the premodern shaman, is at once socially marginal — having renounced or forfeited "the simple human condition" that would make him a regular member of the community — and culturally central, in that he aspires to speak on behalf of the whole community.[18]

~

Any attempt to speak on behalf of others raises a host of ethical issues concerning cultural imperialism and appropriation. These issues have dogged Snyder on and off throughout his career, in terms both of his use of Native American and East Asian materials — ostensibly an appropriation of others' words — and his shamanistic effort to speak in his poetry not only for himself but also for a community. It would be plausible to interpret this attempt to speak on others' behalf as an illegitimate bid for power, an unwarranted form of self-aggrandizement on the poet's or shaman's part. Conversely, however, we could interpret speaking for the community as entailing a dramatic subordination to collective well-being of the poet's or shaman's individuality — a form of self-dispossession rather than self-aggrandizement. The degree to which the poet is obliged to become "a more or less pliant instrument" for "the other voice" suggests that we should not assent too readily to the interpretation that views a poet's speaking for others as a misuse of his power. Instead, we might regard the truly shamanistic poet as one who is used — even abused — by a power greater than himself. This is a crucial yet difficult issue for any impersonalist aesthetic, and it cannot be resolved easily. I intend to illuminate this question by reconsidering the four stages in the narrative of vocation.

As indicated above, the initial call in the quadrature of vocation involves a summons from the world beyond to an individual in the here-and-now — a summons that cannot be ignored or refused.[19] A god or spirit may call the individual selected to be shaman in various ways: by illness or another physical sign, or through a dream or vision. This intervention of the non-human in the human world disrupts quotidian reality, disordering human consciousness through fevers, fugues, hallucinations, dreams. There is something of this consciousness-altering shift at the very beginning of "Endless Streams and Mountains," the opening poem of Snyder's book — "Clearing the mind and sliding in / to that created space" (M&R 5) — as well as in more explicitly hallucinatory dream-poems in the book's first section, such as "The Elwha River," a poem that, dating from 1958, was one of the first to be composed of *Mountains and Rivers Without End*. It is this impersonal summons that Paz is referring to when he speaks of "the *other* voice," a voice whose call initiates poetic and shamanic vocation alike.

The radical otherness of this voice is dramatized especially well in "The Hump-backed Flute Player," where the speaker receives messages across enormous distances of time and space. This poem's representing the origin of voice in prose form indicates Snyder's awareness of the ordering of poetic vocation:

> In Canyon de Chelly on the north wall up by a cave is the
> hump-backed flute player lying on his back, playing his flute.
> Across the flat sandy canyon wash, wading a stream and breaking
> through the ice, on the south wall, the pecked-out pictures of
> some mountain sheep with curling horns. They stood in the icy
> shadow of the south wall two hundred feet away; I sat with my
> shirt off in the sun facing south, with the hump-backed flute
> player just above my head. They whispered. I whispered. Back
> and forth across the canyon, clearly heard.   (M&R 80)

Here the speaker is summoned to be a poet — a flute-player — by the symbolic power of the sheep carved into the canyon wall (these sheep reappear in the poem "Arctic Midnight Twilight" [M&R 92-95]). The vocational call is impersonal, coming not from a person or even a personified figure but from a nonhuman form. This call's origin in "the pecked-out pictures of some mountain sheep" seems to me doubly significant, since it points to both the animal realm and the realm of art: both the petroglyphs of sheep and the ancient Chinese painting that initiates the poem "Endless Streams and Mountains" represent other artworks as the origin of vocation. This

suggests that our relations to the natural realm and to art may take prece-
dence over interpersonal relations. In an aesthetic where the vocational sum-
mons hails from ancient petroglyphs of sheep, we can see the coordinates
for what Snyder describes as "an ethic that goes beyond intrahuman obli-
gations and includes nonhuman nature" (APIS 77). With vocation comes a
new kind of ethical relationality.

The vocational scene of "The Hump-backed Flute Player" imagines the
poet's summoning in the form of a whisper, which suggests that considerable
attentiveness is necessary to hear the call of poetic vocation, since it usually
comes impersonally, from the nonhuman world — from the sea, from a bird,
or from sheep. A mere whisper from the nonhuman realm requires substan-
tial reorientation of one's listening in order to catch; it requires an openness
to voices other than the human and therefore entails an enlarged conception
of voice, an expanded sense of who or what might have something signifi-
cant to say. This kind of openness to the nonhuman or impersonal repre-
sents a first stage in transforming human relations with the world around us.

Snyder's imagery of whispering recalls Whitman's great poem of voca-
tion, "Out of the Cradle Endlessly Rocking," where the poet's mission is
conveyed also by a "whisper," this time from the sea. In his response to the
call of poetic vocation, Whitman gives us some of the most powerful lines
in American poetry, lines that illuminate the distinct call-and-response pat-
terns of *Mountains and Rivers Without End*:

> For I, that was a child, my tongue's use sleeping, now I have
>   heard you,
> Now in a moment I know what I am for, I awake,
> And already a thousand singers, a thousand songs, clearer, louder
>   and more sorrowful than yours,
> A thousand warbling echoes have started to life within me, never
>   to die.[20]

Whitman's speaker makes clear that the second vector of vocation's quad-
ripartite structure involves the solicited individual's calling back to the
power that singled him out — "now I have heard you, / Now in a moment I
know what I am for." Recognizing that the inarticulate sounds he has heard

constitute a summons, he sings antiphonally, back to the mysterious source. This singing or whispering back to an impersonal realm is the decisive act that transforms the individual from an ordinary member of the human community into a poet or shaman — recall Eliade's report on shaman Tüspüt's initiation, "he began to sing, and felt better."

Whitman's characterization of his response to vocation is particularly striking in its picturing all the speaker's poetry as "warbling echoes" of that original call. If all his poems come into being as echoes of a voice other than the individual poet's, then even his most personal lyrics retain a fundamental impersonality. Furthermore, this "other voice" inscribes the narrative of vocation into every poem. Snyder's speaker whispering "[b]ack and forth across the canyon" offers an image of this poetic principle in action, as well as a model of the structure of his book as a whole, since *Mountains and Rivers Without End* comprises a complex set of calls and responses between different voices, cultures, and nonhuman beings.

It is crucial to register heterogeneous vectors of this call-and-response structure, because the poem's polyphony of antiphonal voices depends on the authorizing whispers of nonhuman beings — the pictographs of sheep and ancient bristlecone pine, in "The Hump-backed Flute Player," and the Mountain Spirit, in the poem of that title (M&R 140–47). In my account of Snyder, I avoid critically fashionable explanations of this verbal phenomenon, such as those deriving from Bakhtin's theory of dialogism, because such explanations typically fail to distinguish horizontal from vertical vectors of call and response. By contrast, Grossman's account of vocation argues that its third and fourth vectors repeat on the horizontal, secular level the vertical dialogue of vocation and invocation previously described. Having been summoned by nonhuman reality (vocation — vector 1) and tacitly accepted this summons by responding to it (invocation — vector 2), the poet calls out to the people, to human reality (vector 3), and receives from them a commission (or not) by way of reply (vector 4).

Likewise, the shaman sings first of his encounters with spirits and his journey to the world of the dead (vocation and invocation); then he sings to the human community and, specifically, to human souls. The narratives of shamanism's and poetry's origins are thus homologous; and, indeed, Eliade views the shaman's descent into the underworld as cognate with the

Orpheus myth, that prototype of poetic origins in the Western world.[21] In "The Mountain Spirit," his book's climactic poem, Snyder follows this pattern in that his dialogue directly engages the spirit world — though the explicitly supernatural status of his interlocutor isn't revealed immediately. Having traveled to a certain elevation at the western edge of the Great Basin to find ancient bristlecone pine trees, the poem's speaker is confronted by a voice in the wilderness:

A voice says

"You had a bit of fame once in the city
for poems of mountains,
      here it's real."

What?

"Yes. Like the lines

    Walking on walking
    under foot   earth turns

But what do you know of minerals and stone.
For a creature to speak of all that scale of time — what for?
Still, I'd like to hear that poem."

        I answer back,
" — Tonight is the night of the shooting stars,
Mirfak the brilliant star of Perseus
    crosses the ridge at midnight

I'll read it then."

      Who am I talking to? I think,
walk back to camp.   (M&R 141–42)

Here the mysterious voice quotes back to the poet his own lines in the form
of a challenge — "what do you know of minerals and stone . . . ?" Urged thus
into singing, the speaker reproduces a poem called "The Mountain Spirit,"
which appears typographically set off by different fonts in the larger poem
of that title (M&R 143–46). Immediately following the interpolated poem,
we read:

> The Mountain Spirit whispers back:
> "All art and song
> is sacred to the real.
> As such."
>
> Bristlecone pines live long
> on the taste of carbonate,
>   dolomite,
>
> spiraled standing coiling
> dead wood with the living,
> four thousand years of mineral glimmer
> spaced out growing in the icy airy sky
> white bones under summer stars.   (M&R 146–47)

The reply to the speaker's poem comes in the form of a whisper, which con-
firms, among other things, the significance of whispering in the earlier voca-
tional scene at Canyon de Chelly. Furthermore, this reply comes from the
Mountain Spirit herself, as if the poem had conjured her into being analo-
gously to how the unidentified voice provoked the interpolated poem's rec-
itation. And this exchange of voices takes place in the neighborhood of the
bristlecone pines, whose great age (some of them are over four thousand
years old) makes them representatives of natural immortality. While in "The
Hump-backed Flute Player" the bristlecone pines "whisper" like supernat-
ural beings, in "The Mountain Spirit" they stand as venerable witnesses to
whispering by a more overtly supernatural agent.

The words spoken by the Mountain Spirit constitute a kind of aphorism, riddle, or kōan marking judgment on shamanic practice: "All art and song / is sacred to the real. / As such." By specifying art and song together, these lines emphasize the performative dimension of aesthetic practices over their merely representative functions. And by designating *all* such art as sacred, the Mountain Spirit generously sanctifies — and thus authorizes — a vast sphere of performance quite independently of any hierarchy of aesthetic or cultural forms. If, following Eliade, sacralization depends upon singularization, then the Mountain Spirit's announcement multiplies singularization in the paradoxical guise of a distinctly nonsecular pluralism. The paradox of this inclusive sacralization is only intensified by the second half of the kōan: not only is all art sacred, but it is so "to the real. / As such." Rather than the sacred and the real being mutually exclusive, they appear as mutually supporting and, indeed, thoroughly imbricated. In this view, the sacred is not metaphysical but materially present in the physical world; therefore, the Mountain Spirit implies, it would be pointless to try to transcend the material in search of the spiritual. The sacred isn't even concealed within physical phenomena — as in a pantheistic conception of the universe — so much as it is coterminous with physical phenomena, once we approach the natural world with the right attitude.

This antidualistic perspective characterizes Snyder's treatment of the bristlecone pines, which, as the oldest living beings, he regards as sacred. Though an organic life form, these trees appear immortal, godlike, by virtue of their great age — "four thousand years of mineral glimmer" — which locates them in a planetary rather than human timeframe. Nevertheless, these trees' sacred status does not exist somewhere beyond or apart from their tangible existence; rather it lies in their very materiality — "spiraled standing coiling / dead wood with the living." This image of intertwining "dead wood with the living" resonates with the notion of the sacred and the real imbricated on a single ontological plane. It also provides an image of the deep continuity — between all living beings, as well as across generations — that represents such an important theme in *Mountains and Rivers Without End*.

∽

The bristlecone pine appears also in "The Hump-backed Flute Player" to show the crucial role that vocation plays in sustaining this kind of deep continuity — what Grossman calls the "master-story . . . of the maintenance of the intelligibility of the human world by symbols." Reprising the whispering motif from earlier in the poem, the final section of "The Hump-backed Flute Player" reads:

> Up in the mountains that edge the Great Basin
>
>> it was whispered to me
>> by the oldest of trees.
>
>> By the Oldest of Beings
>> the Oldest of Trees
>
>> Bristlecone Pine.
>
>> And all night long sung on
>>> by a young throng
>
>> of Pinyon Pine.   (M&R 82)

In this passage we can distinguish different vectors of antiphony, different directions of call and response, since unlike earlier in the poem we are not presented with a scene of whispering "back and forth" between the nonhuman world and the speaker. Instead, the poem's speaker is here simply a relay point between other voices. Hence we do not learn what was whispered, only that "it was whispered to me": we are told the vector, not the content, of this communication.

Correlative to the speaker's registering these sounds as a message is his emphasizing the trees' venerable status by capitalizing "Oldest of Trees" the second time around, so that this phrase becomes not merely descriptive but honorific, a title. These lines mimic the phenomenon they describe, in that the repetition of "the oldest of trees. // By the Oldest of Beings / the Oldest of Trees" creates an echo akin to the echo of whispering throughout the night that the poem relates. Furthermore, the intensified sonic qualities that characterize these closing lines — the alliteration, as well as the internal rhymes and echoes set ringing by the monosyllabic "[a]nd all night long sung on / by a young throng" — generate a sense of the pinyon pines' song. It is the trees rather than the poet who sings, even though he functions as a vector of their song.

The significance of the call-and-response arrangement's involving more than two parties — bristlecone pine, pinyon pine, and poetic speaker — lies in how this multiplication of vectors enables the dissemination outward of a certain knowledge, beyond the self-enclosed mirroring relation of self and other. Since what is whispered comes from "the oldest of trees" and is "sung on / by a young throng," we have here an image of transmission across generations, in which the human speaker is only tangentially the agent of transmission. In this instance the call-and-response structure is far from intersubjective or dialogic: it concerns not the speaker's relationally constructed identity, but the counter-recognition that nonhuman forms exist in responsive relation to each other independently of human intervention. Hence the speaker's role in this relational web entails not so much creating responses as scrupulously noticing "calls" and witnessing others' responses to them.

This modified version of antiphony provides the structural principle for Snyder's book as a whole, since *Mountains and Rivers Without End* can be read as a series of responses — "warbling echoes," in Whitman's words — to the original mute call of the twelfth-century Chinese scroll painting that initiates the book. The poet's work consists in making apparant — by taking other people's words, framing and juxtaposing them — how certain ideas, images, and utterances *are* responses. This compositional principle explains Snyder's commitment to quoting the colophons on the Chinese scroll, following his ekphrastic meditation on the painting itself. The painting, titled *Streams and Mountains Without End*, has accumulated a series of responses, some of them poems, which Snyder quotes in his book's proem:

> At the end of the painting the scroll continues on with seals and poems. It tells a further tale:

> " — Wang Wen-wei saw this at the mayor's house in Ho-tung

town, year 1205. Wrote at the end of it,
    'The Fashioner of Things
        has no original intentions
    Mountains and rivers
        are spirit, condensed.'

    '... Who has come up with
        these miraculous forests and springs?
    Pale ink
        on fine white silk.'   (M&R 7)

This colophon provides the identity of its author and the location of its inscription, conscious of how these identifying details contrast with the essentially anonymous provenance of the original painting—"Who has come up with / these miraculous forests and springs?" Snyder's note on the poem observes that "[a] hand scroll by this name showed up in Shansi province, central China, in the thirteenth century. Even then the painter was unknown, 'a person of the Sung Dynasty'" (M&R 9). Since in the model of vocation I've outlined the inaugural call originates anonymously and hence impersonally, it seems fitting that we know who responds to the painting but not who made it in the first place.

    In the collectivist aesthetic tradition from which the painting derives, the poems that follow it are understood to be *part of* the painting. According to Snyder, "the painting is not fully realized until several centuries of poems have been added" (M&R 159). Structured antiphonally, the impersonalist work of art calls out for responses, and *Mountains and Rivers Without End* itself constitutes a fully measured response, almost half a century's worth of meditation on the continuing significance of this artwork for a very different historical, geographical, and cultural context. Snyder takes his cue from Wang Wen-wei, a poet in the classical Chinese tradition, who contributes not only a poetic response, but one that is itself structured antiphonally, as a sort of poetic Q & A:

    '... Who has come up with
        these miraculous forests and springs?

Pale ink
    on fine white silk.'

Raising then deflecting the question of origins, this poem ingeniously points by way of answer to an image at once of writing and of painting. The haiku-like phrase "Pale ink / on fine white silk" provides an image of calligraphy that underscores the artifactual status of "these miraculous forests and springs" — the fact that they are a product of representation. Not only this, but the saying so in an antiphonal poem that itself responds to the painting emphasizes how the continuity or endlessness of streams and mountains depends in part on representational continuity — or, in other words, on cultural transmission.

This image of transmission between generations is cognate with that scene in "The Hump-backed Flute Player" where the speaker witnesses the bristlecone pine whispering something "sung on / by a young throng // of Pinyon Pine." In these images of continuity between generations, the poet functions merely as a placeholder, a link in the chain connecting nonhuman forms. The human speaker's place in each instance suggests that, strangely enough, the nonsubjective forms of art and of nonhuman nature occupy comparable — though not identical — ontological status. Furthermore, this process of transmission impersonalizes its human witness, minimizing his personal individuality in favor of a nonanthropocentric web of relations. We might say that the speaker is de-egoized, an outcome that corresponds to one strand of high modernist aesthetic practice, as well as to the spiritual discipline of Zen Buddhism.

Along with the human speaker's de-egoization, it is striking how nonhuman forms in these poems resist personification — though there remains a hint of anthropomorphism in attributing to trees activities such as whispering and singing. Of course, we speak of birds singing without thereby necessarily personifying them; and *whispering* is a semantically capacious verb that can describe literally the sounds made by non-sentient beings, as well as by humans. My hesitation on this question stems from a reluctance to adjudicate too quickly whether the attribution of voice is necessarily anthropomorphizing. This is a persistent issue in Snyder's work, since his attempts to give nonhuman nature dignity, parity, and full consideration continually come

up against the challenge of how this may be accomplished without human-
izing the natural world in the manner of, say, Romantic poetry.

Part of the difficulty here lies in the idiomatic assumption that according
any entity a share in political processes is tantamount to giving that entity "a
voice." Yet the larger difficulty involves an anthropocentric presumption that
only personifiable entities warrant human consideration in the first place.
Snyder addressed these challenges directly in a 1976 interview:

> When [Whitman] says there should be more democracy, I go
> along with that. We all see what more democracy means, too. It
> means that the Navajo should get their own nation, that Rosebud
> and Pine Ridge maybe should be a separate nation, that the
> Indians of Puget Sound have fishing rights, that trees and rocks
> should be able to vote in Congress, that whales should be able to
> vote — that's democracy.   (TRW 74)

The startling idea that political enfranchisement be extended to the natural
world is one outcome of the desire to give nonhuman forms a voice. At this
point in the interview Snyder's interlocutor, Paul Geneson, quite reasonably
asks, "But who votes for them? How do they vote?" In response Snyder con-
siders two intriguing possibilities, one juridical, the other poetic:

> Well, Christopher Stone, in his essay "Should Trees Have
> Standing?" said legalistically it's very simple — the court appoints
> someone to be their representative. Like someone to be the
> spokesman for the yellow pine-black oak communities of
> Northern California and Southern Oregon. That's a possibility.
> Legally, this is not out of line: it would be analogous to the court
> appointing someone, a lawyer, to speak for a minor. . . .
>
> Actually, that's not so interesting. We can see it has been one
> of the jobs of poetry to speak for these things, to carry their voice
> into the human realm. That it *is* in poetry and in song and in
> ritual and in certain kinds of dance drama that the nonhuman
> realms have been able to speak to the human society. There are
> large numbers of people who don't have an ear for that anymore,
> although once we all had an ear for it.   (TRW 74)

Here again the implicit model of poetry is shamanistic and comports with the notion that a poet-shaman functions as intermediary between nonhuman nature and the human community. In this model of poetry it is not so much a matter of self-expression as it is of opening channels of communication and articulating the otherness of nonhuman nature. Rather than self-expression, we would have something akin to other-expression. Giving voice to the other rather than to oneself need not be anthropomorphizing, so long as otherness is conceived outside an intersubjective perspective — so long, that is, as the other is not conceived as another person. From Snyder's point of view, we need to learn how to treat nonhuman nature as an equal participant in our world without having to personify it. His poetry facilitates our seeing from a nonanthropocentric perspective and exploits impersonalist poetic techniques in pursuit of this ethical goal.

Poetry remains central rather than incidental to this project for at least two reasons. First, as suggested, poetry involves accessing "the other voice." Second, poems provide models of attentiveness by dramatizing the process of attending to one's surroundings. The practice of reading poems carefully, line by line, also dramatizes the process of paying acute attention to a web of relations between voices and their verbal environment. In this respect, the activity of reading a Snyder poem shares much in common with the activity of making that poem, since Snyder's elliptical, paratactic, quietly allusive style compels his readers to discern relations and make hitherto unseen connections between entities in the poem. Reading Snyder we begin to inhabit a point of view in which neither the author nor any other human figure is necessarily central. Ecological consciousness can thus be understood as profoundly impersonal.

∾

Yet the line of argument I'm pursuing here fails to resolve fully the issue of speaking on behalf of others. Far from being a new problem, this feature of poetic practice nevertheless has been viewed with growing suspicion in recent decades. "[T]he poet is representative," declared Emerson in his mid-nineteenth-century idealist meditation on the nature of the poetic function:

> He stands among partial men for the complete man, and apprises
> us not of his wealth, but of the commonwealth. . . . The poet is
> the person in whom these powers are in balance, the man
> without impediment, who sees and handles that which others
> dream of, traverses the whole scale of experience, and is represen-
> tative of man, in virtue of being the largest power to receive and
> to impart.[22]

Emerson, like Snyder, conceived the poet's representative function in explic-
itly sociopolitical terms. Though he never went so far as to recommend
giving the vote to animals, rocks, and trees, Emerson did view the poet's cul-
tural role as inherently political. But what in the nineteenth century Emer-
son considered poetry's chief political advantage, in the twentieth century
we have grown increasingly to mistrust. The claim that the poet speaks
on behalf of the rest of us sounds dubious to postmodern ears, because it
appears riven with potential for abuses of power. We see the white, hetero-
sexual, male poet and wonder how he could possibly speak for constituen-
cies other than his own. Contrary to Snyder's point, in the interview quoted
above, concerning an expansion of democracy, this idea that the poet speaks
for us seems exclusionary and therefore decidedly undemocratic. Unfortu-
nately, insisting on the good faith and unimpeachable character of this or
that particular poet is largely irrelevant to the problem, just as the personal
deficiencies and noxious politics of modernism's greatest poetic innovators
also remain ultimately irrelevant to this issue.

The problem is not individual, but structural. It is a question not of per-
sonalities — honorable or deplorable — but, precisely, of impersonality. I've
tried to suggest that the value of shamanism as a model for understanding
impersonalist poetics lies in its emphasis on the structural feature of *speak-
ing through*, instead of the more conventional enunciative structure of self-
expression. A shamanist or impersonalist conception of poetic utterance
involves finding "the other voice" rather than one's own. Hence it is not
so much a question of speaking *on behalf of* the other as it is of opening a
conduit through which the other — including the otherness of nonhuman
nature — may speak. This distinction helps explain why, in some cultures,
shamans have access to far greater verbal and symbolic resources than other

members of the population. Eliade notes that "[t]he poetic vocabulary of a Yakut shaman contains 12,000 words, whereas the ordinary language — the only language known to the rest of the community — has only 4,000."[23] The shaman utters things that other people are incapable of saying, and hence, in his dramatically enlarged poetic capacity, the Yakut shaman embodies Emerson's ideal poet.[24]

We may get a sense of how this structural distinction between *speaking on behalf of* and *speaking through* plays out in Snyder's work by observing that more than one third of the poems in *Mountains and Rivers Without End* close with somebody else's voice. Sometimes this is indicated explicitly by means of quotation marks — for example, the line "'Your Bubbs Creek haircut, boy'" (M&R 38) that ends the early poem "Bubbs Creek Haircut" — and sometimes it remains implicit. In some cases, the whole poem is cast in another's voice, whether in the form of a persona — for example, the girl who speaks "The Elwha River" (M&R 32) — or in the form of a "found poem" such as "Mā" (M&R 57–60), which takes the guise of a letter and begins "Hello Boy—," thus counterpointing the ending of "Bubbs Creek Haircut." In these and other instances, it appears that one aspect of Snyder's poetic impersonality consists in the ethical imperative to let somebody else have the last word.

Nevertheless, this conception of poetry remains open to the charge that incorporating within a poem voices other than the author's own constitutes misappropriation or cultural thievery. This objection seems especially plausible when the relation between the poet's and others' voices is characterized by an imbalance of power — when, for example, the other voices that a white male poet includes in his work are those of Native Americans and East Asians. In such a case, it can be hard to distinguish between an ethically salutary commitment to letting others *speak through* the poetry, on one hand, and an ethically troubling tendency to *appropriate* nonwhite cultural traditions, on the other.

Here the impersonalist aesthetic verges on the issue of cultural imperialism, a form of aggression that could be understood, in the U.S. context, as repeating on a verbal and symbolic plane the geographical and economic expansionism that propelled North America's colonization in the first place. From this point of view, the impulse to regard poetry in shamanist terms would be just one more instance of cultural imperialism, an extension of the ethnological project of "collecting" (read: misappropriating) artifacts and knowledge from indigenous cultures. As Native American critic Geary Hobson put it when attacking "white shamanism" in the 1970s, "[t]he current fad in some small magazines of poets calling themselves 'poet-shamans' or even 'shamans' is another counterpart of the Indian craft exploiters, the imperious anthropologists, and the buffalo hunters."[25] Furthermore, the very model of shamanism I've used in my account thus far is often guilty of colonialist assumptions vis-à-vis the "primitive" cultural practices it purports to explain. We might even say that the discipline that teaches us about shamanism is inextricably bound up with the history and ideologies of colonialism, and that Western ways of knowing this material are irrevocably contaminated. Disparities of power between whites and the indigenous populations they investigate inevitably compromise the epistemological models generated by such investigations, be they anthropological, ethnological, literary, or artistic. According to this perspective, any interest in "the primitive" is suspect.[26]

Versions of this critique have been leveled, albeit often clumsily, at Snyder and his work. There has been more discussion of his use of Native American materials than of his East Asian commitments, though Hobson charges that the two often go together — that when one encounters white shamanism, the additional menace of Orientalism isn't far behind: "the contemporary writers, especially the 'white shamans,' too often perceive Indian cultures through not only the rose-colored glasses of a white, Anglo-Saxon Protestant viewpoint, but the day-glo spectacles of a hastily assumed Oriental (Buddhist, Taoist, etc.) outlook" (103). In other words, the attraction to Native American and to East Asian cultures usually stems from the same exoticist impulse: a drive to romanticize other, more "primitive" cultures and to use mystified images of them in consolidating one's own Westernized identity, rather than attempting to understand the mundane reality of other cultures in their own terms.[27]

Now the fact that Snyder spent a decade in Japan training in a Zen Buddhist temple renders him immune from the charge of having "hastily assumed" his Buddhist outlook. And, indeed, Hobson largely exempts Snyder from his fierce polemic, suggesting that even though it spawned the problem of white shamanism, Snyder's work should not be understood as part of that problem:

> The "white shaman" fad seems to have begun inadvertently with Gary Snyder in his "Shaman Songs" sections of *Myths and Texts*, in which the poet speaks through the persona of an Indian shaman, and his words become calls to power, of a sort, which in and of itself is innocuous enough, since poetry of this kind does seek to transcend the mundane in such a way that people's lives are revivified. The poems contain great vitality and are, I believe, sincere efforts on Snyder's behalf to incorporate an essential part of American Indian philosophy into his work. Importantly, nowhere does Snyder refer to himself as a "shaman." But, along came the bastard children of Snyder who began to imitate him, especially in the Shaman Songs section, and not being content with that, began to call themselves shamans — which, as I understand it, Snyder still refuses to do.[28]

Snyder's sincerity on this issue can hardly be in doubt. He began experimenting with shamanism as a model for poetry early in the 1950s, over a decade before the white shamanism fashion emerged, and he's pursued this poetic mode for almost half a century, long after it ceased to be in vogue. However, Snyder's indubitable good faith doesn't resolve the broader questions raised by Hobson's critique. Along with Leslie Marmon Silko, whose "Old-Time Indian Attack" singled out Snyder's *Turtle Island* shortly after it won the Pulitzer Prize, Hobson claims that only Native Americans can write legitimately about Native American matters, and that white writers should stick to exploring their own cultural heritages and their own Caucasian identities.

Though she refrains from discussing shamanism, Silko's critique is particularly germane to my account of impersonalist ethics and aesthetics. She connects Snyder's poetic allusions to Native American myths with turn-of-the-century white ethnologists' collecting verbal artifacts from Native American tribes, and she points out the racist assumptions at work in those ethnographic collection projects. "Fifty years later," Silko claims, "this racist assumption is thriving; it flourishes among white poets and writers who romanticize their 'power' as writers to inhabit souls and consciousness far beyond the realms of their own knowledge or experience."[29] Here the very basis of aesthetic impersonality is dismissed as racist — though impersonality demands not that its practitioners inhabit but that they be inhabited, even possessed, by other "souls and consciousness far beyond realms of their own knowledge and experience." This distinction aside, Silko's charge of racism makes clear what's at stake in both her critique and Hobson's: the authority of experience, the idea that one can speak and write authoritatively only of things that have befallen him or her — and, by extension, befallen the community or tribe to which he or she most immediately belongs. It isn't hard to see why disenfranchised groups have recourse to this argument when they see their cultures being described with greater authority — though often less knowledge — by "outsiders," and when, adding insult to injury, they see their own "insider" accounts disparaged for failing to confirm the images promoted by "outsider" accounts. As Michael Castro observes, "[c]ultural arrogance, neo-romanticism, literary careerism, and a failure to recognize and respect the Indian's contemporary reality have been part and parcel of American writers' interest in the Indian throughout the century."[30]

Having acknowledged the validity of such critiques, I nevertheless cannot fail to register the absurdity of their implications, since if one were to adhere to the stricture of writing primarily from experience, all literature would be reduced to an autobiographical function, and nobody would be able to write authoritatively about temporally distant cultures.[31] This kind of ethnic essentialism — which we see in a comparatively crude form in Hobson's and Silko's essays from the 1970s, but which is widespread in more sophisticated forms today — views literature as a vehicle for self-expression and thereby denies the possibility of any encounter with otherness in poetry. To argue in the face of these critiques that Snyder has extensive experience with Zen Buddhism and is steeped in Native American mythology completely misses the point, since this way of arguing doesn't challenge the basic assumption that poetry is simply a heightened form of self-expression and therefore is necessarily composed from its author's experience. According to this way of thinking, writing and reading literature are exercises in self-exploration and can be understood as cultural practices that consolidate one's individual or group identity. This view of literature is found in not only marginal and disenfranchised populations, but is so pervasive today as to qualify as hegemonic.

By contrast, aesthetic impersonality entails a quite different view of the literary, one in which the author's individual or group identity is subordinated in favor of opening the self to others — and, more broadly, to realms of otherness, including nonhuman nature, that have no function whatsoever in shoring up one's self-identity. I find this contrasting view ethically preferable because it treats the literary as a realm in which otherness is given airtime — in which nonhuman nature gains a voice — rather than as a realm in which my own voice, identity, and self are fortified.[32] Impersonalist aesthetic practice is not about incorporating, romanticizing, or otherwise appropriating otherness in order to constitute the self. Indeed, an authentic encounter with otherness may well prove thoroughly inimical to the project of identity-construction. Hence Silko drastically misconstrues the purpose of Snyder's impersonalist poetics when she concludes that "[t]he writing of imitation 'Indian' poems[,] then, is pathetic evidence that in more than two hundred years, Anglo-Americans have failed to create a satisfactory identity for themselves."[33] Snyder is not remotely interested in identity, and his work makes little sense in terms of the proliferating theories of identity currently popular in both academia and the wider culture. Unlike a lot of contemporary literature, his writing is not about selfhood.

Instead, Snyder's work exhibits a deep concern with forms of continuity among living beings, and it treats even the nonsentient natural world as part of a web of interdependence that connects human beings to nonhuman nature. Preoccupied with continuity and connection, Snyder does not see the world in terms of bounded — or even mobile — identities. Rather than the enhanced self-definition that comes with personal and cultural identity, his poetry encourages a kind of self-dispossession that comes with opening the self to otherness, particularly the radical otherness of the nonhuman. This self-dispossession should not be understood in terms of a postmodernist dissolution of the Cartesian subject among the simulacra of cultural forms. Rather, what I'm calling self-dispossession represents simply the precondition for transforming human relationships with nonhuman nature. Snyder is interested in transforming not only particular relationships — for example, land management in the Pacific Northwest — but relationality as such. He wants us to see our place in the world completely differently than we usually do.

Equivocally instrumental though it may be, poetry remains central to this transformative project, because poems entail accessing otherness — or what Paz characterizes as "the other voice." Snyder pushes this dimension of poetic practice further than most contemporary poets, because he tries to access voices of not only other persons but also nonhuman forms too. Speaking of Japanese epic literature, Snyder has referred to this practice as "interspecies communication," a term that suggests just how radically he aspires to transform relationality. "In the tales of the Ainu, who were the indigenous people of Japan and who still live in the north, gods and animals speak in the first person as well as human beings, and the several worlds of sense experience and imagination are knit together" (APIS 95). When nonhuman forms speak in the first person — not *like* humans, but *as well as* us — human perspectives on nature alter drastically and, consequently, our relationships with the world around us shift seismically too.

Far-reaching as this nonanthropocentric notion of interspecies communication is, Snyder has proposed an even more radical transformation of relationality in his idea of "trans-species erotics":

> The worldwide myths of animal-human marriage, or supernatural-
> human marriage, are evidence of the fascination our ancestors
> had for the possibility of full membership in a biotic erotic
> universe. I suspect that many of the problems within the human
> community — racism and sexism, to name two — reflect back
> from confusion about our relation to nature. Ignorance and
> hostility toward wild nature set us up for objectifying and
> exploiting fellow humans.   (APIS 210–11)

Snyder's suggestion regarding trans-species erotics intuits that to exchange sexual love and intimacy with nonhuman forms would be to admit nature to full participation in our world. We see particularly striking examples of bodily intimacy between humans and animals in the poems "Under the Hills Near the Morava River" and "The Bear Mother" (M&R 96 and 113). If the idea of trans-species erotics sounds outrageous or risible, then such responses indicate just how far we are from treating nonhuman nature with equality.

The notion of trans-species erotics furnishes us with an image of what fully impersonal relationality would look like, and it suggests a mode of connecting with the nonhuman based not on meaning — with its lingering potential for personifying the natural world — but on being. It's not by humanizing nature or personalizing our relationships with it that we treat nonhuman nature ethically, but, on the contrary, by impersonalizing our relationships with it and thus effectively dehumanizing (or "de-egoizing") ourselves. The idea of trans-species erotics conjures up a form of relationality that is simultaneously impersonal — since it involves relating to something that isn't a person — and yet fully intimate.[34]

Although Snyder's explanation of racism and sexism, in the passage quoted above, appears superficial, it nevertheless carries the profound implication that our ethical relation to other persons is predicated on our ethical relation to an impersonal realm — in this case, nature — rather than the reverse. Snyder's commitment to aesthetic impersonality is, at bottom, ethical. In *Mountains and Rivers Without End* we encounter an aesthetic mode, that of poetic impersonality, put into the service of negotiating the kind of ethical questions that religious philosopher Emmanuel Levinas wrestled with — namely, how to accord full respect to the other without humanizing it, without making the other just like me. This is why Snyder's de-anthropomorphizing perspective remains so valuable, since his long poem exemplifies the principle that one accords respect to others not because they're other persons, just like him- or herself, but precisely because they're not.

NOTES

1. I am grateful to the Stanford Humanities Center, and its director, Keith Baker, for the residential fellowship supporting my research, and for sponsoring the Mountains & Rivers Workshop. The participants in that workshop, especially its convenor, Mark Gonnerman, formed an ideal community in which to study the poem and its multiple contexts.

2. Octavio Paz, *The Other Voice: Essays on Modern Poetry*, trans. Helen Lane (New York: Harcourt Brace Jovanovich, 1991), 151.

3. "The unconscious is the discourse of the Other" is one of French psychoanalyst Jacques Lacan's best known axioms, his formula for redefining the Freudian unconscious in terms of language.

4. William Butler Yeats, "A General Introduction for My Work" (1937) in *Essays and*

Introductions (New York: Macmillan, 1961), 501. Here we should recall that Yeats, like Snyder, was influenced significantly by Nō theater, particularly the use of masks, whose function lies partly in emphasizing that the words spoken by the actor or poet are not his own. This fact is obvious in theater, if not in poetry; so perhaps we should stress that the mask functions to remind the audience that, more fundamentally, the actor's or poet's *voice* is not his own. The mask represents both a vocal technology and a material sign differentiating the actor's body and voice from the voice and words that, by means of the mask, speak through him. In his notes on the poem, Snyder connects Nō theater to shamanism and to his own poetic technique: "Nō is a gritty but totally refined high-culture art that is in the lineage of shamanistic performance, a drama that by means of voice and dance calls forth the spirit realms. I began to envision *Mountains and Rivers* through the dramatic strategies of Nō" (M&R 155).

5. Snyder quotes this line differently elsewhere: "Though the nation is lost, the mountains and rivers remain" (TRW 74).

6. Snyder's long note on Kokop'ele provides a good deal of useful information without making the figure's connection to poetry explicit: "Ancient rock art — petroglyphs — of a walking flute-playing figure, sometimes with a hump on his back, are found widely in the Southwest and into Mexico. These images are several thousand years old. There is a Hopi secret society that takes the Flute-player as its emblem" (M&R 160). This information suggests just how widespread, ancient, and resonant the figure is. Like the shaman, Kokop'ele fulfills a range of functions and thus represents the expanded sense of poetic role that Snyder derives from premodern cultural traditions. In those traditions and in Snyder's poem Kokop'ele is iconic, and Snyder has punctuated *Mountains and Rivers Without End* with pictographs of this figure, his own version of the petroglyph.

7. Snyder's work has been discussed in terms of shamanism appreciatively by Tom Henighan, "Shamans, Tribes, and the Sorcerer's Apprentices: Notes on the Discovery of the Primitive in Modern Poetry," *Dalhousie Review* 59/4 (1980): 605–20, and critically by Geary Hobson, "The Rise of White Shamanism as a New Version of Cultural Imperialism," in Hobson, ed., *The Remembered Earth: An Anthology of Contemporary Native American Literature* (Albuquerque: University of New Mexico Press, 1981), 100–08 and Leslie Marmon Silko, "An Old-Time Indian Attack Conducted in Two Parts," in Hobson, ed., *The Remembered Earth*, 211–16. I engage these critiques toward the end of this paper. Neither those who praise nor those who blame Snyder for his ostensible shamanism consider the issue of poetic impersonality.

8. Mircea Eliade, *Shamanism: Archaic Techniques of Ecstasy*, trans. Willard R. Trask (New York: Bollingen, 1964), 27 (emphasis added).

9. Eliade, *Shamanism*, 28. See also Claude Lévi-Strauss on the medical efficacy of singing in shamanic cultures in "The Effectiveness of Symbols," *Structural Anthropology*, Vol. 1, trans. Claire Jacobson and Brooke Grundfest Schoepf (New York: Basic Books, 1963), 186–205.

10. J. L. Austin, *How to Do Things With Words* (Cambridge: Harvard University Press, 1962).

11. On the injurious power of words, see, for example, Judith Butler, *Excitable Speech: A Politics of the Performative* (New York: Routledge, 1997) and Elaine Scarry, *The Body in Pain: The Making and Unmaking of the World* (New York: Oxford University Press, 1985).

12. Allen Grossman, "My *Caedmon*: Thinking about Poetic Vocation," in *The Long Schoolroom: Lessons in the Bitter Logic of the Poetic Principle* (Ann Arbor: University of Michigan Press, 1997), 7.

13. Grossman, "My *Caedmon*," 7–8.

14. Eliade, *Shamanism*, 32.

15. Eliade, *Shamanism*, 23.

16. In a related account of English lyric poetry, Susan Stewart shows how poems may be said to be possessed or haunted by the metrical forms of their predecessors. Though her interpretive model is psychoanalytic (deriving from Nicholas Abraham and Maria Torok's theories of psychical encryption) rather than anthropological, Stewart's brilliant account of formal possession illuminates the problem of shamanic singing as well as that of singing in the Western ballad tradition. See her essay, "Lyric Possession," *Critical Inquiry* 22/1 (1995): 34–63.

17. T. S. Eliot, "Tradition and the Individual Talent" (1919), in *Selected Prose of T. S. Eliot*, ed. Frank Kermode (New York: Harcourt Brace Jovanovich, 1988), 38.

18. Although the issue of Eliot's proto-shamanism is too complex to pursue further here, I have explored it at length in "T. S. Eliot, Famous Clairvoyante," in *T. S. Eliot: Essays on Gender, Sexuality, Desire,* ed. Cassandra Laity and Nancy N. Gish (Cambridge: Cambridge University Press, 2004), 43–65. Among the many unexpected affinities existing between Eliot and Snyder, I would note also how Eliot's axiom, in his primer on impersonality, that "art never improves" ("Tradition and the Individual Talent," 39), is repeated by Snyder in his meditation on prehistoric cave art, "Entering the Fiftieth Millennium," in *The Gary Snyder Reader: Prose, Poetry and Translations, 1952–1998* (Washington, DC: Counterpoint Press, 1999), 393.

19. "A shamanic vocation is obligatory; one cannot refuse it" (Eliade, *Shamanism*, 18).

20. Walt Whitman, "Out of the Cradle Endlessly Rocking" (1859), in *Complete Poetry and Collected Prose*, ed. Justin Kaplan (New York: Library of America, 1982), 392.

21. Eliade, *Shamanism*, 391.

22. Ralph Waldo Emerson, "The Poet" (1844), in *Essays and Lectures*, ed. Joel Porte (New York: Library of America, 1983), 448.

23. Eliade, *Shamanism*, 30.

24. It bears mentioning that while his account of the poet is idealist in the philosophical, neo-Platonic sense, Emerson also is picturing an ideal in the colloquial sense: he's describing an ideal type rather than any particular poet, himself included. "I look in vain for the poet whom I describe," he laments toward the close of his essay (p. 465), having not had the historical opportunity to consider shamanic phenomena.

25. Hobson, "The Rise of White Shamanism," 101. In a related critique, Leslie Marmon Silko puts this point in even stronger terms: "The second implicit racist assumption still abounding is that the prayers, chants, and stories weaseled out by the early white ethnographers, which are now collected in ethnological journals, are public property. Presently, a number of Native American communities are attempting to recover religious objects and other property taken from them in the early 1900s that are now placed in museums. Certainly, the songs and stories which were taken by ethnographers are no different. But, among white poets — Rothenberg and Snyder, to mention the most prominent, the idea that these materials should be left to those tribes and their descendants is unthinkable. White poets cash in on the generosity which many tribes have and still practice; white poets delight in saying 'Indians believe in sharing,' and so they go on 'sharing,' collecting book royalties on plagiarized materials" (Silko, "An Old-Time Indian Attack," 212).

26. For representative critiques that conform to this way of thinking, see Michael Taussig, *Shamanism, Colonialism, and the Wild Man: A Study in Terror and Healing* (Chicago: University of Chicago Press, 1987) and Marianna Torgovnick, *Gone Primitive: Savage Intellects, Modern Lives* (Chicago: University of Chicago Press, 1990).

27. The standard account of this impulse is given in Edward Said, *Orientalism* (New York: Random House, 1978).

28. Hobson, "The Rise of White Shamanism," 105.

29. Silko, "An Old-Time Indian Attack," 211.

30. Michael Castro, *Interpreting the Indian: Twentieth-Century Poets and the Native American* (Albuquerque: University of New Mexico Press, 1983), 162.

31. The classic critique of the authority of experience may be found in Joan W. Scott, "The Evidence of Experience," *Questions of Evidence: Proof, Practice, and Persuasion across the Disciplines*, ed. James Chandler, Arnold I. Davidson, and Harry Harootunian (Chicago: University of Chicago Press, 1994), 363–87. On the issue of how identity-based accounts of literary writing tend to reduce literature to autobiography, see John Guillory, *Cultural Capital: The Problem of Literary Canon Formation* (Chicago: University of Chicago Press, 1993), chapter 1.

32. While it is not possible to develop the connection here, I should note that my alternative conception of literary purpose derives from the ethical philosophy of Emmanuel Levinas. For a helpful introduction to this terrain, see Jill Robbins, *Altered Reading: Levinas and Literature* (Chicago: University of Chicago Press, 1999).

33. Silko, "An Old-Time Indian Attack," 213.

34. My thinking along these lines has been influenced by the theory of impersonal relationality developed in Leo Bersani and Ulysee Dutoit, where relationality is conceived in terms not of the communication of meaning, but the communication of being. See *Caravaggio's Secrets* (Cambridge, MA: MIT Press, 1998).

3

Dharma Shoot-out at the OK Dairy

Some Angles and Aspects of Imagination in Gary Snyder's *Mountains and Rivers Without End*

JIM DODGE

At the risk of flogging the obvious, I've found that the pleasure of reading — particularly reading Gary Snyder — resides in engaging another person's imagination through the medium of language. I would even go whole hog and claim that art, like love, is essentially a collaborative act of imagination, a co-creation. That's why writers, despite fervid delusional ego-insistence to the contrary, eventually come to understand they cannot be better than their best readers. Irascible old Kenneth Rexroth claimed, "The imagination is the organ of communion." The root of *communion* is literally "to share," "to hold in common"; *communication* and *community* spring from the same root. I think *Mountains and Rivers Without End* is, to an important extent, a long meditation on the manifold possibilities of communion with the natural world and offers a "model of mind" for such imaginative explorations.

I take it as a given that it is damnably difficult to talk about imagination, but I've found it useful to employ Jung's schema of centers of perception, or elements, or modalities — and the imagination, if nothing else, is a polymodal proposition. So it's worth noting that these perceptual centers are hardly monolithic categories; there's considerable overlap, collateral associations, intricate feedback loops, unpredictable integrations, leaps and swoons and pratfalls and, as is often the case with the human psyche, more exceptions than rules. Those disclaimers in mind, here's the quick schema of Jung's four centers of perception: the *sensational*, which is physical sensory information — sight, sound, taste, smell, and tactility (if you'll indulge a short digression, I would point out that as I've aged I've come to understand that as a writer, the senses are the one area of perception we most reliably share with an audience, and thus is essential to communication, and in the same vein, direct sensory information, as opposed to hearsay, is the most trustworthy source of high-quality information — after all, as an old ranch hand buddy liked to point out for my edification, the closer you get to the source, the less likely someone has crapped upstream). Anyway, direct sensory info is the first center, followed by the *intellectual*, where raw sensory information and the experiences of others, through experiments or reading or campfire conversation, is organized, tested, and integrated into knowledge; the *emotional*, that whole wild and writhing crossfire realm of feelings, which when — or if — integrated with knowledge produces understanding; and the *spiritual* (Jung also calls it intuition and soul), that realm of natural (or supernatural) essence, the source of immaterial sentience/animation/vitality that when added to understanding gives us wisdom. Simple, really: wisdom only requires the astute integration and proper proportioning and dynamic balancing of all the centers, to which most folks would add that you have to know *when*, since timing is critical, and what's wise today is often tomorrow's folly — though not nearly as often as folly that results from bad information and errors of integration. I'm told there's an axiom among truly accomplished criminals that in the commission of any crime there are always at least fifty variables that must be considered and controlled, and you're a genius if you can imagine twenty-five. But back to cases, since we're really not considering *Mountains and Rivers* as the perfect crime.

While the imagination is most often allied with the spiritual center, to my sense of its capacity for communion it is best configured as the psychic nexus of the four centers, drawing from each and all. Or, since the imagination allows such freedom in the pursuit of communion, think of it as a circle without a center, or a center of cascading synaptic summations, a river threading through the clouds that shroud the mountains' peaks, rain on your face, or a created space called "Endless Streams and Mountains," all constantly unfurling.

I don't think it's accidental that *Mountains and Rivers Without End* begins with the directive "Clearing the mind and sliding in / to that created space . . ." One of the things that Snyder is up to — and this goes obliquely to Tim Dean's notion of poetic impersonality — is refreshing the shamanic approach to imaginative communion, an ancient model of regard that essentially involves getting the self out of the way, of "clearing the mind and sliding in . . ." Rilke, in *Letters to a Young Poet* and other places, talks about the "penetration of things." This sounds decidedly male, but it's clear that Rilke means finding a dynamic poise, or call it an aggressive receptivity, the kind of alertness that I first experienced as a young man while hunting and fishing. This particular state of alertness basically involves making yourself available through strongly concentrating outside of yourself — in simple terms, paying attention beyond the immediate bubble and babble of your own being, especially the mind, which is a monkey. If you're hunting, say, you might be focused on discerning any subtle movements in the landscape, breaks in the perceptual flow, interruptions in the rhythm of patterns, a smudge of color where it doesn't belong, a tag of shadow the sun's position renders senseless. Jack Spicer talks about this in his own way, about defeating your intentions and desires, getting outside the self. And this is not some whoop-to-the-Lord transcendental breakthrough into over-soul ultra-alert, but just a still vantage from which to see what you might see. Snyder attended some of Spicer's Magic Workshops in San Francisco, and even though Spicer had the reputation of being a bit of the "poets' poet," and a thorny teacher at best, one can sense, as Snyder surely did, given his interests in Zen Buddhism and the Great Spirit traditions, that a shaman's imaginative purpose is similar to Spicer's conception of the poet's — to "clear the mind" of perceptual sets, intentions, and general expectations in order to forge or reveal new connections, broach other possibilities, and to experience (however briefly) voluntary incarnations of other beings or things, a psychic simultaneity, that extension of identity we call communion. To do so is delicate and difficult work — dangerous, too — easily distorted by delusion and projection, and constantly open to the pitfalls of psychic woo-woo and the narcissism of bad magic. The proof is finally in the poem, or, if a hunter, in meat on the table, or in any sustenance, metaphorical or otherwise, one might prefer. And it's certainly worth noting that, to the great good fortune of many of us, anyone can occasionally get lucky on a wobble.

Having established this scheme of centers and their relationship to imagination, let's see how they play out in Snyder's poetic practice, keeping in mind that *Mountains and Rivers* was forty years in the making. When I first read *Riprap* back in 1965, I was immediately impressed that the poems carried such exact, accurate sensory information, and I think you'd be hard-pressed to read any two pages of *Mountains and Rivers* without appreciating the incredible precision and detail in the physical realm of the poem. Snyder's clear, solid attention to the sensuous is a hallmark of his work and, for me at least, the primary source of its sustaining delight. That goes for the prose as well. In fact, I cannot think of a single instance in all of Snyder's writing where there isn't a palpable, albeit effortless, sense of him working to get the physical details right, to capture the such-ness and is-ness of being alive in a body. That deep regard for the sensuous realm, that care in beholding the other and communicating it with a strict clarity, conveys a respect for the natural world that is fundamental to all subsequent acts of imagination. For example, I opened *Mountains and Rivers* and let my finger fall randomly to this description, from "The Flowing," of an Indian man fishing:

> Long sweep dip net held by a
> foam-drenched braced and leaning man
> on a rickety scaffold rigged to rocks
>
> the whole Columbia River thunders
> beneath his one wet plank
> the lift and plume
> of the water curling out and over,
>
> Salmon arching in the standing spray.   (M&R 69)

Such consistently accurate and lovely descriptions of the sensory realm aren't a matter of luck, but of sustained attention and clear, passionate regard. No wobble there.

   This sensuous clarity leads directly to the second of Jung's centers of perception, the intellect, since knowledge, not surprisingly, is predicated on good information. I tend to assign people I deem beyond ordinary intelligence to one of three categories: really smart; super bright; and holy shit. Snyder is one of the few people I've met that occupies this "holy shit" category. I gather from your response that I'm not alone in that assessment, am I? Reading *Mountains and Rivers Without End*, aren't you just blown away by the breadth and depth of Snyder's knowledge, everything from Eastern religion to ecology to chaos theory and geomorphology and mountaineering? And even more astonishing is his ability to connect them. Wallace Stevens offered a useful distinction between invention and discovery in his comments on surrealism, a distinction to the effect that you can always make a connection by arbitrarily putting two (or more) things together, like I just did by opening Webster's *Instant Word Guide* and randomly linking "muskrat," "Uruguay," and "hatchery." I doubt if there is a muskrat hatchery in Uruguay, or anywhere else for that matter, but as a sheer invention it's not without a certain goofy charm. Discovery inhabits a different order and operates in a different way, finding connections that seem like they were always there. In "The Blue Sky," to take one example from *Mountains and Rivers*, Snyder, as he modestly puts it in the Notes, explores "some of the lore of healing as found in Mahayana Buddhism and in Native North America." In poetic fact, it's a dazzling display of wit and erudition, radically mixing prose and poetry, etymologies, Eastern and Western folklore (and folk songs), dreams, healing prayers, lapis lazuli, mildly psychedelic varieties of morning glories, eagles — everything but the land of sky-blue waters made popular in Hamm's beer ads from the late '50s TV commercials. Reading "The Blue Sky" is akin to watching an alchemical process wherein information precipitates into knowledge; and it's a testament to the power of the integrative intelligence at work in the poem that you'll never look at a blue sky again without thinking of that poem's discoveries.

As a cautionary aside, some readers like myself can go down in the blaze of associations. When I first read *Mountains and Rivers* in manuscript, it seemed like every other poem mentioned buttermilk, and I sent a note to Gary — that I hope he's lost — "What's with these constant buttermilk references?" In "The Blue Sky" a character shows up in a dream, an old guy "with a grizzled face — neither eastern or western; or both" (M&R 43). The old man has a glass of buttermilk in his hand, and the dreamer, who has been looking all over for buttermilk, asks him where he got it. The old man replies, "At the OK Dairy, right where you leave town." Since I'm not a Buddhist scholar, I didn't learn until later that a farm girl gave Buddha some buttermilk to strengthen him in his quest for enlightenment, but as an American kid who went to the movies I knew that the Earp brothers and their cohorts had engaged in a famous gunfight with the bad-ass Dalton brothers at the OK Corral, also located at the edge of town. So I naturally concluded, and in my considered estimation not altogether incorrectly, that the OK Dairy and OK Corral were parallel east/west sites of some ferocious dharma combat, an interpretation that Gary met with a look that openly wondered where my spacecraft had crashed. Such are the perils — and fun — of co-creation when the poet doesn't anticipate a possible angle of a reader's imagination, or the extent of his ignorance. More seriously, *Mountains and Rivers Without End* is a poem of complex philosophic and mythic intelligence, wonderfully so, and assuming most readers are like me, they'll have to work at it. In my experience, the more you dig, the richer the yield; that is to say, it's not an easy poem, but easily worth it.

The third center of perception, the emotional, is the weakest element in *Mountains and Rivers*. Because I know I'm going to take grief for that judgment, let me hasten to clarify it. First of all, *Mountains and Rivers Without End* belongs to the epic tradition, or more exactly, as Snyder himself notes, it is "a sort of sūtra — an extended poetic, philosophic, and mythic narrative of the female Buddha Tārā" (M&R 158) — but it doesn't have a traditional narrative structure with characters to carry the freight of sustained emotional conflict. In a sense, the very structure of the narrative precludes embodied emotion. Moreover, because the "I" has been surrendered in favor of an extended identity and a more detached voice — which allows for greater intellectual range and sensuous clarity — there's no narrator to assume the emotional center. In traditional storytelling terms, you lose the immediacy and intimacy of a first-person narrator, which is the heart-wrenching difference between "I made love to Angelina Jolie" and "He made love to Angelina Jolie." Also, the more radically imaginative aspects of the narrative — giving voice to animals, trees, landscape, and traditions — virtually forbids much emotional expression without risking the more egregious expressions of anthropomorphism and wallowing in the pathetic fallacy — that is, forcing the non-human to take on human feelings. Further, it's not that *Mountains and Rivers* lacks emotion, but that it lacks the sort of sustained emotional conflicts that move their resolution to the dramatic center. On the contrary, the sustained emotional notes in the poem are a deep delight in existence, a profound acceptance of impermanence and the wrack and welter of change, and an abiding love for Tārā — and since those feelings appear fully developed at the start of the poem, already earned, they are never seriously threatened with loss or compromise; they *abide*, and thus slide into the background and become part of the poem's narrative assumption rather than its focus.

Yet in an intriguing way, *Mountains and Rivers Without End* moves *toward* emotion. The poems at the end of the book seem more personal — poems like "Cross-legg'd," "The Mountain Spirit," "The Dance," and especially the last poem, "Finding the Space in the Heart" (M&R 149–52), which aims directly at the heart of compassion: "*O, ah! The / awareness of emptiness / brings forth a heart of compassion.*" Within this high desert emptiness — "mile after mile, trackless and featureless" — an extended family has made camp: "old friends, old trucks, drawn around; / great arcs of kids on bikes out there in darkness . . ." In that emptiness, with "nothing in the way," the only connections left are those we can make among ourselves — friends, family, community. At the edge of my intuition, I sense the poet's clear mind, quiet heart, and distant eye — all necessary for the forty years' work *Mountains and Rivers* required — loosening their claim, and the poet rejoining the circle he never really left, taking his place in the "foolish loving spaces // full of heart." May it be so! This isn't to suggest that with his next book Snyder will become a confessional poet — confessional haiku, now there's a thought — but it should be interesting to see what flowers bloom from the seeds sown in the "awareness of emptiness" so evident at the close of *Mountains and Rivers Without End.*

Finally, I want to briefly consider Jung's fourth center of perception, the spiritual, and how it relates to Snyder's use of imagination. Recalling the schema of integration, the addition of spiritual imagination should cap the progression of sensory-information-to-knowledge-to-understanding with wisdom, but my problem is that I'm not sure I'd recognize wisdom if it shinnied up my leg and bit me on the ass. However, a couple of connections seem worth pointing out, even if they don't point at wisdom. As already noted, Snyder says he's come to think of *Mountains and Rivers* as a sūtra, a "narrative of the female Buddha Tārā, 'She Who Brings Across.'" Her role as the female Buddha of both compassion and wisdom is to bring you, ferry you, across the river of experience to the shore of enlightenment. Coincidentally (and I believe it was Arthur Koestler who called coincidences "spiritual puns"), "to bring across" is also the Greek etymological root of metaphor: *meta* (across); *pherein* (to bear, to carry). Because spirit, by most definitions, is immaterial, the work of the spiritual imagination is to embody spirit, to carry its force into form, to give its subjective power an objective correlative (shades of T. S. Eliot!), to bring it across as a way of bringing it on. It may be that the ability to make metaphors is the best way to manifest spirit, and thereby make it available. The art of metaphor resides in making accurate associations, clear connections, powerful links. Through metaphor, poets aim to tie things together, to join and unify. The Sanskrit root of "yoga" is "union," and the poet and yoga share, through disciplined practice involving intense and complete concentration, the goal of attaining "identity of consciousness" with the object of concentration. What Tim Dean describes as "poetic impersonality" could also be seen, in the shamanic or pantheist sense, as extended or shared identity through the agency of imagination. If the role of the sensory imagination is to perceive the other, the intellectual imagination to know the other, and the emotional imagination to understand the other, the role of the spiritual imagination is to become the other, to experience that shared identity and in a very real sense erase the distinction — or at least appreciate that each and all are as inextricably linked as compassion and wisdom.

Gregory Bateson, in *Steps to an Ecology of Mind*, notes that organisms have two essential urges: to assert their individuality and to integrate into something larger. In twentieth-century American culture the emphasis has been almost exclusively on assertion — rugged individualism, personal liberty, independence, and so on. What *Mountains and Rivers Without End* offers is a more balanced and integrated model of personality, and with it a wider — and wilder — sense of freedom.

The last thing I'd like to say is that I think *Mountains and Rivers Without End* is, in itself, an ecosystem, a model of what it addresses, full of intricate, intimate, and interdependent relationships that, like streams and mountains, never stay the same. I've read it five times now, and it continues to open, offering a dense web of interpenetrating angles, ideas, tastes, textures, and ceaselessly shifting connections. Yet for all those amazing connections, the breathtaking erudition and sensual clarity and wild play, there's almost a haunted sense of loneliness, of existential alienation, of something missing. And I realized last night what this poem lacks is a dog. I think Gary needs a faithful canine companion. I do. It's my solution. And not one he can use to attract mountain lions. A companion he can take on the walk with him when he's walking on walking.

~

The world is our consciousness, and it surrounds us. There are more things in the mind, in the imagination than "you" can keep track of — thoughts, memories, images, angers, delights, rise unbidden. The depths of mind, the unconscious, are our inner wilderness areas, and that is where a bobcat is *right now*. I do not mean personal bobcats in personal psyches, but the bobcat that roams from dream to dream. The conscious agenda-planning ego occupies a very tiny territory, a little cubicle somewhere near the gate, keeping track of what goes in and out (and sometimes making expansionistic plots), and the rest takes care of itself. The body is, so to speak, in the mind. They are both wild.

— Gary Snyder, *The Practice of the Wild* (1990)

4.

Gary Snyder and the Renewal of Oral Culture

DAVID ABRAM

W hat a pleasure to have this chance to ponder this marvelous, and marvelously strange, poem cycle, *Mountains and Rivers Without End*, by our friend, Gary Snyder.

I should admit that this enigmatic series of poems had me flummoxed when I first entered and wandered in its pages. After a short while, however, I found myself caught in the shadowed wonderment of this work, snagged by its juxtaposed textures — here flowing and smooth, there striated, here flint-knapped and honed to an edge, there splintered and prickly. Soon I was striding back and forth through the book, stopping now and then to sit back and listen into the wordless silence, immersed in the participatory, animistic quality of the earthly cosmos revealed by this work. This shifting, metamorphic realm wherein *everything* is animate — not just mountains and rivers, but everything. Not only bristlecone pines, and mountain sheep, but also office buildings, and objects — even a sag-assed rocking chair in the basement of Goodwill has its own struggling life.

Of course, most cultures that are deeply animistic in this way, for whom everything is alive — for whom every material presence has its own dynamism and agency, and even the capacity for meaningful speech — such cultures are traditionally *oral* cultures: cultures that have developed, and flourished, in the absence of any highly-formalized writing system. So I want to reflect a bit on the ways that Gary's work, and this very literate poem in particular, aims us toward a renewal of oral culture.

In his notes on "The Making of *Mountains and Rivers Without End*" (M&R 153–58) we read how, when Gary was living in Japan, he was "given a

chance to see how walking the landscape can become both ritual and medi-
tation." This notion of walking the land as ritual made me think of the ritual
tradition, among the aboriginal peoples of central Australia, of the "walk-
about." In the walkabout, a traditional aboriginal male — let's say a young
Pintubi man, or a Pitjantjara man, or a Warlpiri man — will make a ritual
journey along the dreaming track, or songline: the meandering path first
traveled by his totemic ancestor in the Dreamtime.

Gary's long cycle of journey poems is, for me, primarily a bundle of such
songlines, of dreaming tracks. Now, the Dreamtime, for the indigenous
peoples of Australia, is a kind of time out of time, a time hidden beyond, or
rather, *within* the manifest presence of the land. It is that time before the
world itself was entirely awake — a time that still exists just below the surface
of wakeful awareness — that dawn when the totem ancestors first emerged
from their slumber beneath the ground, and began to sing their way across
the land. The earth, of course, was still in a malleable, half-awake state.
And as the Dreamtime ancestors — Kangaroo Man, or Tortoise Woman,
or Honey-Ant Man, or Wallaby Woman — as they first wandered, singing,
across the surface of the earth, they were shaping the land as they traveled,
forming valleys where they lay down, creating creeks or waterholes wherever
they urinated, and forests where they kicked up dust, etc. . . . So today, when
an aboriginal man goes walkabout, traveling along his ancestral songline, he
chants the verses originally sung by his dreaming ancestor, singing the land
into view as he walks through it. And, in this manner, he renews not only
his own life, but the very life of the land itself.

Because it is not humans alone who dream, and not just the other ani-
mals and the plants, but rather *the land itself dreams, continually.* The
Dreamtime is not something that happened once and for all in the distant
past; rather the Dreaming lies in the same relation to the open presence of
the land around us as our own dream life lies in relation to our conscious
or waking experience. It is a kind of depth, ambiguous and metamorphic.
Indeed, it is a sense of both the past and the future *not* as dimensions that
reside somewhere else, but as realms that are hidden, secretly, within the
depths of the present moment. A sense of time as *depth*. Deep Time, itself
the primary theme, I'd suggest, of this mysterious poem cycle.

Dreaming, of course, is an event that flows like a subterranean stream throughout these *Mountains and Rivers Without End*. This is obvious not only from the explicit dream sequences like the poem called "Journeys" and the amazing "Elwha River" poem, or in the great Ghost Dance dream of Wovoka, the prophet who figures in several of these poems, or the magic dream in the heights above Death Valley that immediately precedes the startling face-to-face conversation with the Mountain Spirit. It is also evident in the continual dissolving of linear, historical time into a sense of the inexhaustible depth of the present moment, wherein all moments are accessible here and now — the present moment a kind of threshold, or opening, into the vast dreaming of the earth. Into that depth wherein all things, even the mountains, are in continual metamorphosis, all things shape-shifting, transforming into one another. Everything shape-shifting. As in the "Night Song of the Los Angeles Basin," when the flowing freeway of cars suddenly becomes a river of fish, and a rain shower becomes the tall flowing dress of the Goddess, who tosses a handful of cornmeal into that river, making the fish roil and swarm. Or, in a very different poem, when a mother macaque monkey, leaping from one tree limb to another, with her baby hanging onto her belly, suddenly becomes the Milky Way filled with stars arching overhead, crossing from realm to realm. These are *not* metaphors. They are *metamorphoses*. Real transformations. The Milky Way arching overhead is not a metaphor for the leaping monkey. Rather, the monkey *becomes* the Milky Way, full of stars, with all of us swinging beneath it. Which then transforms back into the macaque monkey, once again.

Dreaming. Deep time. Metamorphosis. Shape-shifting. Even in that lovely kayaking poem called "Afloat" (M&R 130–32) where various kinds of people: judges and carpenters and speechmakers, suddenly take off their human masks and turn back into water birds. Let me read just a bit of this poem:

> Floating in a tiny boat
> lightly on the water, rock with every ripple,

Umm — I'll interrupt for a moment to say that Gary and his partner are floating, I take it, in a double sea kayak, and this is a realm and a set of images and smells and sounds that are very familiar to me since I've done a lot of kayaking in Alaska, and one experience that is very vivid when you are floating there, is that sometimes it can be utterly still, and then, out of the distance comes a flapping (at first a very gentle rhythm, it gradually gets louder and louder): "*phhh phhh phhh phhh phhh **phhh phhah phhah phhah phhah** phhah phhh phhh phhh phh phh phh*" — and it recedes into the distance, and then other, whirring wings: "*hrrhh hrrhh hrrrh hrrhh hrrhh hrrhh hrrhh hrrhh hrrhh*" — or the sound of webbed feet running upon the surface — "*pteh pteh pteh pteh pteh ptah ptah ptaah ptaah ptaah pteh pteh pteh*" — these water birds, skimpering and flying by, just above the surface of the water, emerging out of the depths of the great mysterious, crystalizing into solid shapes as they get close to you and then dissolving back into the depths beyond:

> twin kayak paddles turn and glint like wings
> casting spume,
> there is no place we are
> but maybe here
>
>   . . .
>
> wind ripples westward, the tide goes east,
> we paddle east southeast
> the world a rush of wings and waters,
>
> up the slopes, the mountain glacier
> looses icemelt over gravel in a soft far roar
> that joins the inlet-basin world of cries and whistles
>
>   . . .
>
> the glaciers shift and murmur like the tides
> under the constant cross-current
> steady drum of bird-wings
> full of purpose, some direction,
> all for what
> in the stroke
> in the swirl of the float
> we are two souls in one body,

two sets of wings, our paddles swing
where land meets water meets the sky,

where judges and speechmakers, actresses and carpenters,
drop their masks and go on as they were,
as
petrels, geese, oystercatchers, murrelets,
and small fish fry . . .

That is material right out of the Dreamtime, or what the Koyukon call the Distant Time. That depth, or distance, wherein the humans take off their masks and reveal themselves as the animals that they really are. Or where the other animals take off their masks and reveal themselves as human-like folk: Kangaroo Man, or Emu Woman, or Lizard Woman. So let me now bring this back to the native Australian tradition of the walkabout. Because it's not just these metamorphoses that lead me to look at Gary's poem through the lens of this particular Aboriginal tradition, and not just the centrality of dreaming ("sheep dreaming" and all the rest), it is also, and even more importantly, the *relentlessly place-specific* character of almost everything that happens in this long poem.

Every event, every vision, every encounter in this poem, is located in a carefully identified place. I mean, for a set of poems essentially about movement, about traveling, about journeying, this work is almost weirdly obsessive about telling us exactly *where* in the land every event or insight occurs. Think of "Night Highway 99" (M&R 11–24). Here we are in Ferndale, Washington, drinking coffee, and we're off. Now we're in Mount Vernon, fifty Indians asleep in the bus station. *Whoop*! Now in Everett — this is what happened here: Wobblies run out of town. Hmmm . . . Seattle: now dried shrimp, smoked salmon. Tacoma now, night rain, wet concrete, headlights blind. Then in Portland, buttermilk. And on and on, through Salem, Eugene, Dillard. All the way down to San Francisco. Each place with its own stories. *Each story with its own place.*

Then the next poem: "Things to Do Around Seattle"; "Things to do Around a Lookout"; "Things to do Around San Francisco"; "Things to do around Kyoto." Places, again. Or, in the poem, "The Market" (M&R 47–51).

Here we are in a San Francisco market:

> Heart of the city
>   down town
> the country side.

> John Muir up before dawn
> packing pears in the best boxes . . .

Then, here's the market in Saigon — what's happenin' here? Here's the market in Kathmandhu. Here's what we notice at the market in Varanasi. The beautiful poem called "The Flowing" (M&R 68–72) begins:

> headwaters, Kamo
> River back of Kyoto . . .

Then we are at the Columbia River. Then a river in the Sierra Nevada. "The Hump-backed Flute Player" (M&R 79–82) starts out sitting

> on the boulders around the Great Basin
> his hump   is a pack . . .

Meanwhile Hsüan Tsang, with his pack, is returning to China from India, crossing "the Pamir the Tarim Turfan / the Punjab." Then we're back with Kokop'ele, crossing the "Sweetwater, Quileute, Hoh / Amur, Tanana, Mackenzie, Old Man, / Big Horn, Platte, the San Juan." Then we're in Canyon de Chelly. Then back in India, "In the plains of Bihar, near Rajgir, are the ruins of Nalanda."

I mean, he's relentless! All these place names, these specified locations. And then Kokop'ele is back in the mountains at the edge of the Great Basin. And so it goes, through the whole sequence, which ends, of course, back at the Great Basin edge. Even the painting of *Endless Streams and Mountains,* which frames the whole cycle of poems, is precisely located. Where? "At the Cleveland Art Museum, which sits on a rise which looks out toward the waters of Lake Erie" (M&R 8).

Now, this may all seem very innocuous to you. "I mean — so there's a lot of places named or indicated — so what? It's only to be expected. The poem is by Gary Snyder, for heaven's sake! The guy's big on the notion of *place* — we've always known that. Big deal!"

But I think there's something way more interesting going on here. For this insistent locating of storied events and experiences in particular places is common to virtually all indigenous, oral (or traditionally non-writing) cultures. Indeed, it is central to the discourse of so many oral peoples. For instance, the Navajo people — or the *Diné*, as they call themselves. Even when they are talking about the most minute occurences, the *Diné* always say *where* those events happened. If they don't say where something happened, then the event loses its significance. Why might this be? Why this insistence on locating every event or encounter in a particular place, at a specific site or locale?

Well, here is the key question: how, in a culture without a formal writing system — a culture without books — how is all of the ancestrally gathered knowledge to be preserved? All of the knowledge about how to survive in the land without destroying each other, and how to find the particular plants that are good to eat, and the knowledge of which plants are useful as medicines for which particular ailments, and how to detoxify and prepare those plants, as well as how to successfully hunt particular animals, and the best way to skin those animals and to prepare them as food, and for clothing and shelter, and all the rest.

So how is all of this place-based savvy preserved? How is all the ancestrally accumulated knowledge preserved and handed down? For us, it is easy; we simply go to the library or to the bookstore, find the right book, and look up the information that we need. But in a culture without writing, how is all this preserved?

All those who have pondered this question for a while have realized, quickly, that the knowledge must be held in stories. All of this information is stored, as it were, in stories. Perhaps we call them "stories" because all this stuff is *stored* in them! The stories are like the living encyclopedias of an oral culture. But the question remains: how is it, then, that the *stories* are preserved? How is it that the stories are remembered? And it is not simply that they are repeated, again and again, because the stories can only be told at certain seasons, and indeed some story cycles repeat themselves only once every several years, sometimes once every ten years. In Indonesia I was present at a cycle of stories that is recounted once every one hundred years! How are such stories preserved in a culture without writing?

Well, one important key is that the stories are often associated with particular local animals, like Jackrabbit, or Bear, or Coyote, who figure as central characters in the story. Then, whenever you encounter that animal, you remember some of the teaching stories linked to that critter. But, even more crucial is that the stories are commonly associated with particular places. And whenever you come upon the place where those events happened (or where this part of the story is supposed to have happened), it triggers the memory of the events that ostensibly happened there.

As you walk through the land, then, the places you meet and the sites you encounter are continually sparking the memory of the particular stories associated with those places and sites. *The land, in other words, is the primary mnemonic, or memory trigger, for remembering the oral stories.* So while ancestral knowledge is held, as it were, in the stories, the stories are held in the land. The landscape is alive with stories!

We might think, here, of the Western Apache teaching stories recorded by Keith Basso in his book, *Wisdom Sits in Places*.[1] The *'agodzaahi* tales, each of which is told only after naming the place where it happened: you announce the place-name, then tell the story, and then you tell the place where it happened once again. "It happened at 'White Rocks Tumble Down in a Big Heap'..." Or, "it happened at 'Big Cottonwood Trees Stand Spreading Here and There' ..." And so on. The Apache individuals whom Basso listens to and learns from say things like: "... the land still looks after us. We know the names of the places where everything happened. So we stay away from badness."[2] An Apache man who went off to live in the city, returns to the reservation after a year-and-a-half, explaining that he forgot how to live right in the city. Since he no longer saw the places where the stories happened, he forgot all the necessary guidance held in those stories. "It was *bad*. I forget about this country here around Cibecue. I forget all the names and stories. I don't hear them in my mind anymore. I forget how to live right, forget how to be strong..."[3]

Here is another, perhaps more relevant, example. Gary Snyder tells this interesting story in *The Practice of the Wild,* about the time when he was visiting Australia, with Nanao, I believe, in 1981. And he was traveling in a pickup truck, in the central desert, with an Aboriginal elder, a Pintubi man named Jimmy Tjungurrayi. And as they were driving through the outback, this Aboriginal man starts talking to Gary very quickly, telling him some stories from the Dreamtime, about some Wallaby People who met up with a couple of Lizard Girls at that spot over there, and some major mischief happened, so the Lizard Girls went up on top of that hill over there, but then they got into some real trouble because they bumped into Kangaroo Woman, and oh, that was a problem, so those girls had to go off over there and straightaway he is telling another story, and then another one, very, very quickly, and Gary can't keep up. He wants him to *slow down, slow down!* Until finally Gary realizes, with a start, that the stories are meant to be told while walking. But they are riding through the outback in a pickup truck! So they are passing, very rapidly, each of the places where these stories occurred (see PW 81–84).

This anecdote makes vividly evident the deep intimacy between language and the land in an indigenous, oral culture — an intimacy so intense that you must pace the speed of your speaking to the speed at which you are moving through the terrain! We might say that *the land, for indigenous, oral cultures, is the very matrix of linguistic meaning.* So, to force a traditionally oral people off of their ancestral lands — perhaps because you want to drill for oil on those lands, or you want to flood those lands with a new hydroelectric dam project, or to clearcut their pristine forests, as in Indonesia and Malaysia, or for whatever other purpose — to shove an oral people out of their ancestral homeland is, effectively, to shove them out of their mind. Because the land is what they think with.

Now, you can see what happens when writing begins to come into such a culture, and the stories begin to be written down. Writing is usually brought in by Christian missionaries carrying the Good Book. But as the stories begin to be written down, they are teased off of the sites that traditionally carried those stories, pried off of the clustered rocks and streambeds and creeks, and replanted on the page. So the stories can now be carried elsewhere. They are not held to that earthly locale. They can be read in distant cities, and even on distant continents. And the original place-based specificity in the stories, all the practical knowledge and savvy regarding those actual places is readily forgotten, and is often written out of the stories entirely. So now the folks in the city read these stories about the "little people who live in the fields," for instance, these tiny persons who live down there among the grasses, and they think, "Gosh, what wild imaginations those unlettered peasants have!" But, if you lived back on that land a couple hundred years ago, and your grandmother was tugging you out into those fields, saying: "Now look at that wee little one there. You have to look at her real careful, just under the mushroom there, do you see? Ah here she comes, real slow. She's a wise one, y' know!" And peering closer, you glimpse something moving, and suddenly recognize that that is Slug-Woman there, sliding out from under that mushroom! Except that now you're seeing her as another shape of intelligence, weirdly different from your own, and you realize that she has all sorts of insights to offer you ... And so you realize that these stories carry real, practical knowledge about real things happening in the actual terrain — knowledge that is place-based, savvy and specific.

But once the stories are written down, the *page* begins to become the primary mnemonic, or memory trigger, for the originally oral tale. The inked traces made by the pen as it traverses the page begin to replace the tracks made by the animals, and one's animal ancestors, as they moved across the land. So the land itself is no longer necessary for remembering the stories; it is no longer necessary for remembrance. We no longer need the land to think with. Now the books carry the stories, and the land can begin to seem rather superfluous, unnecessary. Gradually the living land begins to recede into the background, flattening into a kind of backdrop for our more pressing human concerns.

For all of the literate artistry in Gary's poems, for all of the rich scholarship and the density of literary allusions in *Mountains and Rivers*, one of the things this poem cycle is doing is renewing oral culture. Reawakening that ancient, oral intimacy between language and the land. Remembering language to its oral ancestry. Think of all the moments when the language of the poem suddenly breaks into a chant. Or into a rhyming song, like this one:

>   — nutrient minerals called together
> like a magic song
> to lead a cedar log along, that hopes
>   to get to sea at last and be
>   a great canoe.   (M&R 70)

Or where it breaks into an incantatory prayer, or spell:

> Old Ghost ranges, sunken rivers, come again.   (M&R 9)

  Chants, spells, songs, all drawing us back into that ancient oral modality of place-based participation, renewing oral culture. Not to the exclusion of literate culture, but *alongside* our literate culture. Or not really alongside, but rather, *underneath* the culture of literacy, grounding the cosmopolitan culture of the book — and now, also, the globalizing culture of the computer and the internet — in a thriving, oral culture.

  This, I think, is what Gary Snyder is secretly up to in this poem, this bundle of journey poems: offering us a set of songlines, a bundle of dreaming tracks, of songs and visions precisely located *out there.* Precisely located. And that is why the events and visions and encounters in these poems are so carefully planted in the places where they happened. Mr. Snyder is showing us where we may find these stories for ourselves, *not on the page, but out there in the breathing earth.* On that sidewalk in Manhattan, or San Francisco, or in that stand of bristlecone pines, at the edge of the Great Basin. He's showing us how we may begin to find again the songs and stories hidden in the land, including those stories that we don't write down. Because they only live out there.

  When we read these beautiful and quirky pages, we should not fail to notice what they quietly, inadvertently tell us about *not* writing, about what we don't write down, about what exceeds and cannot be held on the written page. Like in the very opening poem, when at one point

> The watching boat has floated off the page.   (M&R 6)

Or, in "Walking the New York Bedrock":

> — Peregrine sails past the window
> Off the edge of the word-chain . . .   (M&R 101)

Or at the end of "The Flowing," the poet standing in the river mouth, the river making love to the poet:

> Mouth
> you thick
> vomiting outward sighing prairie
>   muddy waters
>   gathering all and
>   issue it
>   end over end
>   away from the land.
> The faintest grade.
> Implacable, heavy, gentle,
>
> — O pressing song
>   liquid butts and nibbles
>   between the fingers — in the thigh —
>   against the eye
> curl round my testicles
> drawn crinkled skin
>   and lazy swimming cock.
>
> Once sky-clear and tickling through pineseeds
>   humus, moss fern stone
>   but NOW
>
> the vast loosing
>   of all that was found, sucked, held,
>   born, drowned,

sunk sleepily in
to the sea.

  The root of me
  hardens and lifts to you,
  thick flowing river,

  my skin shivers. I quit

  making this poem.   (M&R 71–72)

The fluvial erotics of this poem carry a quiet teaching for us, about what we *don't* write down: *"my skin shivers. I quit / making this poem."*

 Or also and especially in the last words of the final poem in the book — words that seem at first to offer a new and fitting metaphor for an author's mortality and the inevitable closure of a life lived in the thick of things, but that can also, less ponderously, be taken as a little teaching about restraint, about setting aside the pen and the written word on behalf of other non-verbal conversations always already going on:

  The space goes on.
  But the wet black brush
  tip drawn to a point
   lifts away.   (M&R 152)

           ~

Why is it so important, finally, to renew oral culture? Because there is simply no way of alleviating the ecological crisis, I suspect, without rejuvenating oral culture, fast.

 Oral culture is local culture. The title of this conference, "Ethics and Aesthetics at the turn of the Fiftieth Millennium," is instructive. "Aesthetics" comes from Greek *aesthesis,* which really means the work of the senses: touching, hearing, seeing, smelling, and tasting. Feeling the world with our senses. Well, the sensuous world is the world of oral culture. Because the sensuous world is always local. It is not what is happening on the other side of the planet, but right here. And it is never strictly human, since it is made up of the ground on which we walk, and the gravity that holds us to that ground, and the air that we breathe — this air that is breathed out by all the green and rooted folks around. The sensuous world is the face-to-face world that we inhabit with our sensing, animal bodies — the world in which we are corporeally immersed. And in which we bodily participate, simply by the very fact of being here.

Now, it seems to me that "ethics" is not primarily a set of mental injunctions, but is something that we only really learn, first, with our breathing bodies, as our bodies come up against *other* bodies, against other beings: turtles, and lichen-encrusted rocks, and spiders delicately weaving their webs across our path, and robins wrenching worms out of the ground, and people, lots of people, and cottonwood trees, and rivers swelling and drying up with the seasons. Ethics is what we begin to practice as we encounter these others *in the flesh,* face to face, and learn to orient and to dwell in the same world that they inhabit, learning to move with restraint, and playfulness, and an appropriate boldness. It is only there, in the thick of the palpable, sensuous world, that we really learn how to be with others, and how to move with others.

Ethics, from this angle, is a felt sense within our muscles. We don't learn ethics, really, from books, and we certainly don't learn ethics from the screen of the computer. It is a bodily thing. And it is learned in carnal reciprocity and relationship with other bodily beings in a particular place, a particular terrain or watershed. We cultivate ethics only by remembering the sensuous, local, more-than-human world, and by taking this world as primary, as the secret source and heart of all those other, more abstract worlds in which we now find ourselves — whether the global marketplace, or the subatomic spaces of quantum physics, or the transcendent spiritual domains to which our New Age friends lure us, or the multiple virtual realities that now beckon to us through the dazzle of the digital screen — it's only by taking the sensuous world of our direct unmediated interactions with other bodies and beings as the touchstone and guide for all these other worlds.

Taking our primary guidance from spider and blackbird and rainstorm. Only then do we have a chance of growing the ethical savvy needed to orient and to navigate in the multiple technological realms that now open before us at the turn of the fiftieth millennium. This, then, is one of the key things I have learned from Gary Snyder, and from this wild sequence of meandering songlines: *Rejuvenate oral culture, fast.*

NOTES

1. Keith R. Basso, *Wisdom Sits in Places: Landscape and Language Among the Western Apache* (Albuquerque: University of New Mexico Press, 1996).
2. Nick Thompson, quoted in Basso, *Wisdom Sits in Places,* 96.
3. Wilson Lavender, quoted in Basso, *Wisdom Sits in Places,* 97.

MAKING PACIFIC RIM
CONNECTIONS

≈

the *buzoku* style
    "we are the primitives
         of an unknown culture --"
    — Gary Snyder (27 October 1991 GSJ)*

* Paraphrase of a 1911 statement by the Italian Futurist sculptor, Umberto Boccioni. *Buzoku* means "the Tribe," a loose-knit countercultural group in Japan in the 1960s and '70s. Nanao Sakaki (1923–2008) was a founder and Gary Snyder a member who carried knowledge of countercultural movements between Turtle Island and Yaponesia. See Katsunori Yamazato, "Snyder, Sakaki, and the Tribe," in *Gary Snyder: Dimensions of a Life*, ed. Jon Halper (San Francisco: Sierra Club Books, 1991), 93–106.

5

Mountains and Rivers Without End and Japanese Nō Theater

A Quest for a New Humanity

KATSUNORI YAMAZATO

I.

After graduating from Reed College in 1951, Gary Snyder went eastward to attend graduate school at Indiana University. He quit Indiana after a semester and later entered the University of California, Berkeley for graduate studies in Chinese and Japanese. As Snyder has repeatedly stated, he did this partly to prepare for disciplined study of Zen Buddhism in Kyoto. Snyder's journey to Japan also supported another far-reaching purpose. On December 9, 1953, he wrote his friend Philip Whalen and said he would like to combine his own Western cultural tradition with Far Eastern traditions. From the early stages of his career, Snyder thus dreamed of combining traditions in revolutionary ways and creating an alternative to a civilization that appeared to him to be self-destructive. This, I think, was the underlying motivation for Snyder's going to Japan in 1956, and it is important to remember this when discussing Snyder's relationship with Japan. Here I would like to focus on some Japanese elements that influenced Snyder's writing of *Mountains and Rivers Without End*. By doing so, I hope to show ways Snyder's years in Japan shaped his career as a poet and thinker.

One of the powerful influences on *Mountains and Rivers Without End* is Japanese Nō drama, which Snyder studied extensively during his years in Kyoto (1956–68). Snyder bought season tickets, attended many Nō plays, and always took the *utaibon* (Nō text) with him. This interest nourished various images and ideas for bringing Nō into North America. On September 30, 1956, four months after his arrival in Japan, Snyder wrote a letter to his close friend Philip Whalen in which he discussed his dream of an American Nō theater. Nō fascinated Snyder, and he studied it carefully while keeping the possibility of an American way of expressing Nō in mind.

By 1965, Snyder must have seen *Yamamba* (The Old Woman of the Mountains) several times, and it began to influence his thinking about *Mountains and Rivers Without End* as he envisioned the possibility of applying "the dramatic strategies of Nō" to the "Turtle Island landscape" (M&R 155). For example, Snyder went to the Glacier Peak wilderness area on October 1, 1965 and, during his hike, attempted to relate *Yamamba* to the North American landscape (see EHH 94–95).[1]

To organize the poems included in *Mountains and Rivers Without End*, Snyder was studying principles from Chinese landscape painting and Japanese Nō. He does not, however, rigidly adhere to the prescribed structure of a Nō play, but uses it rather loosely and creatively to suggest his poetic and cultural vision. In order to see what Snyder has done in *Mountains and Rivers Without End*, we need to understand Nō.

Nō drama originated in medieval Japan in the late fourteenth century. Although remotely connected with *sangaku*, which was introduced from China in the early Nara period (c. 850), it is said that Nō primarily developed out of the two ancient performing arts known as *dengaku* and *sarugaku*. Nō, in the form we see today, owes its formation to Kannami Kiyotsugu (1333–1384) and his son, Zeami Motokiyo (c. 1363–1443). Zeami contributed more than anyone else to the refinement of Nō.[2]

Kannami adapted *kusemai* (a medieval song-dance) to Nō, emphasizing the rhythmic accompaniment and movement in a manner that rendered the genre more attractive to the audience. By incorporating the *kusemai*, which enabled the performer not only to dance, sing, and mime at the same time, Kannami made it possible to compose Nō texts that encapsulate the central narrative in this portion of the play.[3] Thus Kannami's introduction of the *kusemai* into traditional Nō produced striking dramatic effects that had a great impact on Nō dramaturgy.[4]

What is known as the *jo-ha-kyū* principle applied to all medieval arts in Japan. Thanks to Zeami, Nō was no exception, and this basic principle governs its overall structure.[5] Each play is to have three parts: *jo*, the introduction, *ha*, the development or exposition, and *kyū*, the climax or rapid finale. This principle applies to the structure of an entire day's program, to an individual play, and even to a brief passage. Traditionally, a day's program consists of a series of five plays. The five-part structure also applies to the individual play, which is supposed to be divided into five sections. As Zeami himself points out in *Nōsakusho* (The Book of Nō Composition), however, not all plays strictly adhere to this scheme. He states that sometimes there might be plays with four or even six sections.[6]

Mountains and Rivers Without End has four sections, not five, and this long poem adheres only loosely to the traditional structure of the Nō drama. Section I is the *jo* part of *Mountains and Rivers Without End*, and within this section the *jo-ha-kyū* structure may also be observed. "Endless Streams and Mountains" (M&R 5–9) serves as the *shidai* (the entrance song) for the entirety of *Mountains and Rivers Without End* and for section I as well. "Old Bones" (M&R 10) may be read as the *nanori* (a character's self-introduction, which usually follows the *shidai*) for both the entire work and for this section. "Night Highway 99" (M&R 11–24) is the *michiyuki* (a travel song that follows the *nanori* and depicts both the places one travels and the process of one's journey) for both the entire work and for Section I. The rest of the poems in this section except "The Blue Sky" (M&R 40–44) can be thought of as constituting the expository *ha* part. "The Blue Sky," the last poem in this section, serves as the *kyū*. Section I consists mainly of travel poems, and, therefore, this section as a whole corresponds to the opening songs of a Nō play.

Sections II and III constitute the *ha* part of *Mountain and Rivers Without End*. Snyder places "travel songs" such as "Journeys" and "The Circumambulation of Mt. Tamalpais" at the beginning of Sections II and III. Poems of the *ha* parts of the two sections then follow these travel songs. These narratives spiral into and out of Turtle Island while simultaneously developing and deepening themes the poet has meditated on for forty years.

Section IV is the *kyū* part of this four-part poem. The entire work reaches its climax in "The Mountain Spirit" (M&R 140–47), a poem that contains a poem within a poem corresponding to the *kusemai* of a Nō play (M&R 143–46). This poem also serves as the *kusemai* for the entirety of

Mountains and Rivers Without End. "Finding the Space in the Heart" (M&R 149–152) is then the *kyū*, the ending dance not only of this section but of the entire book as well.

II.

As a whole, *Mountains and Rivers Without End* can be taken as Snyder's quest for a new humanity that embraces various world traditions. The poems reflect his search on a planetary scale for myths and wisdom traditions that will bring about a new humanistic vision. In his poetry and prose, he repeatedly asks what it means to be human, and he grapples with this perennial question here. Never has Snyder averted his eyes from this central question; what we see in *Mountains and Rivers* is a body of work that reflects his struggle for a vision of a new humanity that bridges East and West in unprecedented ways. Here the whole planet is conceived of as one place where myths and dreams from various cultures are evoked and fused into a cohesive whole and where humans and the more-than-human world coexist in one interpenetrating web. Snyder thus shows the reader how to live on a planet that is One Big Watershed.

Section I of *Mountains and Rivers Without End* begins with "Endless Streams and Mountains." With it ritualistic tone, this poem introduces the central motif of the entire work and establishes a Nō framework by introducing movements and sounds from the Nō stage: "stamp the foot, walk with it, clap! turn" (M&R 8).

"Old Bones" depicts ancient indigenous people of North America who lived by hunting and gathering. These are the ancestors of the people who now live on Turtle Island. As mentioned above, this poem is the *nanori*, one of the opening songs that reveals the identity of the performer. Thus, *Mountains and Rivers Without End* can also be read as a poem that envisions a future for these ancient inhabitants of Turtle Island still alive inside their present-day descendants. Moreover, it is also possible to see *Mountains and Rivers Without End* as dealing with the whole planet in the poems depicting places outside Turtle Island. "Earth Verse" (M&R 148), for example, which was written in Australia, suggests the chronological and geographical framework within which the entire work was conceived. "Old Bones" thus harkens back not just to Turtle Island, but to the whole planet, depicting the Dream-time of *Homo sapiens* in the Paleolithic world.

As the *michiyuki* (travel song) of Section I and the whole of *Mountains and Rivers Without End*, "Night Highway 99" begins in the Pacific Northwest and ends in San Francisco. "Journeys" (M&R 52–56) records a series of real and dream journeys. Genji in the first line of this nine-part poem is the name of the cat who lived with Snyder during his Berkeley period. It was named after the protagonist of *The Tale of Genji*, which Snyder studied at that time. The bird the cat catches becomes a woman, and, in the second part of the poem, the narrator reaches a place "where no one had ever been." He goes "across dark stony ground" and then feels overwhelmed by "the flaming pulsing sun." The narrator places a strange episode at the end of this series of internal journeys: standing on "a point by a cliff," the narrator and Kō-san, his companion, see "the farther peaks stony and barren, [and] a few pine trees." Kō-san explains that this is "the world after death." Kō-san then pulls the narrator over the cliff and, after falling and hitting the ground, they both die.

To awaken to a new dimension of consciousness, one has to transcend the mundane world, and only after the destruction of the mundane ego is one capable of finding "'the way to the back country'" (M&R 56). Thus, "Kō-san," as friend and mentor, guides the narrator to this awakening through a typically "rough" Zen method of instruction.

"Kō-san," who also appears in "The Blue Sky," is a name for Sōkō Morinaga, Snyder's close colleague during his formal Zen study in Kyoto. He was the head monk at the Daitoku-ji Meditation Hall and later became a *rōshi* who was given a temple, Daishu-in, a sub-temple of Ryōan-ji. Zen monks in Japan call each other by the last syllable of their first names and attach *san* (a suffix showing respect or politeness) to that syllable. (Incidentally, Snyder, whose Zen name is Chōfū [Listen to the Wind], was called "Fū-san" by his colleagues in Kyoto.)

In "The Hump-backed Flute Player" (M&R 79–82), Snyder introduces Hsüan Tsang (600–64), a Chinese priest who traveled to India to obtain original Sanskrit texts. After long, difficult travels and rigorous studies in India, he returned to China, bringing back with him, among many other important sūtras, "the famed 'Heart Sutra'" (M&R 160), a teaching on the

Buddhist idea of "emptiness." This is the first sūtra Snyder learned by heart during his initial year in Japan.

The first poem in Section III, "The Circumambulation of Mt. Tamalpais," is an example of cultural absorption and transmission. Snyder, Allen Ginsberg, and Philip Whalen circumambulated Tamalpais "to show respect and to clarify the mind." According to David Robertson, they "opened" the mountain on October 22, 1965.[7]

In a letter written to Philip Whalen in 1960 now housed in the Reed College Library, Snyder describes in detail a staff-top with metal rings he found in a second-hand store in Kyoto and mentions his intention of doing a walking meditation practice all over California, especially around Mt. Tamalpais. Snyder likens Tamalpais to Hiezan (Mt. Hiei in Kyoto). In a 1961 letter, he also tells Whalen that someday he would like to "sacredize" Tamalpais.

The three poets chose places to perform rituals and "sacredize" the mountain. First they stop in Muir Woods ("Stage One"), and recite the *Prajñāparamitā-hṛidaya-sūtra*, the "Dhāranī for Removing Distasters," and "Four Vows." The *Prajñāparamitā-hṛidaya-sūtra* is another name for "the famed 'Heart Sutra'" Hsüan Tsang brought from India and translated into Chinese. Snyder and his friends then carried "emptiness" from Japan to North America, so to speak.

The Wooden Fish, a pamphlet edited by Snyder and Gutetsu Kanetsuki, explains that *dhāranī* are magical invocations in Sanskrit. They also point out that the "Dhāranī for Removing Disasters" is part of sūtra chanting in the meditation hall each morning. The three pilgrims on Tamalpais recite this *dhāranī* at every "stage" where they stop, exorcising "evil spirits" and rendering the place sacred. At the first "shrine," the three poets also recite the "Four Vows" in order to "dedicate their lives to work for the benefit of every other being on earth."[8] Here I quote three versions of the "Four Vows." The first version is D. T. Suzuki's translation, printed in his *Manual of Zen Buddhism*, compiled in Kyoto in 1934:

However innumberable beings are, I vow to save them;
However inexhaustible the passions are, I vow to extinguish them;

However innumerable the Dharmas are, I vow to master them;
However incomparable the Buddha-truth is, I vow to attain it.[9]

The second version is from *The Wooden Fish*, published in 1961 and trans-
lated into English by Ruth Fuller Sasaki:

Sentient beings are numberless; I take a vow to save them.
Deluding passions are inexhaustible; I take a vow to destroy them.
The gates of the Dharma are manifold; I take a vow to enter them.
The Buddha-way is supreme; I take a vow to complete it.[10]

The third version was translated by Snyder, and I quote it from the pam-
phlet entitled *Daily Tasks in the Zen Woods* used at the Ring of Bone Zendo
on the San Juan Ridge where he now lives:

Beings are numberless: I vow to enlighten them.
Obstacles are countless: I vow to cut them down.
Dharma gates are limitless: I vow to master them.
The Buddha-way is endless: I vow to follow through.[11]

In these three versions of the "Four Vows," then, we see a process of cultural
confluence, transmission and refinement.

The circumambulation ends, "— standing in our little circle, blowing
the conch, shaking the staff rings, right in the parking lot" (M&R 89). The
conch reminds one of the Yamabushi tradition, and the staff rings are cer-
tainly those Snyder mentions in his letter to Philip Whalen.[12] "The Circum-
ambulation of Tamalpais" is thus not only about a journey into and around
a mountain to make it sacred, but it is also about cultural transmission on
a planetary scale.

III.

In Section IV, the narrator takes the reader into the mythic world of Izanami,
Amaterasu, and Ame-no-uzume, three goddesses prominent in the Japanese

creation myth told in the *Kojiki* (Records of Ancient Matters).[13] "The Dance" (M&R 133–36) tells how the world began with Izanami, a Great Mother figure like Tārā, and the letter writer in "Mā" (M&R 57–60), whose creative power is shared by Amaterasu, "Goddess of the Sun," and Ame-no-uzume, "Outrageous Heavenly Woman" (M&R 133).

In the Japanese myth, Amaterasu shuts herself in a cave and makes the world dark because of her brother's outrageous acts. The gods entreat her to come out of the cave and fill the world with light again. Ame-no-uzume then dances an extraordinary dance in front of the cave. She stamps her feet and almost exposes her genitalia. The gods cheer, laugh and shout and the dance draws Amaterasu out. The Japanese critic, Shunsuke Tsurumi, calls Ame-no-uzume "a stripteaser in Japan's national myth."[14]

This striptease is also connected with the origin of Nō. In fact, Zeami states that Ame-no-uzume is the originator of Nō when her "divinely inspired" dance brings out the hidden Sun Goddess. What is striking in this poem is that Snyder directs the reader's attention not to Amaterasu, who is usually highlighted in this famous myth, but to Ame-no-uzume. Her stamping and stomping is compared to the water cycle as Snyder juxtaposes mythic episodes with realistic depictions of nature.

Snyder's Ame-no-uzume, a goddess identified with rivers and creeks, dances amid the desolate landscape as if through her dance she is attempting to bring back sunshine to the impoverished "land of darkness" (M&R 133). But when will it be? How do we do this? Where is our contemporary Ame-no-uzume with the power to bring light back to this world? The narrator ends the poem with questions, as if to invoke Ame-no-uzume's fluid and creative energies.

"The Dance" brings us to "We Wash our Bowls in This Water" (M&R 137–39), a meditation on water in its various forms. Rafting one day on the North Pacific Coast, the narrator sees "sea lions" under the surface of the sea and suddenly remembers some lines from "a Zen training-hall meal verse": "*We wash our bowls in this water / It has the flavor of ambrosial dew —*" (M&R 137, 162). This verse, called *Sessui Ge* (Verse of the Wastewater) in Japanese, is recited as monks wash their bowls after meals. In *The Wooden Fish*, Snyder and Kanetsuki quote D. T. Suzuki's translation in his *Training of the Zen Buddhist Monk*, published in 1959:

This water wherewith the bowls were cleansed,
Has the taste of heavenly nectar;
I offer it to you hosts of the spiritual realms,
May you all be filled and satisfied!
Om, Ma-ku-la-sai Svāha![15]

Snyder later translates this verse into English, and it is interesting to compare his translation with D. T. Suzuki's earlier version:

We wash our bowls in this water
It has the flavor of ambrosial dew
We offer it to all demons and spirits
May all be filled and satisfied.
Om makula sai svaha[16]

Here again we see an excellent example of cultural confluence, transmission, and refinement.

After this immersion in water comes "The Mountain Spirit," the climax of Section IV and the *kusemai* of the entire book. For a 1997 Tokyo reading, Snyder wrote a short essay entitled "Myth, Poetry, Landscape." I quote from the English text:

My residence in Japan, and many a walk in the hills and mountains of Kansai and Nagano-ken, gave me the courage to try and bring her [Yamamba's] story to North America, where I link her (in my poem, "The Mountain Spirit") with my youthful intuition of mountain spirits (I was a fanatic snowpeak mountaineer in my youth) and the Apache Indian idea of the Mountain Spirits whom they call the "Gahei." But more than that, I have the sense that it is a story the American landscape is ready for, whether the people are ready for it yet or not.

"The Mountain Spirit" thus results from a cross-fertilization of Japanese folklore and literature and the indigenous folklore of the North American landscape.

"The Mountain Spirit" retells the story of the Nō play *Yamamba* in

North American terms. Zeami's Nō play unfolds with three characters who take a short trip to a temple. One of the three is Hyakuma Yamamba. The first attendant explains to the audience: "The urchins have given her this name, because she has composed a song for a *kusemai* dance on the theme of the Yamamba's wandering from hill to hill and performs it herself."[17]

The reader who compares and contrasts "The Mountain Spirit" with Zeami's *Yamamba* at once notices similarities and differences between the two. Snyder basically follows Zeami's plot and characterization, but in "The Mountain Spirit" it is a lone male traveler who faces and dances with the Mountain Spirit. The theme of Zeami's play is the Buddhist doctrine of transmigration. Forever caught in this cycle of births and deaths, Yamamba roams from hill to hill, and Zeami foregrounds this religious theme in the climax of the play. In "The Mountain Spirit," however, it is not just the religious theme that the poet brings to the fore. What is striking and original in Snyder is his bold cross-fertilization of Far Eastern and North American traditions. The poem thus again shows a mixture of Buddhism, ecology, and indigenous North American cultures.

Japanese elements are most evident in the structure of the poem. "The Mountain Spirit" unfolds with an opening song that imparts the Buddhist doctrine of transmigration, the ecological concept of the cycle of life, and the American landscape in which the poem takes place. This corresponds to the *shidai* (entrance song).

In this connection, it is interesting to remember what Snyder envisioned in Kyoto in the 1950s. Concerning the possibility of American Nō, he wrote in his journal on September 30, 1956: "American Nō stage: background painting a desert and distant mountains? chorus on a long low bench. Maybe one larger real boulder" (EHH 37). "The Mountain Spirit" is thus a poem in which Snyder's long-held vision is finally realized. In this poem, the western American landscape represented by "red sandstone and white dolomite" is juxtaposed with lines that evoke religious and ecological themes.

Let me quote another passage that clearly shows Snyder's blending of Western American and Far-Eastern landscapes:

> Evening breeze up from the flats
> from the valleys "Salt" and "Death" —

Venus and the new moon sink in a deep blue glow
    behind the Palisades to the west,
needle-clusters shirring in the wind —
listen close, the sound gets better.   (M&R 142)

This is a landscape from the dry, arid American west. The landscape consisting of deserts and mountains fading in the distance is an American backdrop for the Nō stage. The last line in the quotation ("listen close, the sound gets better"), however, is taken from Snyder's own translation of Han Shan (RCMP 43). (Snyder's Zen name, Chōfū, is based on this line.)

IV.

As one of the salient Nō influences in *Mountains and Rivers Without End*, "The Mountain Spirit," a poem within a poem, tells of the creation of mountains and rivers in geological terms. As the poet recites his poem, the Mountain Spirit dances and the central thesis of the whole of *Mountains and Rivers Without End* finds expression as Snyder envisions the whole history of planet Earth, showing dynamic geological and biological movements as the planet forms itself.

    Snyder's Mountain Spirit differs from Zeami's Yamamba in that whereas the former represents the fusion of ecological and spiritual forces that shape the world, the latter emphasizes the Buddhist fate that forces her to roam from hill to hill. Snyder's American Mountain Spirit is free from Zeami's medieval Japanese lamentation over a person's inability to transcend the karmic cycle. Instead of lamenting, the narrator of Snyder's poem celebrates the shifting world:

    old woman mountain hears shifting sand
    tell the wind
        "nothingness is shapeliness"   (M&R 145)

This, I think, is the central statement in the poem, and it succinctly sums up Snyder's religio-ecological convictions.

    "Nothingness" is used here in a Buddhist sense. Buddhism holds that things in this cosmos are all mutually dependent and interconnected. In this sense, therefore, no phenomenal entity has any fixed or permanent form, and thus "no nature" is "true nature." The "shapeliness" of mountains and rivers, that is, the form of this world, is born of "nothingness," and this religious insight cross-fertilized with Western ecological science has informed Snyder's works and ideas. In this poem, the sand, a symbolic entity of formlessness, tells the wind about the ontological reality of this world.

After reciting his poem within a poem, the poet from the City and the Mountain Spirit dance together among the bristlecone pines (M&R 140). In this climactic scene, the differentiating line between nature and the human is obliterated. In this dancing scene, the syntax does not support a dualistic view of the world. Under the bright stars, the speaker dances with the Mountain Spirit, and the pine trees (now dancing with/as the Mountain Spirit) also dance with him. The dancers become one, and, at this moment, the pine trees scatter seeds on the ground — an ecstatic vision of fertility and life continuity nurtured by mountains and rivers. The dance ends when, as in a Nō play, the main dancer stamps down her foot. The Mountain Spirit then disappears, and the poet-narrator returns to his bedroll. Unlike Zeami's play, which ends with a tone of resignation on the part of Yamamba about her inability to escape the karmic cycle, Snyder ends his poem with a note of promise, fertility and continuation of life on this planet. Here, in this climactic scene, ethics and aesthetics are inextricably and convincingly entwined.

"Finding the Space in the Heart" (M&R 149–52) is the *kyū* ending of the whole book. It is a poem that celebrates the vastness and openness of the North American landscape, and the Buddhist idea of "emptiness" overlies the depiction of the physical vastness of the wilderness in the United States. The physical emptiness of the Western desert interacts with the human mind, leaving indelible impressions of a natural landscape that forces humans to ponder and debate their reasons for being there. This is a place to learn how to be, a place to envision a new future, reminding the reader of the indigenous tradition of a wilderness vision quest. I think the ending of this poem is typical of Snyder in that he combines a depiction of North American wilderness with the central concept of Buddhism.

Who are these people eating "grasshoppers roasted in a pan" and singing sūtras for insects in the wilderness? These are the new people emerging from the North American landscape who are committed to watersheds and bioregions, armed with a new vision for the future, and deeply conscious of how to be on this continent. In short, these are forerunners of Snyder's vision of a new humanity in the American landscape: "Natives of Turtle Island" who learn from "elders" and nurture a compassionate heart born of the vast "empty" space in North America.

Snyder has written, "I would like to think of a new definition of humanism and a new definition of democracy and that would include the nonhuman, that would have [senatorial] representation from those spheres. This is what I think we mean by an ecological conscience" (TI 106). Here Snyder extends Aldo Leopold's idea of a land ethic by bringing in a Buddhist-Ecological-Native American view of life. In *The Practice of the Wild*, Snyder writes:

> The "post" in the term *posthumanism* is on account of the word *human*. The dialogue to open next would be among all beings, toward a rhetoric of ecological relationships. This is not to put down the human: the "proper study of mankind" *is* what it means to be human. It's not enough to be shown in school that we are kin to the rest: we have to feel it all the way through. Then we can also be uniquely "human" with no sense of special privilege. . . . When humans know themselves, the rest of nature is right there. This is part of what the Buddhists call the Dharma.
>
> (PW 68)

Of course this vision of a new humanity transcends the geographical and political borders of North America. As we dwell in the midst of a planetary ecological crisis faced by all beings, the importance of our ability to understand and realize our posthuman prospect only increases.

NOTES

1. *Yamamba* sometimes appears as *Yamauba*. See Zeami, *Yamamba* [The Mountain Crone], in *Japanese Nō Dramas*, ed. and trans. Royall Tyler (New York: Penguin Books, 1992), 309–28; "Yamamba," in *Japanese Noh Drama: Ten Plays Selected and Translated from the Japanese* (Tokyo: Nippon Gakujutsu Shinkokai, 1959), 159–79.

2. Hiroshi Koyama, ed., *Nō kanshō annai* [A Guide to Nō] (Tokyo: Iwanami Shoten, 1989), 50. [For a scholarly introduction to Nō and Zeami's artistry, see Thomas Hare, *Zeami's Style: The Noh Plays of Zeami Motokiyo* (Stanford: Stanford University Press, 1986). This book contains an excellent glossary of technical Nō terms.

Tom Hare, a regular member of the Mountains & Rivers Workshop, presented on "Reclaiming Orientalism" at the Stanford Humanities Center on 26 January 1998.–ed.]

3. Toyoichiro Nogami, "Nōkoku no kosei" [The Structure of Nō] in *Nōgakuzensho* [A Complete Book of Nō], ed. Toyoichiro Nogami (Tokyo: Sogensha, 1980), 6.

4. Koyama, *Nō kansho annai* [A Guide to Nō], 35–36.

5. Motokiyo Zeami, *Kansho* (Kyoto: Sumiya-Shinobe Publishing Institute, 1968), 39.

6. Motokiyo Zeami, "Nōsakusho" [The Book of Nō Composition], in *Jurokubushi Hyoshaku*, ed. Asaji Nose (Tokyo: Iwanami Shoten, 1940), 624.

7. David Robertson, "The Circumambulation of Mt. Tamalpais," *Western American Literature* XXX/1 (1995): 4.

8. Robertson, "The Circumambulation of Mt. Tamalpais," 7.

9. D. T. Suzuki, *Manual of Zen Buddhism* (New York: Grove Press, 1960 [1934]), 14.

10. Gary Snyder and Gutetsu Kanetsuki, ed., *The Wooden Fish: Basic Sutras & Gathas of Rinzai Zen* (Kyoto: The First Zen Institute of America in Japan, 1961), 15.

11. *Daily Tasks in the Zen Woods* (Nevada City, CA: Ring of Bone Zendo, n.d.), 4.

12. Snyder introduces and discusses the Yamabushi ("those who stay in the mountains") in "Walking the Great Ridge Omine on the Womb-Diamond Trail," *Kyoto Journal* 25 (1993): 71–77.

13. See *Kojiki*, trans. Donald L. Philippi (Tokyo: University of Tokyo Press, 1968).

14. Shunsuke Tsurumi, *Ame-no-uzume-den* [Legends of Ame-no-uzume] (Tokyo: Heibonsha, 1991), 11.

15. D. T. Suzuki, *Training of the Zen Buddhist Monk* (New York: University Books, 1959 [1934]), 32.

16. [See Snyder's discussion of Zen meal verses in "Grace," a section of "Survival and Sacrament" in *The Practice of the Wild* (San Francisco: North Point Press, 1990), 182–85). —ed.]

17. "Yamamba" in *Japanese Noh Dramas*, 162.

6.

Mountains and Rivers and Japan

NANAO SAKAKI

My story starts at the end of the Pacific War, 27 March 1945. In response to the ardent demand of the crew, an American movie was shown on the upper deck of the *Yamato*, a Japanese battleship. The movie: *One Hundred Men and a Girl* (1937). The cast: Deanna Durbin, fifteen-year-old soprano singer with Leopold Stokowski and his musicians. The *Yamato* was the biggest ship in WWII and the only battleship left in the Japanese fleet at that time. The day after they saw the movie, the *Yamato* headed for Okinawa to fight back the American fleet. On 7 April, after two hours of hopeless fighting against one thousand American airplanes, the *Yamato* and its crew of three thousand went to the depths of the East China Sea.

One hundred and seventy kilometers southeast of the *Yamato*'s graveyard, there lies a small island named Suwa-no-Se. On 9 April, two days after the fighting, thirty dead bodies of the crew drifted ashore on the island. With sympathetic fingers and arms, the islanders cremated these bodies and built a grave for them. A week later, the rumor of the *Yamato*'s suicidal ending sneaked into my ears on the Kamikaze Air Base in the south of Japan. As a radar analyst, I couldn't harbor any illusions about the destiny of Japan. My concern at the moment was not over the battle, but over the coming days of peace if God would save my life in the war. In the air raid shelter, with long shiny black hair and a beard, I was listening to J. S. Bach's music and reading Shakespeare, the haiku poet Issa, and Kropotkin.

July 1967. From Industrial Empire, Japan. Thirty long-haired and long-bearded refugees drifted ashore on Suwa-no-Se Island. There they started a commune. Gary Snyder and Nanao were there.[1]

So now, I will talk a little bit about the situation of forests and rivers in Japan. Seventy percent of the land in Japan is mountain forest, and seventy percent of the forest is cedar. Several thousand black bears live on the mainland. One thousand brown bears live on the northern island of Hokkaidō, but no river otters. Many wild boars and fox, raccoon, and rabbit. No coyote. The rivers and the lakes are terribly contaminated. All around the second largest lake in Japan, named Kasumigaura, east of Tokyo, you can read signs that say NO SWIMMING. There is no fishing either; nobody even wants to go there. So now, I am helping to save two rivers. One is named Nagara River, between Tokyo and Kyoto. Every year my group walks the full length of the river (160 kilometers). Already we have walked it seven times, and this year will be the eighth. We start 21 July, so if you want to join, please talk to me. I am walking another river on Shikoku Island named Yoshino. The local people are starting to fight back against government projects.

Here is a little story about what is going on, from my poem "April First 1997":

> The Ministry of Construction who
> Already filled up Tokyo Bay
> With earth & rocks of Mt. Fuji
> Will build up another Mt. Fuji
> With ferro concrete for a tourism complex.
>
> > (from *Let's Eat Stars*, 88)

Now I will read two poems about a river. The first one, "Somewhere on the Water Planet," is for Nagara River. There is a very exciting animal still living in this river called the Giant Salamander, which can grow to be one-and-a-half meters long. So huge! I have met it two times already.

> In the beginning
> There was a forest, a beech forest.
> The forest gathered rain & divided rivers.
> Rivers that nourished all breathing creatures.
>
> Through long summer days
> We, honorable descendants
> Of *Yamamba*, mountain witch *Kappa*, river goblin

Walk down-river to the ocean.

On the path, scorching sun-beams
& sometimes torrential downpours.
In the bush, gnats, mosquitoes, ticks, newts & vipers.
At day's end, the darker the night, the brighter the moon & stars.

Our first meeting — *Megalobatrachus japonicus*
A giant salamander, who knows nothing
Of the extinction of dinosaurs or the end of the atomic age,
At ease in a pool by himself.

Next, a piece of Neolithic jar,
Shattered by a summer thunderbolt,
Buried deep in river-bank for five thousand years,
Waiting for some-one to pick it up.

In the blue sky, something dazzling drifting —
White porcelain, or fair weather cumulus?
Far away . . . typhoon;
Sound of a swallow skimming over a big dragon-fly
Resting on a trembling reed.

Ripples & children — the sun's dew drops —
Play in the same flow.
Diving, swimming, chattering together.
Cooking brown rice with driftwood on dry river-bed —
Dear sweet smell of campfire in years long-gone!
Dear living memories of a forest life in Neolithic times,
Under a roaring tsunami of golf balls
Many time-honored beech forests are drowning today.

This is a flow —
Binding forest to ocean or yesterday to tomorrow.
Look — fisherman's arms, fishing-pole, fishing-line, fishing hook!

There at the end of the line, brilliant silver light reflecting.
Is that a sweet-fish or a bubble of toxic waste-water?

One day from the ocean, from yesterday, I'm sure
A lost hump-back whale will swim up this river.
And someday, from the ocean, from tomorrow,
Countless whales will swim up the river
To revisit the ancient beech forest,
Whales swimming up the river, up the river.

August 1992
Nagara River, Japan (from Let's Eat Stars, 32–33)

I know there was one young whale swimming up the Sacramento River many years ago. See?[2]

Now, another river. The government in Tokyo wanted to build a huge, enormous dam. So, another poem: "Don't Cry Yoshino River":

Somewhere on the Water Planet
Somewhere in Yaponesia
Somewhere in a rice-rich country
Along the Median Tectonic Line

There is holy water.
People call it a river:
People call it Yoshino River.

Earth's muscle — the mountains high.
Earth's bloodlines — the gorges deep.

The Yoshino River
Gathers snow, rain and beech tree sap,
Cascades numberless falls, and
For a short while
Hanging in the terracing rice paddies

Reflects beautifully thousands of moons
Through late spring nights.

In the olden days
When the Yoshino River was dreaming
The twenty-first century
A golden wooden-horse was crossing
In a desert of concrete blocks and plastic trees.

A mysterious figure,
With an attaché case and a portable phone,
Was sitting uprightly on that golden saddle.

Today the Yoshino River
Is a flow of spirits
Offering generously
Its beauty, its strength and its richness
To all beings.
At the end of an epic journey
The water is returning
To the mother ocean
Now and always.

Look there!
At the estuary
A golden monolithic dam
Rises up!

Under the foot of the magic dam
All disappears . . .
From the tidal flat   the fiddler crab
From the beach   the whimbrel
From the binoculars   the osprey
From the future   the birdwatcher.

Living in his concrete cave
Third Stone Age man,
Just like a fiddler crab,
Brandishes triumphantly
His one-sided tremendous claw.
What destiny awaits him tomorrow?

Don't cry, Yoshino River!
    You are holy water!
    People call you a river!
    People call you Yoshino River!
Don't cry Yoshino River!

November 1996
(from *Let's Eat Stars*, 81–83)

Thank you.

DISCUSSION

RICK FIELDS: Nanao, where do your poems come from?

NANAO: Very good question. But first, tell me why such a question comes from you. Why? From where?

FIELDS: I have another question. What do you think about the future of the environmental movement? Do you think we have a snowball's chance in hell of reversing the destruction of the planet and if you do, how can we go about that?

NANAO: I have a mostly happy feeling of the twenty-first century. I read a miserable poem yesterday. It's too pessimistic, I feel. You must believe. Never give up. That's all. Never give up! If you give up, you can't write a poem. You can't sing a song. I still sing songs always. It means there is hope. But it's not so easy.

MARK GONNERMAN: Gary would like to say a few words.

GARY SNYDER: I don't have very much to add except to affirm how much Japan has meant to me. This string of islands far west across the Pacific from where we are here at the eastern shore of the Pacific: Yaponesia, Wa, Yamato, its many names, its many islands.

In learning how to get past the first rigidities of being in a new culture and in a new nation, I was helped enormously by Nanao, but was also helped by habits I had already established before I went there in 1956, which were habits of looking at the land. So the first thing I did on the third day I was in Kyoto was to go to the western end of the city. With very little Japanese I figured out how to get the bus and climb to the four-thousand-foot summit of Mount Atago. I found a trail and went up there because whenever I was in a new place it was my practice, my habit by that time, to go to the highest point available and look it over. And what are we looking at? We're looking at the mountains and the watersheds, the drainages and the ridges and the hills. That Chinese word, *shan shui*, mountains and waters, actually means "landscape" in Chinese. And so I was able to begin to learn from the landscapes.

Yamazato-san has very skillfully brought forward some of the esoteric interconnections in my poems with my Buddhist training and teachers in Kyoto. And Nanao was my teacher in another realm within Japan — his post-war realm of thinking, traveling, and learning with his circle of friends who are that "other" Japan that is looking for a new humanity. This business of looking for a new humanity, a new post-humanity is a mutual exercise, and there is an entirely mutual exchange back and forth across the Pacific.

NOTES

1. See Gary Snyder, "Suwa-no-se Island and the Banyan Ashram," in *Earth House Hold* (New York: New Directions, 1969), 135–43.
2. In October 1985, a humpbacked whale dubbed Humphrey made a wrong turn into San Francisco Bay while migrating south from his Alaskan feeding grounds. He traveled sixty miles up and back the Sacramento River, lured back to the ocean by Bernie Krause's recordings of feeding humpbacks (see Bernie Krause, *Notes from the Wild: The Nature Recording Expeditions of Bernie Krause* [Roslyn, New York: Ellipsis Arts, 1996], 53–77).

~

After it was acquired by the Cleveland Museum, the scroll was the subject of one of the first monographic studies of a single Chinese painting in a western language, Sherman Lee and Wen Fong's collaborative *Streams and Mountains Without End*, first published in 1955, just a year before the inception of Snyder's poem cycle. Those authors dated the painting to the early twelfth century, in the late Northern Sung period. Other scholars have argued for a somewhat later, mid-twelfth-century date during the Chin dynasty, based mostly on stylistic qualities of eclecticism of the composition and abbreviated treatment of the landscape motifs in terms of volume and surface texture. More recently, a still earlier, mid or late eleventh-century date for the scroll was proposed rather than a later one (that's not usually the way things go in art history). Susan Bush has summarized the varous proposed chronologies and supporting arguments in an article titled "Yet Again 'Streams and Mountains Without End'" [*Artibus Asiae* XLVIII, 3/4 (1987): 197–223]. Her study, which conveys something of another kind of endlessness, of art historical controversy and reassessment surrounding the painting, argued for a return to the early twelfth-century dating proposed by Lee and Fong, but for different iconographic and cultural-historical reasons.

> — Stanford art historian Richard Vinograd in his 27 October 1997 Mountains & Rivers Workshop presentation, "Words on Paintings on Words, & the Aesthetics of Endlessness"

EXPLORING POETIC ROOTS

~

As poets, our politics mostly stand back from that flow of topical events;
and the place we do our real work is in the unconscious, or myth-
consciousness of the culture; a place where people decide (without
knowing it) to change their values.

  — Gary Snyder, Letter to Wendell Berry (3 November 1977)

7

Some Interim Thoughts about Gary Snyder's *Mountains and Rivers Without End*

WENDELL BERRY

ountains and Rivers Without End is an ambitious poem, and it fulfills its ambition partly by going about its task with a kind of modesty. Gary Snyder knows well what his work is or must try to be, and from start to finish he is busy doing his work. At no place in these 152 pages does one feel the poet calling attention to his skill or watching to see if he is being admired.

The poem takes shape within the tradition of Zen Buddhism, which Mr. Snyder has long studied and practiced, and it is informed by his extensive reading of geology, astronomy, biology, history, and the literature of Asian and American Indian cultures.

Many readers by now take for granted that Mr. Snyder's mind and art have an Oriental ancestry, and this poem originates authentically in meditation on Chinese scroll paintings of endless mountains and rivers and in Dōgen's *Mountains and Waters Sūtra*. However, one cannot read this poem without feeling also the presence of its Western ancestors. It owes much to *The Cantos* and *Paterson*, though it seems to me a far neater poem with a more workmanly sense of purpose. *The Bridge* is back there in the pedigree somewhere, somehow, though I don't think Mr. Snyder's poem has a smidgeon of Crane's sentimental patriotism or his symbolistical confusion. And though it may be an understatement to say that Gary Snyder and John

This essay was composed in 1996 and first appeared in *The Sewanee Review* (Winter 1998) and was reprinted in *Imagination in Place* (Berkeley: Counterpoint, 2010), 103–10.

Milton are not alike, *Mountains and Rivers Without End* recalls and converses with the passages on the emerging world in *Paradise Lost*, Book VII.

I am confident that this poem has faults, and that it is no more definitive than any other poem — Milton's, for example — has been or will be. But this may be its fundamental proposition. If it should even for a moment forget its own condition of impermanence and claim to be the last word, it would be involved in a self-contradiction that would amount virtually to self-cancellation: It would disappear.

Mountains and Rivers Without End is not an endless poem because it cannot be — it ends, in fact, with perfect propriety and grace — but it is a poem about an unending subject: the great making of which we are the products, to which we contribute (not always or necessarily in our best interest), and to which the poem itself belongs. It is a poem about the poiesis of topography, cultures, cities, stories, dances, poems; about orogenesis, erosion, sedimentation; about composition; about travel.

Travel, in fact and metaphor, is its formal principle. The mountains are walking, says Dōgen; they are traveling on water. And we, says Mr. Snyder, are walking on the mountains that are walking; we are floating down the rivers:

> *Walking on walking*
> *under foot   earth turns*
>
> *Streams and mountains never stay the same.*
>
> (M&R 9 and *passim*)

People who think that "poetry makes nothing happen" will have to reckon again in reading this poem. Gary Snyder has been under the influence of his thought and work on this poem for forty years, during which he has not only worked to make things happen himself, but has influenced others who have been working to make things happen. And not only that. His poem is suffused, imbued, steeped in happening, the unending event of this world. How, as an effect of that event, with which it is totally preoccupied, could the poem not be in turn a cause?

Everything is in motion, everything is under influence, is being moved by something else, or by much else. Everything is "traveling." The great scroll painting *Endless Streams and Mountains*, now in the Cleveland Museum of Art, is a painting full of travelers on trails and waterways; the painting itself has traveled from place to place, from owner to owner; Mr. Snyder traveled to Cleveland to see it; he has borne it in mind during his other travels. And everything that happens happens in its time and in all time, and is never finished.

In Milton's version, the world was made at the beginning, once and for all; after that, human history would be the thing to watch. In Mr. Snyder's version, we are living in a world that is still and always being made; human history is not being made "on" or "in" the world, but is involved by intricate patterns of influence and causation in the continuous making of the world. This is an extremely important difference — morally, practically, and prosodically.

I am not dismissing Milton, whose work is eminent in my thoughts, and who is as instructive, dissident, and disturbing to intellectual conventions in our day as he was in his own. Read his lines on nature spirits (*Paradise Lost*, IV, 677–88) or on "knowing in measure" (VIII, 111–30), and you will see what I mean. His account of the creation of the world is an astonishing realization; I can't imagine that it will ever cease to matter. But one of the interesting things about Milton is his entanglement in the modern, dominantly urban and political world. Past the great Judaic legend of the acts of creation, Milton took the world for granted, as modern urban people and modern politics have steadfastly continued to do. The difference between John Milton and Gary Snyder is not primarily that between Western and Eastern cultures, or that between Europe and America, but that between a man who took the world for granted and a man who does not.

Mr. Snyder is by no means ignorant of the modern urban and political world, as several sections of this book amply show. But one thing that most distinguishes him as a poet is the extent to which he has accepted the influence of his experience of actual landscapes and cities, mountains and rivers. Milton was preeminently a scholar, and in his most productive years as a poet, by necessity of his blindness, he was a sedentary scholar; his task as a poet was to summon his great learning into imagination — to see inwardly what no human had seen before. Mr. Snyder too is a scholar, but he has always been a scholar walking and looking, telling us at times of things beyond sight, but telling us too what we will see in our everyday world if we will have the kindness to look. His poem is full of what is sometimes called "information," but it is information that has become real knowledge, knowledge worn in by experience. Much of what he has read about he has also seen, walked across, floated over. Several of the landscapes he has lived in he has also worked in.

Mountains and Rivers Without End is a poem keenly and amusedly conscious of participating in its subject. Its subject is ever-changing. By being about its subject, the poem assumes a certain power or responsibility to change it — perhaps for the better. The poem thus refuses to be measured exclusively by literary or critical or scholarly standards. It freely and good-humoredly offers itself also to the measures of nature and experience. The statement implied by its publication is not an assertion but a question: not "This is the way it is" or "This is the way it seems to me" but "Is it not something like this? Does it not seem so to you?"

This poem is instructive. Whether or not it is "didactic" probably does not matter. It certainly is not didactic in the bad sense; it does not grab at your lapels or rant or condescend. What it teaches and indeed insists upon is the fluency of the world and therefore the pervasiveness of human influence and the moral problem of that influence. The world is always being changed, partly by us. We are always being changed by the world — and by the world as we have changed it. We cannot escape these forceful patterns of influence. The world cannot escape our influence or our effluents, including our poetry.

Since we are members of the natural world, what we do is "natural" — as cynics and technological determinists like to say. A beer can is as natural as a leaf, an atomic explosion as natural as a volcanic eruption, etc. Mr. Snyder concedes the point:

> trucks on the freeways,
> Kenworth, Peterbilt, Mack,
> rumble diesel depths,
> like boulders bumping in an outwash glacial river   (M&R 66)

But he points out, further, that these natural doings of ours can be dangerous to ourselves, not to mention the natural neighborhoods in which we must live. It is possible for humans to fabricate a human condition that obscures their natural condition:

> us and our stuff just covering the ground.   (M&R 67)

so that we can know neither the mountains nor the Mountain Spirit. The solution to the moral problem (which is always more than moral) is to "become born-again natives" (M&R 161) of the places where we live.

Mr. Snyder's poem will be disturbing also to people who think of the English sentence as an ultimate or adequate model of reality. What we have here, instead, is a syntax of verbal strokes, gesturing toward a reality that is not linear and directly causative like a conventional sentence, but instead is multidimensional and accumulative, is influential in all directions, like a geological formation, an ecosystem, a city, a culture. The difference is like that between the structure of a factory or a modern school and that of a family or a forest.

A fairly continuous and reassuring thread of merriment runs through this book, and part of it is the almost thematic upsetting of syntactic expectations. Fragments of syntax that at first seem to promise to become sentences lead into lists of items tumbling down the page. This is exactly as if what appears at a glance to be a stable slope is revealed, to a longer look, as a landslide — which is what every slope is, to a look that is long enough.

Mr. Snyder, of course, can write good sentences, and he has the confidence of this ability. His poem does not reject the artifice of syntactical "completeness" and closure — it is itself an artifice and must end — but puts it off, finds ways of procrastinating: lists, sentence fragments, sentences only begun, sentences caught up and carried on in structures that are not sentences. The book ends — humorously and gracefully acceding to its own provisional need to stop — with two plain, perfect sentences:

> The space goes on.
> But the wet black brush
> tip drawn to a point,
>   lifts away.   (M&R 152)

Mr. Snyder does not believe — as Teilhard de Chardin and many others have believed — that humans can "'seize the tiller of the planet'" (M&R 39). *Mountains and Rivers Without End* is about the impossibility of such control — which, in a sense, it may demonstrate by its fragmentary syntax, its lists, its abrupt shifts of thought. And yet the poem does not imitate control-lessness. The poet's intelligence, skill, and artistic judgment are evident throughout, and from the earliest sections to the latest, his abilities increase. I leave the book, every time, with the sense that it is rhythmically and even musically coherent from start to finish. That is hard to demonstrate, obviously, but one of the signs of such coherence is economy, which is unarguably here. A wonderful amount is accomplished in these 152 pages; nothing is wasted. Another sign may be the frequent occurrence of passages that are eminently lyrical or memorable. I hesitate to quote because I will necessarily be quoting "out of context," but consider this prosodic astuteness of these lines:

> boat of the sun,
> the abt-fish, the yut fish,
> play in the waves before it . . .   (M&R 39)

And the section entitled "Afloat" opens with a lyric that spirals down, turning on rhymes and assonances:

> Floating in a tiny boat
> lightly on the water, rock with every ripple,
>
> another skin that slides along the water
> hung by sea and sky
>
> green mountains turn to clouds
> and slip slow by
>
> two-mile saltwater channel
> sucks and coils with the tide . . .   (M&R 130)

Thus it flows.

8

Proceeding by Clues

Reading *Mountains and Rivers Without End*

ROBERT HASS

I.

It's a pleasure to be here, and it was a struggle to arrive in the midst of this amazing storm. The trip made me think of all the journey poems in *Mountains and Rivers*. Traveling, of course, was a literary tradition in Asian poetries. Bashō set out on his treks in imitation of medieval monk-poets like Saigyō. The idea was that passing through was a way of reminding oneself that we are all always just passing through. And this morning was some metaphor for the journey. At one point just before Niles Canyon, traffic stopped altogether. The rain was coming down in sheets and there came to be no point in trying to drive at all. So everyone stopped where they were. The rain drummed on the car so hard it was as if I were pure mind and all of sense experience was just drumming away on the outside of it. So I thought of Bishop Berkeley and of how Buddhists could come to think of the world as pure phenomenal illusion. When the traffic started up again, I could see that the road was filling up with the memory of having been a salt marsh. The wind along the Dumbarton Bridge was so fierce that the gulls that tried to launch into it just gave up and sat on the rail and pulled in their necks. One snowy egret kept trying to rise, and each time sheared off into the wind. Its wings trying to get purchase on the air had the ferocious, awkward look of an Audubon painting. It was really spectacular, an object lesson in the world as pure energy.

I feel I'm not very far along in my understanding of *Mountains and*

This text is based on a transcription of an informal talk delivered to the Stanford Mountains & Rivers Workshop, without notes and with a copy of the poem in hand. It has been lightly edited for coherence but not substantially revised.

Rivers, but would like to begin by locating it in the tradition of the American long poem. The first great long poem in American literature is "Song of Myself." It's rooted in vegetation myth. Whitman was, before there was such a term, an ecological thinker. He read Emerson and he also read the Humboldt brothers, Wilhelm and Alexander. He understood the science of his time and he took from it the idea that the creative principle in nature was diversity and abundance, and the idea that nature is a constant process of birth, growth, death, and regeneration. It is there in the blades of grass in section 6 of the poem, where he projects a series of meanings onto the grasses. He was really trying to invent a new imagination, rooted in this sense of nature, for a new poetry and a new political system on this continent. He was trying to enact how curiosity about life gives us quick powers of sympathy and identification that were or could be the basis for a democratic culture.

There's a way in which you could see T. S. Eliot's *The Waste Land* as a direct reply to "Song of Myself." In fact, Eliot's poem seems to be about the failure of a vegetation myth. At its core is a prayer for rain in a desert place, a call for the renewal of fertility. Eliot had read the book of a folklorist named Jessie Weston who proposed that elements of an old Celtic fertility myth, perhaps a ritual, underlay the Arthurian stories. The mythic story was about the son of a fisher king who had to recover his creative powers and restore health to the land, and Eliot made of it a metaphor for a desiccated, postwar Europe. I think at this moment in the history of the interpretation of the poem, there is a question about the final direction of Eliot's conflicted intentions. There is a reading of the poem in which it imagines the return of rain, the discovery of the Grail, the recovery of fertility, and the reconstruction of society based on these ancient patriarchal and salvific stories that became the Arthurian legends that came to be embodied in Christianity and the grail quest. At least the poem ends with a prayer in the direction of these aims. And there is a reading of the poem that thinks Eliot is saying that we have to see through the illusions of the sensual world, see through, in the famous passage in the first section of the poem, what the girl in the hyacinth garden has to offer — "'You gave me hyacinths first a year ago; / 'They called me the hyacinth girl.'" — to a hard, clear, ascetic light, to the narrator who says he is at that moment, "neither / Living nor dead" and "Looking into the heart of light, the silence." In this reading, the old wisdom of the Vedas that the thunder speaks at the end of the poem leads not back to the world, but away from it, toward a rejection of the myth of flowering. My own sense is that part of the power of the poem is that Eliot didn't know which way the poem was leading him. The point for our purposes is that, fundamentally, it is rooted in ecological thought, an attempt to describe an alignment of natural, political, and personal life by describing a world in which that idea had radically failed and existed only in fragmentary glimpses to be longed toward.

Eliot's use of fragmentation, juxtaposition, allusion, and quotation from traditional sources that seem to embody values no longer available are elements of the poem that came to define modernism, and they very much influenced the young Gary Snyder. In fact, one of his first published poems in the college magazine at Reed is a poem about Sir Edmund Hillary's conquest of Mount Everest, written in imitation, he has said, of *The Waste Land*.

The other enormously important long poem in this American grain was Ezra Pound's *The Cantos*. Snyder's methods depend on Pound in every way. In fact, there is an early parody of Gary Snyder's style — an affectionate parody — by Robert Bly called "Hearing Gary Snyder Read," published as a broadside in 1971. In Bly's version the narrator of the poem describes himself bucking hay with an old guy who lays down his pitchfork, turns to the young man in the poem, and says, "Kid, you should learn to write like Ezra Pound. You'll go a long way."

Snyder did take over a lot of Pound's rhythms and he also took over, as Pound did, the techniques of *The Waste Land*: juxtaposition, fragmentation, associative leap and connection, the constellated image as ideogram, and the use of brief quotations to evoke the lived values of whole cultures. This work done by Eliot was extended by Pound in his poem or set of poems. People get lost in *The Cantos*, but at their center one of their great impulses is clear enough. When someone asked Pound his motive for the poem, he said it was "to return the altar to the forest." This is very interesting in connection with American culture because the effort to reconstruct the terms of myth and push them forward was, as with Whitman, the effort to write a long poem that reconstructs and transvalues the values of what Pound, like Eliot, saw as a corrupted civilization. It's interesting that Pound and Eliot thought of it as a *young* and corrupted civilization and looked for renewal to an old and corrupted European civilization, though they both also made a pivot to Asia, Eliot to the Upanishads and Hindu asceticism, Pound to his long involvement with Confucius. Their notions about the recovery of myth came from Eliot's reading of Jessie Weston, but also and more crucially from Jane Harrison at Cambridge and from Frazer's *Golden Bough*. They willed to the future — and to the young Gary Snyder — a sense of the possibility of renewal in archaic values it had become the task of poetry to recover.

I think there are a couple of other things about *The Cantos* that are interesting in relation to Snyder's work. One is that there is a central mythic ascesis in the poem through the three female deities who appear. Am I using that word correctly? I have in mind an ascent, an evolution upward, achieved through self-discipline. I think you can still think about the poem as organized first around Aphrodite, the figure for beauty in movement and the energy of sexuality. Then around Hera, the Mother Goddess, the harvest queen who becomes the goddess of cities, and, by the end of the poem, Kuan Yin or Kannon, the Chinese or Japanese Buddhist figure — well, not only Buddhist — for compassion toward the suffering implicit in all the movements of desire. This arc is rooted in Pound's critique of the aestheticism in which he was reared and gets some poignancy from the failures and catastrophic errors in his own life and in his acknowledgement of them in the final fragments of his poem.

The other interesting thing is that the time of Pound's formation was the time of the formation of the conservation movement in the United States. It was the period when Teddy Roosevelt went camping with John Muir in Yosemite Valley. In 1909, when Pound was in London trying to write poems that would bring European mythological thinking in poetry back to life, the legislature of the United States was engaged in the creation of the first national parks, the first places where we set aside large tracts of land, Yellowstone and Yosemite, as national monuments and shrines to the natural world that we had settled and were ruthlessly and successfully exploiting.

The thing that makes *The Cantos* different from either "Song of Myself" or *The Waste Land* is that both, in their different ways, are vision quests. Pound describes himself early in his poem as "sailing after knowledge." As anyone who has had any acquaintance with the Ezra Pound scholarship industry knows, Pound proposed a curriculum. He thought to create a sort of alternative, non-Christian reading list of the history of human cultures in order to reorder civilization. The poem aims to transform culture by embodying a different tradition of knowledge. And that is clearly one of the aims of Gary Snyder's poetry. It's certainly possible to argue that *The Cantos* does have a dramatic quest at its center, or that Pound's life gave it that structure in the end. There is a longing for a unifying vision and an acknowledgement of not having got there at the end of the poem. "It coheres alright," he wrote in the last fragments, "though these notes do not cohere," but large stretches of the poem aim to impart and embody knowledge. The extent to which *Mountains and Rivers* is a dramatic poem and a vision quest, and the extent to which it aims to impart and embody knowledge (to use the language of genre, a georgic or a series of georgics) is an interesting question about its organization, one that readers of the poem are going to want to answer for themselves.

Another long poem that bears thinking about in the tradition I've been sketching is Allen Ginsberg's *Kaddish*. One way to make the connection is through the figure of Naomi Ginsberg. In Ginsberg's then-revolutionary autobiographical poem, we get a highly personal account of his mother's madness and his relation to it. If you were so disposed, you could read Naomi Ginsberg as another aspect of the fertility stories, as a Tārā figure. There is enough evidence and enough emotional charge in the poem to support that reading. Tārā covers a lot of ground in Buddhist iconography. In Snyder she is synonomous with Kuan Yin. The goddesses — or the faces of the goddess; in one way of speaking about this, there is one goddess whose faces correspond to the moon's phases, the waxing moon that begins with a virginal huntress like Artemis and moves through the figure of Aphrodite to the full moon of the Mother Goddess, the cereal goddess, Hera, to the waning, thin moon of Isis-Kannon. This is the movement, I think, in the *Cantos,* where Pound conflates the Egyptian goddess with the Asian ones. These readings of lunar phases are an aspect of an old and almost universal mythology of the feminine, of the female principle, the carrier, the bearer and producer of fertility. Tārā, Black Tārā in Tibetan Buddhism, is power, and wrath, Medea, scary nature. She's Tārā in her Kali aspect. Ecologically, I guess she is the decomposer aspect of the carbon cycle. And she is what humans have understood to be female in what they fear about nature and natural cycles. Or about violence done to them. This is the territory also of *The Eumenides*, and very different from the Tārā in *Mountains and Rivers*, where she seems synonomous with Kannon, where she is a figure for compassion flowing back into the world. Black Tārā is the wounding. She's the wounded world and she is its fury.[1]

You could read Naomi Ginsberg this way. The poem ends, you remember, with the young Allen Ginsberg coming away from the hospital where his mother has been incarcerated, given shock therapy, and lobotomized to free her from the terror of the delusions of what we call her paranoid condition. Her son had to sign the permission for these procedures. When he is coming away from the hospital, outside Paterson, New Jersey, he sees in a field a flock of black crows, cawing in chorus. "Caw, caw, caw." And Jewish prayer comes up in him and he calls back to the crows: "Lord, Lord, Lord." And the crows go, "Caw, caw, caw." And the speaker goes, "Lord, Lord, Lord." And the poem ends with "Lord" rather than "caw." "Caw Lord, caw, Lord." But it ends in a kind of unbearable, emblematic anguish between the purely naturalistic and terrifying view of the world and the one in which there is something transforming suffering. It ends right on the gnostic edge between acceptance of the processes of this world and their rejection. All through American literature the poets stumble up against this. That's where we are in 1958, in that field in New Jersey. You can see that Gary Snyder sits right in the middle of this conversation. He takes over its terms and its techniques, and does new things with them.

All this by way of background.

II.

The next thing is for us to read *Mountains and Rivers Without End.* I've been reading bits of it as they have come out over the years, having no idea how or if Gary Snyder would ever finish the poem. So when it came out, I got my hands on it and began to read it with students in a course I was teaching. I've read through it this way a couple of times, just trying to see what's there. I was puzzled and interested, first of all, by what the principle of organization is, and in what sense it is a poem and not a collection of poems. It wasn't clear to me. Snyder's first long poem, *Myths & Texts*, is very highly organized and articulated. It has a first section called "Logging," a second section called "Hunting," and a third section called "Burning." The first section is called "Logging" because it is about his own experience as a logger; it's also about that way of relating to the world. The second section is called "Hunting" because he wants to move into and through Native American and current relationships to hunting practices and evoke the animist root of them found in almost every culture. And the third section is about meditative practices. So in a way it's about building, eating, and praying as three fundamental activities.

In the first essay written about *Myths & Texts*, Richard Howard argued that the organization of the poem was connected to the three categories of human activity proposed by Hannah Arendt in *The Human Condition*. The work of *animal laborans*, writes Arendt, is the stuff we do that disappears with us: grow potato, eat potato, it's gone. *Homo faber*, man the maker, constructs things that may very well outlast him as he constructs a world. And finally, there are intellectual and spiritual activities that at their best have a longer life than chairs or houses. So one can think of this as about our relation to plants, animals, and the mind. Really, it tracks and sorts out the activities Snyder was engaged in — summer work in logging camps, on trail crews, studying Native American mythology, studying classical Asian literature and Buddhism. However it's framed, the structure of *Myths & Texts* is clear; it's interesting, it makes its proposal. With *Mountains and Rivers* it is not so clear what Snyder is doing.

So I want to come at this first in two ways. I know that the date of publication is not necessarily the date of composition, but I want to give you a sense of the date of publication of each part of the poem. I think it's revealing in terms of how the poem was put together. So, the poem was published in 1996. The first two poems, "Endless Streams and Mountains" and "Old Bones" were published in 1995. This was when Snyder turned with a will to finish a poem that was begun forty years before in 1956. "Night Highway 99" was published in 1962; "Three Worlds, Three Realms, Six Roads," 1966; "Jackrabbit" — this looks like an anomaly and I'll tell you why later — 1988; "The Elwha River," 1965; "Bubbs Creek Haircut," 1961; "Boat of a Million Years," 1996; "The Blue Sky," 1968. If you look at what was happening there, you can see that Snyder put in the first section the earliest parts of *Mountains and Rivers Without End,* which were published as a little chapbook with that title in 1965. Then he wrote the beginning of the poem, or the two introductory poems, "Endless Streams and Mountains" and "Old Bones," and then, interestingly, he added toward the end of this section another new poem, "Boat of a Million Years." So one way of trying to understand his intention would be to pay attention to this. It's a way of seeing the maker at work as you read the poem. I can understand not wanting to read this way, to take the poem as it comes, poem by poem, section by section, and let it work on you, but if you care about the structure, looking at this chronology helps.

So here are the dates of publication — not composition — of the poems in the second section: "The Market," 1964; "Journeys," 1965; "Mā," 1974; "Instructions," 1995; "Night Song of the Los Angeles Basin," 1986; "Covers the Ground," 1994; "The Flowing," 1974; "The Black-Tailed Hare," 1968; "With This Flesh," 1994, "The Hump-backed Flute Player," 1971. One thing to note is that he begins still in the early writing of the poem from '64 and '65, and includes the only three poems written in the 1970s that went into the poem — "Mā," "The Flowing," and "The Hump-backed Flute Player." Two poems, "Instructions" and "With This Flesh" belong to the period of the final shaping. So in a rough way you can say that Part I is the poems of the 1950s and '60s, and Part II, poems of the '60s and '70s.

Section three: "The Circumambulation of Mt. Tamalpais," 1966; "The Canyon Wren," 1983; "Arctic Midnight Twilight," 1986; "Under the Hills Near the Morava River," 1993; "Walking the New York Bedrock," 1987; "Haida Gwai North Coast, Naikoon Beach," 1989; "New Moon Tongue," 1996; "An Offering for Tārā," 1995; "The Bear Mother," 1988; "Macaques in the Sky," 1991. So this section begins with an early poem, "The Circumambulation of Mt. Tamalpais," as the second section does, but it contains mostly poetry from the 1980s. Again for clues to the final shaping, the newest poems, "New Moon Tongue" and "An Offering to Tārā," were published in '95.

The final section: "Old Woodrat's Stinky House," 1996; "Raven's Beak River," '88; "Earrings Dangling and Miles of Desert," '92; "Cross Legg'd," '96; "Afloat," '93; "The Dance," '87–91; "We Wash Our Bowls in This Water," '96, "The Mountain Spirit," '96; "Earth Verse," '96; "Finding the Space in the Heart," '96. So one thing you can tell from this about the shaping of the poem is that, whatever his earlier intuitions about the poem and its future he may have had in mind as he added sections in the 1970s and '80s, the organization and construction of the poem occurred somewhere between 1993 and 1995, and the first poems and the last poems were written as he was trying to give final shape to the whole poem.

One of the things this suggests is that the poem invites an autobiographical reading. That is, he put the poems of the '60s in the first section, the poems of the '70s in the second section, the '80s in the third, and the '90s in the fourth. It is not strictly so, but it corresponds roughly to the four decades during which the poem was written. If you are going to think of Snyder's life in this way, I think you probably think of the '50s and '60s as the Beat period, the time of his formal education, his Buddhist training in Japan, the first writing of poetry with its mix of Poundian aesthetics and study of classical Chinese poetry and the new compositional energies of his contemporaries including O'Hara and Ginsberg. The 1970s and early '80s is the period of his settling in Nevada City and raising a family. There's a turn at this point in his work, too. *Turtle Island* won the Pulitzer Prize in 1975, as he was coming to prominence. This was a period, it seems to me, of a turn for Snyder from the time of his putting his ideas together — the poetry of *Rip Rap, Cold Mountain Poems, The Back Country, Myths & Texts,* the early sections of *Mountains and Rivers Without End* — the poetry of somebody who was inventing himself and figuring out what he was going to do — to the work of someone who had settled down to put into practice what he had learned. There's also, I think, a turn, or half turn, from the compression of the modernist aesthetic to a more populist style. The poems of the later '70s — which are not my favorite of his poems — are the ones in which, while he continues to be an observer, he also sets out to be a teacher. They are much more didactic poems, more intended to demonstrate things he's arrived at, rather than forge out of his own conflicts the terms of his vision. By the 1980s he was a much put upon and widely traveled environmentalist, Buddhist teacher, and poet. He took on all three of these roles and, here, in these poems, what the '90s stand for, is the period when he withdrew again — having retired from his position as a university professor at UC Davis — to do the job of finishing this poem. This is a way of mapping the territory.

Another is to see what he himself has said about the making of the poem. When I first read his little essay, "The Making of *Mountains and Rivers Without End*" (M&R 153–58). I thought, "Oh! This is really no help at all." In fact, I thought it was infuriatingly evasive about what he was up to in the poem. And the more I read it, the more I see that that's not true; it's enormously helpful. Let me say what I can about the clues offered there, and then I want to do some reading.

The first crucial thing is his remark in the beginning of the essay that he discovered East Asian painting in college and began to do ink drawings. He says, "I became aware of how the energies of mist, white water, rock formations, air swirls — a chaotic universe where everything is in place — are so much a part of the East Asian painter's world." I want to call attention to the word "energies," to the series of elements, "mist, white water, rock formations, air swirls," and to the paradox of "a chaotic universe where everything is in place." As a premonitory look at one of the subjects of the poem, this is important.

On the next page he talks about going back into the mountains where he liked to watch "the change of mood over vast landscapes, light moving with the day — the countless clouds, the towering cumulus, black thunder storms rolling in with jagged lightning strikes." Maybe this is the place to say that the idea of change is at the core of Buddhist theology, in one way or another. The old term for it in medieval Buddhist thought was one word made out of a series of words: "swirling-petals-falling-leaves." You can't from some angles tell snowflakes from plum blossom petals. The world is in motion, in ceaseless and endless change. And the central meditative act of so much of medieval Buddhist practice and the subject of Buddhist visual art and poetry was "falling-blossoms-swirling-leaves." Another way to say this is "the change of mood over vast landscapes, light moving with the day — the countless clouds." As an image of change, this is also an image of travel. It's an image of a world ceaselessly in movement, and in this case, conjured from the fixed point of view of a perceiver. That turns out to be important in the poem.

At the end of the same paragraph, Snyder says he began to read Chinese and Japanese Ch'an texts, and also Hindu texts, and to take "delight in their scale of imagination and their fearless mytho-psychological explorations." Clearly, *Mountains and Rivers* is about scale, and I want to comment on those "mytho-psychological explorations." He says that it was out of these that he began to write *Myths & Texts*: "This sequence was my first venture into the long poem and the challenge of interweaving physical life and inward realms." Here he names another ambition of his poem.

Then he talks about meeting Alan Watts and through him meeting Saburo Hasegawa and others who spoke of "the East Asian landscape painting as meditative exercise." I think this comes to the heart of what is going on in *Mountains and Rivers*. At one level it is an imitation of landscape painting as meditative exercise. He goes on, "I think he once said that the landscape paintings were, for Zen, as instructively and deeply Buddhist as the tankas and mandalas were for Tibetan Buddhism." On the next page he tells us, usefully, that he began the poem on April 8, 1956, and though he doesn't claim to have finished it on April 8, 1996, he does describe giving a party on that date to celebrate the completion of the project. Like Louis Armstrong's claiming to be born on the Fourth of July, this suggests a desire to see life through mythic patterns, or to make them. It's also an interesting take on Gary's precision and discipline.

Next paragraph: "I came to see yogic implications of 'mountains' and 'rivers' as the play between the tough spirit of willed self-discipline and the generous and loving spirit of concern for all beings: a dyad presented in Buddhist iconography as the wisdom-sword-wielding Manjushri, embodying transcendent insight, and his partner, Tārā, the embodiment of compassion, holding a lotus or a vase. I could imagine this dyad as paralleled in the dynamics of mountain uplift, subduction, erosion, and the planetary water cycle." This is a big clue for us to what he was up to: that the thought of those landscapes came to be blended with a thought about the interplay between two aspects of Buddhist spirituality.

And another clue follows: "I began to envision *Mountains and Rivers* through the dramatic strategies of Nō." The particular poem in the book that is modeled explicitly and directly on Nō drama, almost scene by scene, and line by line, is "The Mountain Spirit." One of my former students at Berkeley, David Lee, wrote an honors thesis that is an intense close reading of this poem in relation to the Japanese text, *Yamamba*, on which Snyder modeled it. Two things about Nō are important here. First, it is shamanic in origin. That is to say, it's about conjured experience, about confrontation with a spirit. And this is in keeping with the whole modernist project of remythologizing and respiritualizing the world positive science had seemed, to many minds in those years, to have rendered dead. Whether and on what terms that project is possible, is more than romantic sentimentality, is one of the burdens of Snyder's entire body of work. Secondly, a Nō play is almost always about a journey. It's almost always in motion. And its formal structure is an almost continuous self-commentary. I think that's going to be very important to the epistemology of the poem. It will come up for readers of the poem in various ways.

And then on page 156: "Although my main reason for being in Kyoto was to do Zen Buddhist practice, . . . I was given a chance to see how walking the landscape can become both ritual and meditation. I did the five-day pilgrimage on the Omine ridge and established a tentative relationship with the archaic Buddhist mountain deity Fudō. [Meeting "The Mountain Spirit" is, of course, the explicit treatment of this theme.] This ancient exercise has one visualizing the hike from peak to valley floor as an inner linking of the womb and diamond mandala realms of Vajrayana Buddhism." Add to this the linearity of looking at the paintings horizontally as another motion of meditation entangled with the up-and-down exercise of walking as a way of linking the two energies of the poem, water and mountain.

When he came back from Japan, he writes, "Poems for *Mountains and Rivers* kept showing up at the rate of about one a year." That's not very many. There was the explosive beginning, and then a few — a periodicity over the middle years of poems he recognized (By what principle?) as *Mountains and Rivers* poems — and then another great burst at the end. I confess I was tempted to pick up the phone and ask him what told him he had a *Mountains and Rivers* poem, but I believe it was D. H. Lawrence who said, "Never trust the artist. Trust the tale." My interest really was in reading the poem, in having the experience of proceeding by clues.

There is a lot else in the essay, but let's come to the end. He tells us that between 1991 and 1995 he turned his attention to the completion of the poem and if you look at the chronology of the individual pieces you can see that. The other important things to say he says in the last paragraph: "I knew my time with this poem would eventually end." This way of conceiving his relationship to his own poem comes into it in various ways. And then the final thing: "The form and emptiness of the Great Basin showed me where to close it; and the boldness of my young people, who ate unlikely manna in the wilderness, how." He doesn't specify what kids he means, his own children, his many young readers, the "great arcs of kids on bikes out there in darkness" that he sees in the final poem of the sequence, but I think of the second half of "Song of Myself" when Whitman suddenly imagines himself addressing disciples, his *eleves*. Snyder, of course, doesn't do that. But he does say, "This poem, which I have come to think of as a sort of sūtra — an extended poetic, philosophic, and mythic narrative of the female Buddha Tārā — is for them."

And what he says at the end of the essay is quite useful. It's evident enough, not just in the dating of the individual poems, that the whole poem has an autobiographical arc. It ends in "Finding the Space in the Heart" with a poem that looks back across his experience of the Nevada desert from the 1960s, when he first visited it, to the poem's present, when he is an older man. In the middle of the poem he revisits the landscape of the 1960s in the 1980s. In the 1960s he visits it with "a dangerous girl with a husky voice." In the '70s with kids he gets stuck in the sand. In the '80s he visits it with his lover; in the '90s, the poem's present, his lover has become his wife. I don't think this is the presentation of a changed person. The poem hasn't moved to some transformed place. It's the same person at the end, changed and not changed. A "mythic narrative of the female Buddha Tārā." That's a big clue, and should send readers to the complex poem, "An Offering for Tārā," which occurs about two-thirds of the way through the book. She comes clear in the Great Basin poem in the desert emptiness where, as in the epigraph to the poem, "The notion of Emptiness engenders Compassion." And there is the fact that he turns the poem over to the young people. That is, like *The Cantos*, it's important to understand about the structure of the poem that it's intended, or came to be intended, as an instructional text, a georgic, or sūtra, with the Sanskrit root implying something stitched together. Like *The Cantos* it aims to be an embodiment of knowledge.

So we can see that one part of the structure of the poem is that it takes its shape from the arc of the poet's adult life, a period of about forty years. It's a poem of experience. And the composition to some extent tracks that process. We also know that it's informed by this dyadic interest in disciplines aimed at transcendence, on the one hand — troubling term, I know, but associated with the idea of non-attachment and figured as upward movement, ascent — and, on the other hand, compassion for the world figured as the downward flow of water. The misty energies he talks about at the beginning of the essay (air rising, water descending, clouds moving) are movements between these things, or, maybe better, the movements that constitute them, contemplated as the eye moves across the landscape of a scroll painting. So walking as a meditative practice, more largely travel as a meditative practice, the eye moving across a represented landscape, and the arc of life informed his idea of what kind of thing he was making.

Another metaphor we know from both the tradition of the scroll and of Nō is commentary, which is a form of teaching, or transmission. It's how spiritual traditions (probably also scholarly traditions and craft traditions) get carried on. Commentary and transmission are what is meant by *culture.* It's in a sense what culture is. Most creatures on earth seem to carry most of what they know as hardwiring, and then learn a few other things by imitation. Human beings do a vast amount of learning by imitation and the actions we imitate are shaped by the values implicit in the other kinds of transmission: stories, songs, oral and written knowledge of wisdom traditions, and ways to see and what to see implicit in visual arts traditions. So part of what Snyder is doing is recovering what he's intuited in East Asian painting. And there is something mysterious about this process that's generative, something that has to do with the unsaid in whatever is sayable about a tradition. This connects in my mind to Snyder's remark on page 153 about "a chaotic universe where everything is in place."

Which brings us to the role of myth in his thinking. This is especially interesting to think about now when myth as a way of approaching literature has more or less disappeared from university curricula. If postmodern thought — or critical theory — means anything, it means radical skepticism about any story of origins. The classical site of this is Nietzsche's remark that there are no facts, only interpretations — which is to say there is no truth because there is no one true world. Snyder had undergraduate training in an anthropological tradition that took myth to be the primary meaning-making activity of the human imagination. Robert Duncan in those years — late 1960s — could write, "Myth is the story told of what cannot be told, as mystery is the scene revealed of what cannot be revealed, and the mystic gnosis the thing known that cannot be known." This was appealing to poets, of course, because the traditions of symbolist and modernist poetry conceived the task of poetry to be saying the unsayable. And this unsayable was imagined to be a kind of truth, not interpretation, but the thing itself, communicated perhaps only gesturally, but communicated and passed on because it reflected the deepest structure — and therefore, according to Jung, say — the deepest tasks of human beings.

What contemporary critical thinking has to say about meaning-making is that there is no one true world, and so people make up narratives. And then certain narratives become master narratives for purely ideological reasons. A story survives because it nourishes and is nourished by various forms of power, and institutions like universities keep the discourse about these stories alive if it protects their interests. So, in reading *Mountains and Rivers Without End*, we also need to ask going in what we are to make of the poem in relation to the animist habit of mind that is at the root of shamanic thinking and the mythic lore that Snyder thinks with and admires. I can tell you very briefly how I tend to navigate these questions, but the point I want to make is that every contemporary reader of the poem is going to have to answer it for her- or himself. I think these issues — what to make, for example, of the idea of "the feminine" as a primary mythic iconography — have to be part of the way we read the poem.

It is interesting in this way to draw a comparison now between Snyder and another poet of his generation, John Ashbery, whose poetry is rooted in a profound and utter epistemological skepticism that it enacts as a form of play, mostly good-natured and open-ended. It would seem for Snyder that there is, in one way or another, an idea of ground, and for Ashbery there isn't. A literary scholar could also look here at the different epistemological propositions flowing out of Pound and Wallace Stevens.

My shorthand way with this set of issues is to look at the word *purely* in the idea that stories survive for "purely ideological reasons." I think it is probably the case that they survive partly for ideological reasons and partly because they do answer to something in the makeup of human consciousness. I don't mean simply to split the difference between a Marxist, or Foucauldian idea about myth, on the one hand, and a Jungian reading (the name

I associate with this way of thought is Joseph Campbell), on the other, but I do think that the cultural landscapes we move through — like Snyder's conjuring of rising mists and falling water, hills and valleys, a world in movement — are a mix of tribal lore, which is to say ideology, and something else that is transmitted while attached to ideology, but isn't ideology purely. It is something older and deeper, or to say the reverse, newer and still always ahead of us, that poetry aims at.

And there's a final, interesting complication I would be inclined to go to the poem with rather than to external sources. It's connected to the question of the difference between a Buddhist and a nihilist. What's the difference between the European critical tradition that says there's no ground, that there's no place to stand from which to say anything is true, and the Buddhist position that also says there's no place to stand to say anything is true because it's all samsara in the first place? Hence the argument of Wallace Stevens's "The Snow Man" in which he says you have to have a mind of winter to see "nothing that is not there" and "the nothing that is." Meanwhile, of course, while poets and philosophers figure out in what sense harbor seals, canyon wrens, coral reefs, and glacier "are," they are wholly at risk from the technologies we live through. Snyder was, of course, one of the first English language poets in the middle of the twentieth century to write from this concern. We are reading his poem, begun in the middle of the century, at the end of it. It makes sense that part of what we bring to the poem at the end of the century is a question about the terms on which the human imagination can project and has projected meaning onto the world.

III.

In some ways, this is a really weird poem if you think about the creation of *Duino Elegies* or "Song of Myself" or *The Four Quartets* or *The Cantos*. This is an odd poem. It was begun in a burst by a very young guy in the late 1950s, announced as a vast, epic enterprise, *Mountains and Rivers Without End*, and then it perked along during the decade of the '60s, with something turned out almost every year that seemed to belong to this project, individual poems that were also seen as part of a larger work, then only a couple of poems in the 1970s, the project in abeyance while he was doing much other work, then more poems in the 1980s. Then, forty years later, in the 1990s, he finished in another burst. There was a question in my mind about whether and in what way this could be one poem under these circumstances. As we've seen, the answer has to be partly autobiographical, something like the way you can say *The Cantos* is one poem, when there are good reasons to read it otherwise. So we bring this question into our reading.

Let's begin at the beginning by noticing that, beginning at the beginning, we are beginning somewhere near the end. Although the initiatory impulse of the poem was East Asian landscape scrolls, it was not until quite late in the process that Snyder sat down to write an introductory poem. The title, *Mountains and Rivers Without End*, may have been as much an exuberant borrowing as an aesthetic premise in the early 1960s, but by the time he wrote "Endless Streams and Mountains" it is evident that it gave him a place to start. That it is a meditative exercise in looking is crucial to the sense of the long poem as a book of instruction and embodiment of knowledge, for its imagination of a transformation of American consciousness, and, implicitly, of our politics, and the ways we interact with the world. Here are the first lines —

> Clearing the mind and sliding in
> to that created space,

This invites us to a deliberate act. It says, literally, "Okay, clear your head." The poet is speaking to himself, probably as watcher, but also to us. It also invites the reader into the poem. *Mountains and Rivers Without End* begins with an account of a mind looking at a scroll called "Endless Streams and Mountains." "Created space," I think, is a term also that begins to be an answer to this question about the ground of the real.

> a web of waters streaming over rocks,
> air misty but not raining,
> seeing this land from a boat on a lake
> or a broad slow river,
> coasting by.

These next three lines have to do with the position of the viewer. The first two lines clear the ground, clear the mind to enter the created space. This space happens to be a work of art, it could be a landscape. What's creation? Who's the creator? Those issues will come up before we're through with the poem. Then the sounding of the central theme and myth: "a web of waters streaming over rocks." As Wallace Stevens says in "Sunday Morning," "We live in an old chaos of the sun." What is it? "a web of waters streaming over rocks." This is a literal description of the world.

"air misty but not raining": To what extent we're asked to read symbolically is one of the things I want to talk about here, so, for the moment, let's read a little bit symbolically. Mist is this condition of a kind of easy breathing relationship between the upper and lower, between ascent and descent. And then the point of view of the observer: he's describing the observer point of view as looking at a thing as if "from a boat on a lake / or a broad slow river, / coasting by." That's the sequence: clear your head, initiate movement.

That there are poems about rivers throughout *Mountains and Rivers* matters, and it's not an accident that the other poem written in the 1990s that's added to this first section is called "Boat of a Million Years." And maybe this is the first clue to the ways in which this poem is a constructed thing. This kind of echo and recurrence is the traditional method of literature to make meaning, right? I'm just going to point it out as we go, and you'll see for yourself all the ways in which recurrence and echo, thematic rhyme, are being used. I want to claim that this boat may very well be connected to Mahayana.

(I know, I know. I'm beginning to sound like the kind of English teacher students are wary of: the symbol finder. But part of a teacher's job and a poet's is to re-teach students their own symbolic imaginations. To do that we have to read slowly and with the whole mind that has, in dream and daily life, a huge, mostly unconscious symbolic vocabulary. Noon is symbolic. Socks and sidewalks are symbolic.)

It's what one first admires about Snyder's writing: it's about someone clearing their head and just taking in what's in front of them. In this case it's the overall mood and central imagery of the painting that is going to be the subject of the poem. It's the typical initiatory ground of a meditative act as a Buddhist discipline, much as the appearance of a crucifix is at the beginning of a seventeenth-century meditative poem. Needless to say, this is true not only for looking at this scroll, but for looking at the poem as a whole. And then the image of "a broad slow river, coasting by" refers to the situation of all of us in time, in relation to a world that we see from inside the boat of our life, inside the greater vehicle.

So, we've begun. Next stanza:

The path comes down along a lowland stream
slips behind boulders and leafy hardwoods,
reappears in a pine grove,

This is pure naturalistic description. It also is an image of descent, the image of the flowing downward of water.

no farms around, just tidy cottages and shelters,
gateways, rest stops, roofed but unwalled work space,
— a warm damp climate;

Is anything going on here besides description? Is anything going on in the painting other than description? This is the place where I want to talk about how you read the poem somewhat symbolically and somewhat allegorically in a hovering sort of way.

The tradition of the Chinese and Japanese literature of travel is really unlike European literary traditions of travel in profound ways. You could argue that it is the sort of central fact of Japanese, Chinese, and, as far as I know, Korean poetry. And this is because the central piety and everyday truth, the thing I imagine you got sick of hearing if you went to schools in East Asia as a kid, was that *ceaseless change* is the central fact of reality. From the earliest monk-wanderers — from Saigyō and Sōgi up through Bashō, and through the wanderers through war-devastated landscapes in post-war Japanese films — the pilgrim in a constantly changing world is engaged in a central spiritual practice. That is, the Buddhist exercise of meditation on these scrolls is a meditation on an endlessly transforming, endlessly changing reality: "what's out there" (save the word *reality*). And inside this tradition, all kinds of things that look extremely casual to us tend to be allegorical.

Let me just give you two quick examples from one of the classic texts, Bashō's *Narrow Road to the Deep North*. The form of *Narrow Road to the Deep North* is a paragraph of prose by this man who is on a typical pilgrimage going to visit the holy places and famous historical sites, and then a haiku at the end. Here's one of them (from my *The Essential Haiku*):

> A huge chestnut tree in the outskirts of this post town and a priest living like a hermit in its shade. Perhaps like Saigyō, "Deep in the mountains, gathering chestnuts." Or so I imagined and took a scrap of paper from my bag to write, "The Chinese character for 'chestnut' comprises 'west' and 'tree' and is, therefore, linked up with Amida's paradise in the West. This is why Gyōgi Bosatsu all his life used the wood of this tree for his walking stick and the pillars of his house."

And then, the little poem:

> Chestnut by the eaves —
> not many people
>   notice the blossoms.

So the blossoms of the chestnut tree are associated with the Dharma, with the teaching. The flowers are also associated with the Western Paradise, and Bashō notices this huge chestnut at the entry to this bustling logging and mining town at the outskirts of civilization. There is one monk living outside the town walls in a hut under the chestnut tree. That's the position of the spiritual truth in relation to the big, busy world.

This connects directly to the quote from Lew Welch that is the epigraph for "Night Highway 99," the third poem in the opening sequence (M&R 11):

> *Only the very poor, or eccentric, can surround themselves with shapes of elegance (soon to be demolished) in which they are forced by poverty to move with leisurely grace. We remain alert so as not to get run down, but it turns out you only have to hop a few feet to one side and the whole, huge machinery rolls by, not seeing you at all.*

That's the position of the religious seeker in relation to the world. And Snyder, later in his collection of poems called "Hitch Haiku," took Welch's remark and made a poem out it. He's hiking on a desert road and the poem goes, "A great freight truck / lit like a town / through the dark stony desert." Right? Standing out somewhere in Nevada between Wendover and Salt Lake, and {whoosh} Western Civilization goes rolling by! First, silent, desert stars, then {whooorrrr} some mammoth trailer truck full of electronics or frozen food, and then silence. And stars.

Notice that this is not an image of the traveler in motion, but of the traveler stilled and the world in motion. They amount to the same thing. Here's a poem that is even more typical. We are inclined not to read these things allegorically, because they look like casual notations. This translation I'm reading here is by Cid Corman, who was in Japan at the same time Snyder was there and was doing the translations in a very telegraphic English that sounds a bit like Jack Kerouac, or Gary Snyder. It is very accurate too, I've been told, to the extremely condensed notational style of Basho's *haibun* prose:

> Intending to ride down the Momamigawa, waited at a place called Ōishida for good weather. Here the seeds of old *haikai* sown, brought back past times and unforgotten flowers, cry of a reed-flute easing heart, gone astray trying to take both ways at once, the new and the old, no one to guide them, left them a collection of no great merit. But as far as *furyū* had till then come.

Here Bashō is making his living, stopping every once in a while and conducting these *haikai* sessions. And he is at an old town in the back country, where people are writing poems that are so old-fashioned and backwards that it reminds him of a song of Tu Fu's about hearing the barbarian flute on the borders of the Chinese Empire. And then he describes talking with them a bit because they had incorporated all of the worst elements of the new style, so he did a session with them — it's the practice of linked verse he's talking about — which wasn't very good, but he took them as far as *furyū*, a certain idea of elegance, could take them.

Then the next part of the *haibun*:

> The Mogamigawa has its source in Michinoku and its upper reaches in Yamagata. With the daunting perils of the Goten

shoals and Hayabusa rapids. Descending north of Mt Itajiki, it empties into sea at Sakata. Right, left, mountains close, up, boat shot down through clustering trees. Boats like this with sheaves of rice probably those called *inabune*. The Shiraito Falls plunges through thick green foliage and the Sennindō stands at river's brink. What with swollen waters, boat ran risks.

The image here is practically out of one of those scrolls. We would not be inclined to read it symbolically but Japanese readers absolutely would. Here's the furious moving river on which daring old boatmen took the sheaves of back-country rice and transported them down to market. This is karma {shkurrshhhh} roaring past. And off to the side, in the mist, a temple. The *Sennindō* is a hermit's hall, associated with someone who retired from the world after an experience of bloody battle. This is exactly the same position as that Buddhist monk on the edge of the town. Over and over again we find this figure of the hermit or sage.

Bashō is not that figure. He's not the monk recluse, nor the hermit in the temple in the back country. He's the wanderer. He's the one who is record-ing these images. This was the other spiritual tradition, the tradition of wan-dering, in which you see the constantly changing, constantly transforming world, and finally grasp the way in which, in a certain sense, there is noth-ing there. All of this is by way of glossing what Snyder is doing in the open-ing images of the poem:

> The path comes down along a lowland stream
> slips behind boulders and leafy hardwoods,
> reappears in a pine grove,
>
> no farms around, just tidy cottages and shelters,
> gateways, rest stops, roofed but unwalled work space,
> — a warm damp climate;

He is describing the scene. He is also, in some sense, describing the world, or this part of the world as a place — here it is! — that is governed by this play of the descent of water, a fluid movement that, as the poem deepens, is going to be associated with an idea of compassion.

The next section — and you'll see how typical this is of the movement of the poem as a whole — is about ascent. First this was about water flowing down. Now the eye climbs:

> a trail of climbing stairsteps forks upstream.

Snyder's music is so wonderful to me and he often begins with a kind of iambic music: "a trail of climbing . . ." and then he just piles up the strong stresses: "stairsteps forks upstream." One, two, three, four, five stressed syllables in a row. The way his lines sound is a whole other order of magic:

> a trail of climbing stairsteps forks upstream.
> Big ranges lurk behind these rugged little outcrops —
> these spits of low ground rocky uplifts
> > layered pinnacles aslant,

Let me go back to that passage I read to you from his essay on the poem:

> I came to see that yogic implications of "mountains" and "rivers"
> as the play between the tough spirit of willed self-discipline, and
> the generous and loving spirit of concern for all beings: a dyad
> present in Buddhist iconography. . . . I could imagine this dyad as
> paralleled in the dynamics of mountain uplift, subduction,
> erosion, and the planetary cycle.

So the male principle in this mythology is the upthrust of rock from the fire at the center of the earth. The female is the descending flow of water to the places of human habitation. It is worth noticing that if the Greek mythological dyad was Father Sky and Mother Earth, this tends to be Mother Sky and Father Earth. That is, the male principle is the earth with its rock-will upthrust and the female principle is the descending flow of water from the sky. So it reverses the gender terms of Western mythos, Greek myth anyway.

> a trail of climbing stairsteps forks upstream.
> Big ranges lurk behind these rugged little outcrops —
> these spits of low ground rocky uplifts

> layered pinnacles aslant,
> flurries of brushy cliffs receding,
> far back and high above, vague peaks.

You can read this as Dantesque. These are the metaphors of ascent to the places of vision, out the valley. And then all of this, as described in the painting, acquires a human context.

> A man hunched over, sitting on a log
>   another stands above him, lifts a staff,
> a third, with a roll of mats or a lute, looks on;
> a bit offshore two people in a boat.

One of the great things about these Chinese paintings is that in the world seen in this immensely spacious way doesn't hierarchize kinds of people. Here is the lord's place over here, here's the guy coming down the mountain over here. (I suddenly realize that I haven't read literature on this. There must be new scholars who have worked out exactly how class relations work in these depictions.) But in my sense of the scroll paintings, their tendency is to disrupt or disperse social categories. And it seems to me that this list of people in the scroll anticipates exactly what goes on, for example, in "Night Highway 99."

> "I had a girl in Oakland who worked
> for a doctor, she was a nurse, she let him
> eat her. She died of tuberculosis
> & I drove back to Portland
> nonstop, crying all the way"   Grants Pass

> "I picked up a young mother with two
> small children once, their house had just burned down"
> "I picked up an Italian tree-surgeon
> in Port Angeles once, he had all his
> saws and tools all screwed & bolted on

a beat-up bike."

"Phoenix . . . Redding . . . Anderson." You see how the hitchhiker, moving through the landscape, hearing these stories, is in exactly the same relation to the human world as the traveling eye moving through the painting.

So how much do we read this symbolically? Well, I don't really want to get into the difference between symbol and allegory. But you know what I mean — how much do you read in those terms? I would say it's nearer to allegory than to symbol here. That is, we have one-to-one correspondences. And I want to call it symbolic because it's held so lightly. The projection of of symbolic, religious, interpretive, moral meanings on this writing is all over it, but without determining it, quite. The things are held in place as things, the people as people, and, really, it is interesting that they are fictive things already. This is not a description of the world, which is going to come later, but a description of a description of the world.

"The trail goes far inland," the next stanza begins. Well, then, once you start to see allegorical movement, or the kinds of metonymy that invite allegorical reading, you want to say what it means for the poem to go inland.

> The trail goes far inland,
>   somewhere back around a bay,
> lost in distant foothill slopes
>   & back again
> at a village on the beach, and someone's fishing.

You know, taken by itself this could be a tanka, a five-line Japanese poem that aims to be a kind of portrait of all of reality. The eye wanders in, loses the road, the road comes back, comes to a beach, and someone's fishing. The content is not quite paraphrasable as a metaphor, but is at the edge of being paraphrasable as a metaphor, for fishing both an economic and contemplative recreational activity. Somebody at the edge of the water, dreaming. The road that goes inland returns to this place of work and contemplation.

When I was first reading this poem I thought, "Okay, okay, he's describing the painting." And it wasn't until two or three readings that I saw, "Oh, every bit of this counts and can be read with this habit — almost medieval habit — of allegorical reading." But it is profoundly in the tradition of Asian, Chinese, at least, aesthetic commentary, and also of the use of the metonym as a main device in Chinese and Japanese poetry.

I'll say one quick word about metonymy. Typical Western poetry is metaphorical transformation: "love is a lion's tooth," or Hart Crane: ". . . and love / a burnt match skating in a urinal." Metaphor takes two terms and lays them across one another, the mind goes dark for a moment, and wakes to surprise at the way they are put together. The typical Japanese way is to say, with Issa, "Noon / orioles singing, / the river flows in silence." There's no metaphorical turn. What's it about? It's about the absolute press of that moment: "Noon / orioles singing, / the river flows in silence." In fact, I could give you an elaborate Buddhist doctrinal interpretation of that poem, but the first thing it is is a metonymy. It's about "is," not about "becoming." But the "is" is always shifting, from one image to the next. The river is a spring river in full flood. I think Wallace Stevens called one of his books *Parts of a World* from the idea that parts of the world, seen intensely enough, are the world.

> Rider and walker cross a bridge
> above a frothy braided torrent
> that descends from a flurry of roofs like flowers
>   temples tucked between cliffs,
>   a side trail goes there;

This is that same thing: the temple tucked next to the waterfall. People going over a bridge. Below it the rapid movement of water. Here it is the force of life. Slowed down, it can be the watery movement of this compassionate flowing toward the world that is associated with the temple roofs and the petal showers of flowers. The Japanese idiom for the froth or foam on a wave is the "blossom" of the wave. And Snyder's line seems to pick up on that.

> a jumble of cliffs above,
> ridge tops edged with bushes,
> valley fog below a hazy canyon.

Read in these symbolic terms, the down-flowing water, the human context of people moving and flowing among these energies, water falling, mists rising, the upthrust energy of the earth, hazy valleys, distances: they all have a faintly symbolic, but not absolutely allegorical, context.

> A man with a shoulder load leans into the grade.

There's our sack-carrying wanderer, a figure for "pilgrim-consciousness," with its load of ordinary karmic suffering that runs all through the poem.

> Another horse and a hiker,
> the trail goes up along cascading streambed
> no bridge in sight —

It's another image of the crossed forces of climbing and falling: climbing will, falling water. "no bridge in sight — " could be read symbolically. This doesn't show the bridge that's going to get this traveler to his destination.

> comes back through chinquapin or
> liquidambers; another group of travelers.
> Trail's end at the edge of an inlet,
> below a heavy set of dark rock hills.
> Two moored boats with basket roofing,
>   a boatman in the bow looks
>   lost in thought.

The first time I read through, I was sort of impatient with this writing, "Okay, okay." Now I see it is an exquisite little poem, just on its own terms. It's a description of one part of the scene of the painting, as the mind is moving from one part to another, but in each case, the shaping activity of the mind using this fundamental symbolism of climbing and falling, is giving us a world.

> Hills beyond rivers, willows in a swamp,
> a gentle valley, reaching far inland.

In his description of the spirit of Tārā, of the female principle, Snyder speaks of "the generous and loving spirit of concern for all beings." Here it's the valley that reaches far inland. That movement seems to me clearly connected, throughout the poems, to an idea of heart, of the world seen lovingly, or, in these lines, gently. The poem settles here. We have about come to the end of the poem's description of the painting, where the painting itself comes to its end. But it doesn't actually end there, doesn't stop. It ends with what I think is a really extraordinary line that finishes the description of the painting's act of description:

> The watching boat has floated off the page.

We're now at the end. The watching boat — that's us, the readers at the beginning of the poem who were "seeing this land from a boat on a lake." And we're still moving. This makes me think of the end of Wallace Stevens's "Sunday Morning," when the pigeons "sink downward to darkness, on extended wings." This is probably the most famous American post-symbolist description of death, or of mortality anyway. They're still going down when the poem ends. (Take a look, in this context, at the last line of Keats's "To Autumn.") Anyway, a quite magical thing happens here: "the watching boat has floated off the page." The eye is through. That is what is going to happen to each of us. But the land hasn't disappeared and the movement hasn't stilled.

So that's the instruction, the guided tour the introductory poem gives us. It's an exercise in slowing down, meditating, looking at the human in the context of this vast sense of space, this larger landscape. Looking at one's own life as a pilgrim life among other lives, busy and various, and mists rising, roads going inland and coming back, all this slowed down with his musical, strong stress lines and with the extraordinary visual clarity of the writing, hovering around symbolic meanings. And, at a certain point, the boat drifts out of the scene.

But the poem is not over. It's going to continue by describing the commentary, the seals and poems that have been affixed to the scroll because, as Snyder says in his essay, the scroll paintings were not thought to be completed, ever.

They called up the poems and commentaries that flowed from them.

> At the end of the painting, the scroll continues on with seals and poems. It tells a further tale:

This is the moment that goes from the act of looking as an act of meditation to the collective transmission of the experience of this created thing. And there are one, two, three, four, five seal poems Snyder incorporates into "Endless Streams and Mountains."

> "— Wang Wen-wei saw this at the mayor's house in Ho-tung
> town, year 1205.
> Wrote at the end of it,
> 'The Fashioner of Things
> has no original intentions
> Mountains and rivers
> are spirit, condensed.'

That's one guy's take. Part of the take is profoundly Buddhist. This is not the Pan-Creator at the top of a Renaissance painting, the Author of All Being. The very terms of a scroll painting don't allow for the hierarchical idea of a Fashioner of Things who intended a particular order. It's "here it is," this stretch of it, and, of course, it's like a life in that it begins here and ends there. Is there more over here? Probably. Is there more over there? Probably. You're not going to see it all.

> 'The Fashioner of Things
> has no original intentions
> Mountains and rivers
> are spirit, condensed.'
>
> '. . .Who has come up with
> these miraculous forests and springs?
> Pale ink
> on fine white silk.'

This is a sensorial world. Maya, a world of delusion, of art and created space. "Pale ink on fine white silk." This is one guy's take. Another:

> Later that month someone named Li Hui added,
>   '. . . Most people can get along with the noise of dogs
>   and chickens;
>   Everybody cheerful in these peaceful times.
>
>   But I — why are my tastes so odd?
>   I love the company of streams and boulders.'

This is a basic, self-congratulatory cliché of the Chinese aesthete, and the American Bohemian.

> T'ien Hsieh of Wei-lo, no date, next wrote,
>   '. . .The water holds up the mountains,
>   The mountains go down in the water . . .'

He's thinking about that relation of ascent and descent, how they depend on each other — old Buddhist thought.

> In 1332, Chih-shun adds,
>   '. . . This is truly a painting worth careful keeping.
>   And it has poem-colophons from the Sung and the
>   Chin dynasties. That it survived dangers of fire and
>   war makes it even rarer.'

As Snyder says in the notes, the commentary is part of the process. That is, the teaching and the transmission are the same thing, and our eye moving through time, listening to these sometimes banal, sometimes interesting responses by various people, is part of the learning. It is part of the thing itself.

In this way the poem models a certain kind of civility, and a certain idea of transmission. And it is a generous and inclusive one. You know, some of these are interesting, some of these are not so interesting. And now it includes us. We are the next stage in this, the people who are sitting around studying Snyder's transmission of these people's transmission of this Fashioner's painting, which had no original intention. In the mid-seventeenth century one Wang To had a look at it:

> 'My brother's relative by marriage, Wen-sun, is learned and
> has good taste. He writes good prose and poetry. My brother
> brought over this painting of his to show me . . .'

This guy is the least interesting of the group, he knows that the appreciation of art has to do with social class.

The next stanza and commentary is Snyder's prose:

> The great Ch'ing dynasty collector Liang Ch'ing-piao owned it,
> but didn't write on it or cover it with seals. From him it went into
> the Imperial collection down to the early twentieth century. Chang
> Ta-ch'ien sold it in 1949. Now it's at the Cleveland Art Museum,
> which sits on a rise that looks out toward the waters of Lake Erie.

This is the stage of the transmission in which the Tao gets planted in North America. In some way, it began with Emerson's reading of the Upanishads, shows up in Whitman's use of Hindu stuff throughout *Leaves of Grass*, in Eliot's use of Sanskrit at the end of the *The Waste Land*, the incorporation of Confucian and, even though Pound disapproved of Taoism, Taoist elements in *The Cantos*, and comes down to us here. It's a sweet moment. It consciously evokes what Snyder has been from the beginning: one of the transmitters of this tradition into North America. And of course this rhymes with what I was saying about Pound: that he conceived of his poem as a way of bringing a refocused set of traditions into Western culture. And Snyder has done the same thing with the introduction of Native American mythologies and Hindu mythologies in *Myths & Texts*, Buddhist teaching traditions into North American writings, and with them altered ways of seeing North American literary arts. So he is commenting on this process, and commenting on it as a natural outgrowth of this commentary tradition. It tells us about the way in which this poem is the transmission and embodiment of a way of knowing and tells us that to introduce into the West this alternative style of looking is part of its intention. How much it is alternative and how much its roots are congruent with English-American Romantic thought is another tale.

Having read the seal poem, he gives the painting another look:

> Step back and gaze again at the land:
> it rises and subsides —

How insistent he is on this theme!

> ravines and cliffs like waves of blowing leaves —
> stamp the foot, walk with it, clap! turn,

I'm not sure, but I suspect this refers to some stylized Nō theater movement.

> the creeks come in, ah!
> strained through boulders,
> mountains walking on the water,
> water ripples every hill.

Here's the same interpenetration again.

I want to bring this back to Ginsberg's "Caw, Caw, Caw." "Lord, Lord, Lord." Note this his feeling of an absolute split that is in Ginsberg's early poetry, this kind of anguished assault on the torment of body-hatred in American culture that shows up in *Howl* and *Kaddish*. Ginsberg was, of course, a lover of Burroughs's treatment of the body as a grotesque joke that needs to have needles stuck into it to get to the mind, to give it visions, and to get out of this detestable physical realm. *Naked Lunch* is an absolutely gnostic book. Ginsberg loved it. And Ginsberg, the great risk-taker of sexual liberation, feeling the hatred of sex at the root of life and the need for the body to get out of the body. Part of him wanted out of the whole thing. "Caw, Caw, Caw, Caw." "Lord, Lord, Lord, Lord." "Caw, Caw, Caw, Caw." "Lord, Lord, Lord, Lord."

Snyder says (it's an easy thing to say), "mountains walking on the water,

water ripples every hill." This fundamental physical process of the universe is not a metaphysical drama. How is meaning made here? I don't know. One can see as equal these two forces of willed self-discipline and compassion in an oscillating relationship of ups and downs. In ceaselessly changing transactions of energies that are the physical world, the poem attends to the sense that what is *is*.

> — I walk out of the museum — low gray clouds over the lake — chill March breeze.

So here we are on the North American earth. And then he meditates on what he has seen, and in some way this is his colophon, his commentary poem.

> Old ghost ranges, sunken rivers, come again

Is he talking about North America, or what he has seen in the painting? Both, I think.

> Old ghost ranges, sunken rivers, come again
>   stand by the wall and tell their tale,
> walk the path, sit the rains,
> grind the ink, wet the brush, unroll the
>   broad white space:

These are instructions to consciousness. He is also imagining the artist sitting down to do this. Himself as artist, sitting down to his poem.

> lead out and tip
> the moist black line.

"Grind the ink." By the way, does everybody know about this? In any art store now you can buy Chinese ink stones and grind the ink yourself. It's inexpensive and totally cool. So are the brushes, each animal hair tip making its own stroke.

> lead out and tip
> the moist black line.

> *Walking on walking*

That could either mean, walking and more walking. Or walking on other people's walking. I don't know which he had in mind. Maybe both.

> *under foot   earth turns.*
> *Streams and mountains never stay the same.*

This would be walking in the *mujo*, the constantly changing realm. And he's going about it as a meditative activity.

The first time I read this poem, I thought, "Oh, okay, description of the painting, and the colophon quotations, and then he kind of does this little, you know, Gary Snyder number in the last line. . . . But I didn't see how powerfully all of this is working, how deeply it's the introduction to the poem and its themes.

So, now, where do we go from there? We are into the painting. I'm sure you have all noticed, but in case you haven't, *Mountains and Rivers* ends when the brush lifts. The very last lines of *Mountains and Rivers* are (M&R 152):

> The space goes on.
> But the wet black brush
> tip drawn to a point
>   lifts away.

So it's the end of the poem. The brush lifted from the silk. The whole poem replicates the scroll and the description of the scroll in the first poem. It's the end of the exercise and a metonymy for endings, for our deaths, the withdrawal of attention. If you pay attention, the poem and the scroll seem to say, at least you can draw your brush to a tip. Which is maybe too phallic for everyone here, but it has as its aim an idea of art as an alive, sensuously vivid and contemplative mirroring of the moving world.

IV.

The next poem, "Old Bones," follows immediately. So it's interesting to see
how Snyder is thinking about the organization of the poem and where he's
going. The first phrase in the first line of the poem, "Out there," turns out
to be epistemologically interesting. It raises the whole question of what you
project onto the world and what's not projected. "Out there," he repeats it
in the third stanza. "Out there." It's the outback of the American desert, but
it's also the "out there." "walking round" is the next phrase: again, the cen-
tral meditative practice of the poem. "looking out for food," As in so much
of human life, what begins as a economic activity, gets turned into a ritual
for vision, in one form or another. Who were the human beings? He begins
with "Old Bones" (M&R 10):

> Out there, walking round, looking out for food,
> a rootstock, a birdcall, a seed that you can crack
> plucking, digging, snaring, snagging,
>   barely getting by,

I assume this is an evocation of our hunter-wanderer-gatherer genes.

> no food out there on dusty slopes of scree —
> carry some — look for some
> go for a hungry dream.
> Deer bone, Dall sheep,
>   bones hunger home.

Scree is glacial rubble. People went to the mountains for vision. They didn't
go there looking for food much at all. When you go into the mountains, you
"carry some — look for some" because there isn't much up where you go for
a dream, which is hunger.

The move from the first poem to the second is also a move from the
extremely refined aesthetic of East Asian painting to the animist origins of
dream quests among Neolithic peoples. "Dall sheep": so we are in North

America. Snyder is going directly to sources he wove into North American landscapes in *Myths & Texts*, to the art of China for a Buddhist aesthetic, on the whole alert and realist, and to Native American myth for another relation to the earth, for animals and dreams.

Dream is going to get to be an important term when we get to "The Elwha River," the sixth poem in the first section. Someone who knows the word *dream* and the notion of dream vision shows up there, where the idea of the real also appears. I'm not going to gloss "bones hunger home." It's one of those lines that each of us must find our way into on our own.

Back to "Old Bones":

> Deer bone, Dall sheep,
> bones hunger home.

> Out there somewhere
> a shrine for the old ones,

The leaving out of the verb is typical of diction from Snyder's early poems, so you don't know whether it means "they used to put" or "we should put" — I think it means both. And this echoes that project of Pound's to "return the altar to the forest."

> Out there somewhere
> a shrine for the old ones,
> the dust of the old bones
> old songs and tales.

This speaks of transmission, about which the little colophon poems were an example.

> What we ate — who ate what —
> how we all prevailed.

That is what the shrine of the bones is. So he places his first temple in this place, and it's the temple of the human story and its transmissions.

In Part III of *Mountains and Rivers*, written, mostly, in the '80s, he adds one poem, "Under the Hills Near the Morava River" from '93, which is interesting to look at in connection with "Old Bones" (M&R 96):

> She lay there midst
> Mammoth, reindeer, and wolf bones:
> Diadem of fox teeth round her brow
> Ocher under her hips
> 26,640 plus or minus 110 years before "now."
> Burnt reindeer-pelvis bone bits
> in her mouth,
> Bones of two men lying by her,
> one each side.

This is a description of one of the most amazing events of the twentieth century, the digging up in southern Moravia of some of the first human remains to give evidence of ritual burial. Many people think humanness in evolution first shows up with ritual burial of the dead. When archaeologists look at the various hominids they dig up it is the first thing they look for. This site in the Czech Republic is now the oldest site with archaeological evidence of a ritual burial. Old bones.

> Burnt reindeer-pelvis bone bits
> in her mouth,
> Diadem of fox teeth round her brow
> Ocher under her hips

This old association of humans with animals and animal magic is going to be one of the continuing arguments of the poem, and it's an argument for animism.

It's interesting that he needn't have gone here to "Old Bones." At first it seemed to me to point to a rather loose, associative organization of the poem, which suggested something about halfway between a collection of poems and a poem-sequence, or a long poem. Having seen now how thoroughly you can read the whole book in the first poem, and how much more moving and exquisitely wrought it is as a poem than I saw at first, I look at "Old Bones" differently. He needed at the outset to evoke the human history of our relation to the "out there" and to connect that history through the idea of "hungry dreams" to the earliest idea of sacred places and our relationships with the other animals. Animal and tutelary spirits are going to show up throughout these poems.

In this connection I want to point out something else. In his notes on "Endless Streams and Mountains," Snyder talks about the history of the tradition of Chinese landscape painting (M & R 159):

> There were very early scenes of hills and woods in China, or silk
> or plastered walls, but they were full of deer and other animals,
> or dream creatures, or people, or some combination. Paintings of
> large vistas did not appear until around the tenth century. This
> was after two and a half millennia of self-aware civilization in the
> basins of the Ho and Chiang. They are at their most vigorous
> from mid-Sung through the Yüan and early Ming — exactly when
> much of China was becoming deforested.

Snyder's notes are also, of course, part of the poem. Here he is constructing a bridge from the art of neolithic China, akin to the early art of Europe and North America, to the refinement of the Sung and Yüan dynasties. He wants us to see that the period of the flourishing of this kind of painting, this way of seeing, which he is trying to transplant in America, occurred during the time of the beginning of the deforestation of China. This corresponds in some ways to the rise of romanticism in Europe and America at the onset of industrialization.

> After the Yüan dynasty large-scale "Mountains and Waters"
> paintings became less important, and the painter's eye moved
> closer; some call them "Rocks and Trees" paintings. Later
> paintings drew even closer to give us picture of "Birds and
> Flowers," *hua-niao*, precise and lovely, and superb sumi sketches
> of insects, gourds, melons, and leaves.

I think this provides another key to the structure of the poem. That its large overall intention has to do with the river and landscape tradition, and then, sometimes, it moves in closer to rocks and trees, which have to do with many of the individual walking exercises within the larger landscape, and then the *hua-niao*, the close-up things of birds, flowers, animals, and so on. And that tells me something else about the organization of the poem, which is that certain of the poems that have to do with animals especially, can be thought of as the *hua-niao*, the little sketches of the animals inside this larger structure. I can tell you which ones it seems to me they are. In Part I, "Jackrabbit." In Part II, "The Black-tailed Hare." In Part III, "The Canyon Wren," "New Moon Tongue," and "Macaques in the Sky." And in Part IV, "Earrings Dangling and Miles of Desert."

What are these little poems doing here if this is not just a book of poems, but a conceptual structure? How come these little poems about animals are tossed in here and there? They correspond to one of the modes of vision in the poem and in the cultural traditions the poem is tracking, of which there are three or four: the archaic body out wandering, hungry for food and for a vision place; the full-blown animist tradition, its rituals and prayers; the great contemplative landscape tradition; and the little objective *hua-niao* poems, an aesthetic turn that points to scientific observation, in the way, say, seventeenth-century Dutch painting fused science and art. Magic, art, science, so the nineteenth-century positivists described human development. There is nothing so neat here. But there is a trying out of these ways and what they have to tell us: the mountains and rivers of big landscape, the somewhat more close-up approach to rocks and trees, and the very close attention to animals. Then, in addition to that, there will be poems connected to hungry dreams and to vision experiences and the viability of animistic and shamanistic ways of seeing. Central to those are "An Offering for Tārā" and "The Mountain Spirit." "The Hump-backed Flute Player" and "The Blue Sky" are perhaps the central poems where he takes on the myth issue.

So, in terms of the organization of the poem, it looks like at the beginning of the poem he's getting his ducks aligned: first the overall theme drawn from the East Asian tradition, then the smaller theme set inside of Neolithic technologies and what we know of the archaic relation of humans to the earth and to animals. Then he's going to take us on "Night Highway 99" and into "Three Worlds, Three Realms, Six Roads" (and we've already noted that "Jackrabbit" is tossed in here as a *hua-niao*). And "The Elwha River" and "Bubbs Creek Haircut" bring us to the originating poems of the *Mountains and Rivers* idea and to, for him, a record of where he was and what his spiritual condition was in relation to this vision in the 1960s. This is going to be that part of the story. Then "Boat of a Million Years" is a later meditation that picks up the metaphor of boat. Then "The Blue Sky," which is from 1968, the period after the first part was published, but in fact during the period when he was writing *Regarding Wave*, the poems that were most involved with the idea of mythologies to do with the mythic feminine, with what he calls in an essay on myth our "archaic matrifocal roots."

One way to think about the poems in the first section is that they're all versions of the journey, that they model certain kinds of consciousness, and that they tell the story of where the poet's consciousness was at that time. They root these materials in North America as his studies in Zen or Hindu thought are beginning to deepen. And they evoke the first animal spirit, "Jackrabbit," and end with his first sustained attempt to introduce to the North American continent female mythologies through the old shamanistic healing colors, blue and the azure. So if you overlay the biographical element with the set of instructional themes within the overall argument plus the two or three epistemological problems around myth, animism, and shamanism at the core, you can see how textured and layered this work is, casual as it seems. Because it's a book of instruction it can take things up in a certain order, but it is also trying to do two or three other things at the same time. So here you get some feeling for the sense I'm beginning to get of the richness of this.

V.

Let's read a little of "Night Highway 99" (M&R 11–24). After China and Neolithic Native America, we come back to the Whitman tradition and to American hitchhiking where the early Snyder of the Beat (*On the Road*, Wobblies, the old American romance of the tramp) Generation, gets connected to the travel pilgrim tradition in Japanese and Chinese literature. At the beginning of *The Dharma Bums* — Jack Kerouac's novel about Gary Snyder (Japhy Ryder) — the Kerouac character, Ray Smith, has been in Mexico and has jumped a freight he is riding with an old hobo up to California. The old bum has a worn copy of *The Flowers of Saint Francis* in his pocket and Kerouac has his Signet paperback of *The Essential Buddhism* or something like that. Suddenly he sees the new beatnik as the grandson of the old hobo. (You can think of Hart Crane's poems.) Here we are deep into an American iconography that Snyder takes very seriously, and he offers it here to the American young as an adventure and as serious spiritual practice in the same way that travel was a spiritual practice of monks. For me now it has the innocence of that time, which of course wasn't innocent at all. Who would hitchhike now?

In the poem he does it on Highway 99, which no longer exists. It was the old north-south road through California's central valley that connected California to the Pacific Northwest. It was the adventure road, to use Jack London's phrase.

> We're on our way
>
> man
> out of town

When I first read this I found it very jarring to go from the style of the '90s to the style of the late 1950s. What's going on here? In terms of the autobiographical ground of the poem as an account of an education, this has to be the older Snyder introducing his themes and then giving us the younger man.

> go hitching down
> that highway 99

That's how he sets us on our way. He means it to rhyme with the movement of the eye in the first poem and the hunter-gatherers out wandering in the second:

> Too cold and rainy to go out on the Sound
> Sitting in Ferndale drinking coffee
> Baxter in black, been to a funeral
> Raymond in Bellingham — Helena Hotel —

> Can't go to Mexico with that weak heart
> Well you boys can go south. I stay here.
> Fix up a shack — get a part-time job —
>   (he disappeared later
>   maybe found in the river)
> In Ferndale & Bellingham
> Went out on trail crews
> Glacier and Marblemount
> There we part.

The interesting thing for me is that this is the beginning of *Mountains and Rivers Without End*. Snyder had published *Myths & Texts* in 1960, which is a poem of place, a poem that tried to take native myths and his early studies in Asian literature and religious thought and drill them into North America in the context of the work of logging and hunting. It's still true that almost everybody in America with an active relationship to the natural world has an economic relationship to it. This is not about Sierra Club folks but about the people who live in it and around it all the time, and all of them are extractors. You know, they're mining, they're cutting down trees, they're fishing, they're growing food, and working on wildcat oil rigs. That was the intersection he was interested in in the 1950s. How working traditions in American culture had some relation to the Native American traditions, which were also active and not national park relationships rooted in conservation and tourism.

"Night Highway 99" begins in the fall with the arrival of inclement weather for all these activities: it's too wet to go out on the Bay, too dangerous to go out on the Sound and fish, there is snow in the mountains, the logging work has closed down, the road clearing work has closed down, the farming is done . . . and then you take off. So this is very self-consciously the moment of where the living-in-place poem stops and the we're-on-the-move poem begins. It's about movement in America. It tries to fuse his early ideas of the Japanese-Chinese spiritual-pilgrim tradition with this American hobo hitchhiking romance that Kerouac got people going on in *On the Road*.

> Tiny men with mustaches
> driving ox teams
> deep in the cedar groves

In "Bubbs Creek Haircut" the barber is going to say (M&R 33):

> "Well I been up there, I built the cabin
> up at Cedar Grove. In nineteen five."

And later in the poem Snyder ends up in Cedar Grove in King's Canyon, the great gateway for hikers into the Southern Sierra. How much to read into these recurrent references? If they were in Eliot you would think they're all on purpose. You're not quite sure with Snyder. But it was very much part of the Poundian aesthetic of his early work. He trusted readers to hear the echoes and pick up the rhymes.

> Tiny men with mustaches
> driving ox teams
> deep in the cedar groves
> wet brush, tin pants, snoose —

Tin pants are waterproof work pants. "Snoose," not in the *OED*, is logger's slang for chewing tobacco, probably Scandinavian in origin.

The ox teams in the cedar grove are hauling out logs. From *Myths & Texts*, "Logging," section 14 (M&T 15):

> The groves are down,
>   cut down
> Groves of Ahab, of Cybele
> Pine trees, knobbed twigs
> Thick cone and seed
> Cybele's tree this, sacred in groves
> Pine of Seami, cedar of Haida

And here we return to the actual, rural Northwest landscape (M&R 12):

> Split-shake roof barns
>   over berry fields
>   white birch chicken coop

I'm not going to read through all of this, but you see how we're now invited to read it as a *Mountains and Rivers* scroll and see the hovering affectionate symbolic play in just the description of the moving, changing human world. That it's now been connected to "What we ate — who ate what — / how we all prevailed." That "Old Bones" was possibly conceived as a transition to "Night Highway 99," and that was intended to get us from our early habitation of the North American earth to the way it looked to a young guy doing a Whitman list to evoke the working world of the American West.

> Put up in Dick Meigs cabin
>   out behind the house —
> Coffeecan, PA tin, rags, dirty cups,
> Kindling fell behind the stove, miceshit,
>   old magazines,

And here's where he invokes the urge to travel from the point of view of a logging operation:

>   winter's coming in the mountains
>   shut down the show
>   the punks go back to school
>   and the rest hit the road —
> strawberries picked, shakeblanks split
> fires all out and the packstrings brought
> down to the valley,
>   set loose to graze.

Grazing in valleys. This, you know, already has a symbolic drift with mountain wild and pastoral valleys as a human (and animal) rhythm.

Gray wharves and hacksaw gothic homes
Shingle mills and stump farms

I grew up in Northern California. The first time I saw the Northwest land-
scape was driving up Highway 99 with friends to see a girlfriend who was
at school in Seattle. I could watch the vegetation change as the weather did
and the architecture with it, but I had no language for it. The next time I
saw the Northwest I'd read Snyder and saw that he was describing it exactly.

Fifty weary Indians   Mt. Vernon
Sleep in the bus station
Strawberry pickers speaking Kwakiutl
        turn at Burlington for Skagit & Ross Dam

under apple trees by the river
banks of junked cars

That could be a haiku.

BC Riders give hitchhikers rides

The next stanza is a notation about Everett, Washington. Here he evokes
the old Wobbly mythology. The way Snyder is thinking about Big Bill Hay-
wood and the Wobblies is very much like Bob Dylan channeling Woody
Guthrie at just about the same moment as West Coast small presses and East
Coast folk clubs were both trying to reach back to a pre-war radical tradi-
tion. I like this stuff so much I cannot adjudge of it.

"The sheriff's posse stood in double rows   Everett
        flogged the naked Wobblies down
        with stalks of Devil's Club
        & run them out of town"

Devil's Club is a Northwest shrub walking sticks and billy clubs were made from. This stanza rhymes with "Logging," section 7 of *Myths & Texts*, which tells the same story (M&T 9):

> Felix Baran
> Hugo Gerlot
> Gustav Johnson
> John Looney
> Abraham Rabinowitz
> Shot down on the steamer Verona
> For the shingle-weavers of Everett
>   the Everett Massacre November 5 1916

By the way, this story gets told in a great new book about the trial of Big Bill Haywood by *New York Times* reporter, Tony Lukas. It's just a fabulous social history of this period of the Wobblies.

> Ed McCullogh, a logger for thirty-five years
> Reduced by the advent of chainsaws
> To chopping off knots at the landing:
> "I don't have to take this kind of shit,
> Another twenty years
>   and I'll tell 'em to shove it"
>   (he was sixty-five then)
> In 1934 they lived in shanties
> At Hooverville, Sullivan's Gulch.
> When the Portland-bound train came through
> The trainmen tossed off coal.
>
> "Thousands of boys shot and beat up
> For wanting a good bed, good pay,
>   decent food, in the woods —"
> No one knew what it meant:
> Soldiers of Discontent."

This references the IWW (International Workers of the World) and the radical union's name for strikers in the first lumberjack strike in the Northwest. Snyder's father was a logger, and this world is romantic to Snyder, who grew up in the Northwest where the Wobblies had legendary status. A little later he will quote another IWW slogan: "Forming the new society within the shell of the old" (M&T 44), which gets at the transformative ambitions of the poem.

Back to "Night Highway 99":

> While shingle weavers lost their fingers
>   in the tricky feed and take
>   of double saws.
>
> Dried, shrimp
>   smoked, salmon
> — before the war old Salish gentleman came
> & sold us kids rich hard-smoked Chinook
> from his flatbed model T
>   Lake City,
>   waste of trees & topsoil, beast, herb,
>   edible roots, Indian field-farms & white men
>   dances   washed, leached, burnt out
>   minds blunt, ug! talk twisted
>
>   a night of the long poem
>   and the mined guitar
>   "Forming the new society
>   within the shell of the old"
>   mess of tincan camps and littered roads.
>
> The Highway passes straight through every town
>   at Matsons washing bluejeans
>   hills and saltwater

The word for road in Japanese is *michi*, and the character for it is the Chinese character for the Tao. So in those poems when Bashō says

> Autumn night —
> on this road
> no one walking.

the road is the empty autumn road. But it is also the Tao, the Way, the Path. When it's being used by Snyder for this purpose, it is the Tao. When it's being used for other purposes, not. And it's very interesting to see how he does it:

> The Highway passes straight through every town
> at Matsons washing bluejeans
> hills and saltwater
>
> ack, the woodsmoke in my brain
>
> (high Olympics — can't go there again)
>
> East Marginal Way the hitchhike zone
> Boeing down across Duwamish slough
> and angle out   & on.

Next section:

> Night rain wet concrete headlights blind   Tacoma
>
> salt air / bulk cargo / steam cycle / AIR REDUCTION
>
> eating peanuts I don't give a damn
> if anybody every stops I'll walk
> to San Francisco   what the hell
>
> "that's where you going?
> why you got that pack?"

This pack is the Hump-backed Flute Player's pack. It's the pilgrim's pack. It's the pack of everybody's karma on their road.

> "well man I just don't feel right
> without something on my back"
>
>> & this character in milkman overalls
>> "I have to come out here
>> every once in a while, there's a guy
>> blows me here"
>>> way out of town.

There's a really nice thing about the milkman overalls, which is the way the theme of buttermilk shows up in the poem. On page 17:

> Portland sawdust down town
> Buttermilk corner all you want for a nickel
>> (now a dime)   — Sujata gave

This is where some of his study of Buddhist myth comes in.

> Gautama buttermilk.
> (No doubt! says Sokei-an, that's all it was:
>> plain buttermilk)

So buttermilk gets associated with the goddess here. On page 19:

> What elegance, What a life.
> Bust my belly with a quart of
> buttermilk
> & five dry heels of French bread

Like William Carlos Williams, Snyder is alert to any evidence that the earth likes and feeds us. It gives him enormous pleasure. And buttermilk serves that function here. So the driver he seems to report on with no particular purpose is splashed with the water of love, punning with the sweet milk of jism, too, I am sure. We are still on the road, hitching the stretch from Tacoma to Portland:

> Stayed in Olympia with Dick Meigs
> — this was a different year & he had moved —
> sleep on a cot in the back yard
> half the night watch shooting stars

Anyway you can see what's going on here and how I want to read this.

The interesting and curious figure on page 17, Sokei-an, was a Japanese Buddhist monk who came to the States in 1906 and walked around Oregon and Washington. He picks up on the theme of the transplantation of the tradition.

> (No doubt! says Sokei-an, that's all it was:
> plain buttermilk)

> rim of mountains
> pulp bark chewed snag papermill
> tugboom in the river
> — used to lean on bridge rails
> dreaming up eruptions and quakes —

Of course he said this before he had this thought. But this is not only the transforming earthquake, but also the theme that is going to be associated with will, discipline, and transcendence. And it's set right next to the buttermilk passage that twins these themes.

> An old book on Japan at the Goodwill

The Goodwill secondhand store is going to become a more elaborate pun in "Bubbs Creek Haircut." This is followed by these lines:

> Bust my belly with a quart of
> buttermilk

So Portland: where used books can be had, and cheap milk and bread. All this is living off the grid and on the Tao in the imagination of the young Snyder. Further down on this page he pauses:

We're on our way

> man

> > out of town

Go hitching down that
> Highway 99

And then a more rapid list:

Oil pump broken, motor burning out   Salem

Ex-logger selling skidder cable
> wants to get to San Francisco,
> fed and drunk   Eugene

Guy just back from Alaska — don't like
> the States now — too much law   Sutherlin

A woman with a kid & two bales of hay   Roseburg

We're now instructed in how to read this, as if it is a series of haiku. As if it is an account of human movement through the landscape.

(Six great highways; so far only one)

99 was the westernmost of six great American highways. (The Eisenhower freeway system was on the drawing board.) Two poems after "Highway 99" we're going to read one called "Six Roads." There's another echo there. There's a town called Bandon in southern Oregon. It calls up for the traveler the Buddhist sense of travel:

> — Abandon really means it
> the network womb stretched loose all
> things slip through

This was the Kerouac/Ginsberg/Snyder *On the Road* dream. And immediately after that comes an image that's pure haiku:

> Dreaming on a bench under newspapers
> I was covered with rhododendron blooms
>   alone in a State Park in Oregon

If you're a good Buddhist reading this, those rhododendron blooms would not just stand for beauty, but would be rooted in the idea of endless change as well. And then you get these other transcriptions I was reading. Page 21, the middle of the poem, is the first place where he actually picks up on the idea that tells us this is a scroll painting:

> Snow on the pines & firs around Lake Shasta
>   — Chinese scene of winter hills and trees
>   us "little travelers" in the bitter cold
>   six-lane highway slash & D-9 Cats —
>   bridge building   squat earth-movers
>   — yellow bugs
>   I speak for hawks. Creating
>   "Shasta" as I go —

> The road that's followed goes forever;
>   in half a minute crossed and left behind.

And this is where he's playing with "You don't have to go on the highway. This is the other highway." It's "The Way that can be followed is not the Way" from the *Tao Te Ching*. All you have to do is walk across the road. This is the 1950s. Allen Ginsberg was still working as an advertising agency writer in a three-piece suit and having a scientist help him overcome his homosexuality. You don't have to go down the highway, just cross the road. Over and over they're saying it. And of course there's this business — Blake's business — of the "mind-forg'd manacles."

> Out of the snow and into red-dirt plains
> blossoming plums

Notice that this is a poem of descent, coming down out of the mountains, out of the north, into the fertile plain of the Bay Area. And when we get there:

> City
> gleaming far away
> we make it into town tonight
> get clean and drink some wine —
> SAN FRANCISCO
> NO
> body
> gives a shit
> man
> who you are
> or what's your car
> there
> IS no   99

To summarize: What he's done in this poem is to evoke the theme and bring it to North America. Then he does the little poem of the sub-theme: humans, animals, living in a place, transmission of the culture's songs, and so on. Those old songs and things — to condense my argument — are going to be his answer to the critique of myth. That is to say, "No, there's nothing originary. What there is is an endless set of commentaries on that ineluctable beginning. And the harvesting, passing-on, transforming of that set of stories, songs, is what we do." Is it reality? Moot point.

From "The Mountain Spirit" (M&R 146):

> The Mountain Spirit whispers back:
> "All art and song
> is sacred to the real.
> As such."

That's right: "sacred to the real as such," which is a mystery. In plain episte-
mology, there's a simple way of saying this. Radical skepticism from Hume
to the present says pretty much the same thing. What you're seeing and
I'm seeing we're both calling a chair. We may be seeing completely differ-
ent things. We're seeing them through more or less one kind of sense expe-
rience. More like each other than an ant's vision or the vision of a bird that
sees spectrums of light different from humans. Different kinds of animals
have different kinds of eyes. So is there such a thing as "objective knowl-
edge"? Not in this sense. What there is is a testable common knowledge. If
I say "Stand up, close your eyes, take three steps, hold out your hand, you're
going to touch something hard" and you touch something hard, that would
happen outside of my consciousness. That's Samuel Johnson refuting Berke-
ley. And it's a repeatable experiment. Is there "a chair" there. No. In Humean
terms, no, there's no chair. Is there something there that we commonly call
a chair? Yes there is. Can we know it? That's a story.

Buddhism has no problem with this. I gather it was one of the aims of
Buddhist thought from the beginning to use epistemological problems like
those in Western philosophy to loosen people's attachment to their world
picture. Not, of course, as an end in itself. And, in my understanding, the
thing that is the end is more or less wordless. I assume it's the wordless thing
that Gary Snyder means by "the real as such." Though it's quite possible he
means the world of common knowledge in which bodies make love to bod-
ies that may or may not have any objective existence and climb trees and
drive cars similarly. I don't think that shamanic thought had much trouble
with this problem either, used as it was to crossing boundaries. Snyder did
wrestle with this problem early in his Buddhist studies in *The Back Coun-
try*. I'm thinking of the poem, "Through the Smoke Hole." When I asked
him about it once, he said, "Well, I was trying out Buddhist metaphysics."

VI.

We have to stop, so I just want to say a word about each of the next sections
in Part I. So what happens in the next poem, "Three Worlds, Three Realms,
Six Roads"? Why does he put this in? Well, it was written around 1966 and
is part of the autobiography of this time, it's an example of his practice of

assimilating Buddhist notions of attention to North America, it presents different ways of walking on the earth, and it is as an embodiment of knowledge, as in "Things to Do Around Seattle." It's literally that: not only things to do, but examples of ways of paying attention in the world that are not purposive in some larger way. Once you say this is both an autobiographical book and an embodiment of knowledge, and understand the way these different parts follow one another, it becomes intelligible as part of a larger philosophic-dramatic myth.

With "Jackrabbit" what you get is the first of the *hua-niao* poems and an example of the animism theme (M&R 31):

> Jackrabbit,
> black-tailed Hare
> by the side of the road,

[By the side of the road is a symbolic place at this point.]

> hop, stop.
> Great ears shining,
> you know me
> a little. A lot more than I
> know you.

This is the exercise with the chair. Finally, we can't know animals in any literal way. It's just simply true. Do plants have feelings? We're never going to know. I've written several poems about what a raccoon is thinking, so I paraphrase myself. But the place of this epistemological mystery is that every species lives in its own sensory world, which is inescapable. And we're one species. Once you make that acknowledgment, certain things can happen. And one of the things that can happen is the permission to make the animist leap, understood in this way.

The Jackrabbit is not a metaphor. It is a being. *Jackrabbit* is a generic term. This particular rabbit — if there was a particular rabbit — has got its own problems. We don't know what they are and can't experience them experiencing themselves. When I first read "Jackrabbit," I thought, "Well, this is not a very good poem. It's one of his mediocre middle period animal poems." And I think by itself it would be one of his somewhat charming, not great, middle period animal poems. But you have to be very careful with this judgment of Snyder, because his touch is so light. Set here, I think it works brilliantly. It's organized by being one of these small things in the larger whole set on the North American continent. The issue of animism is placed beside the road, and it introduces the whole discussion of animals that's going to come by saying "you know me / a little/ a lot more than I / know you." Neither knows the other very well or very much. And it looks back to the issue of "the real" and the "out there" we've been talking about.

I think "The Elwha River" is an amazing poem. It's the first one that breaks up the reality discussion by introducing dream (apart from the dream as hunger in "Old Bones"). I think you have to make the argument about myth through dream. I don't think myth can come into the poem until you break up realistic story time. To break up the time sense reminds us that our travels are not just in a temporal world from town to town, but that we travel in non-spatial, non-logical, non-temporal ways in the dreamtime. That's a condition for myth. You have to go through the gateway of dream, which is a phenomenal experience you can appeal to. The speaker of the poem, gender unspecified, dreams of being a pregnant girl who comes to the Elwha River, which is near her school where she is given the assignment of writing about what she just did and so she writes a composition about coming to the Elwha River at a bridge near some redwood trees. Then, toward the end of the piece, this (M&R 32):

> As I write this now I must remind myself that there is another
>   Elwha,
> the actual Olympic peninsula river, which is not the river I took
>   pains to
> recollect as real in the dream.

And then in the last stanza:

> There are no redwoods north of southern
>   Curry County, Oregon.

Is there a real world? Is it all ideologically determined? The poem can't tell you much, but it can tell you certain things. That, for example, above Curry County, Oregon you start to get Sitka spruce instead of redwood trees. That's as much objective reality as we are going to get. And it tells you there are bridges. And dreams. And dreams inside of dreams.

So we've come to "Bubbs Creek Haircut." It's about going up. "Night Highway 99" is about going down. Notice the structure. After "Night Highway 99" you come to the dream space and then you have a poem about going up: the ascent. So this theme of climbing and falling that is so important in the opening poem gets assimilated to the hobo-romantic thing here in these earliest *Mountains and Rivers* poems. By the end of which — the last line is "'Your Bubbs Creek haircut, boy.'" — the narrator is like a monk getting his tonsure, albeit a kind of American-Hobo-Buddhist-barber-college tonsure. And, literary considerations aside, what I would really suggest is that, if you are physically able, you might think about reading the poem carefully and then driving down to King's Canyon and hiking into the mountains along Bubbs Creek.

Then we get the next poem Snyder wrote in the '90s to give shape to this whole thing: "Boat of a Million Years." And we have in our head the echo of "the watching boat has floated of the page." Boat is already an active metaphor for our lives, for what carries us and is moving (M&R 39):

> The boat of a million years,
>   boat of morning,
> sails between sycamores of turquoise,
>
> Dawn white Dutch freighter
> in the Red Sea — with a red stack —
> heads past our tanker, out toward Ras Tanura,
>   sun already fries my shoulder blades, I
>   kneel on ragged steel decks chipping paint.
> Gray old T-2 tanker and a
>   white Dutch freighter.

> boat of the sun,
> the abt-fish, the yut-fish,
> play in the waves before it,
>
> salty Red Sea
>   dolphins rip sunlight
> streak in, swirl and tangle
>   under the forward-arching wave roll
> of the cleaving bow

Of the boat: it is the boat of our life that's floating past on the Red Sea. It comes from Snyder's experience forty years earlier as a merchant seaman, but it's the boat of the Mahayana tradition, it's the boat of all time floating past the other boat, the tanker, like a kind of magic. Arrested between the two, the narrator says:

> Teilhard said "seize the tiller of the planet" he was joking,
>
> We are led by dolphins toward morning.

It's hard not think that because *The Waste Land* ends with the "Datta. Dayadhvam. Damyata." One of these three admonitions is to "control," and Eliot figures control as use of the tiller of the wind in sailing, which would seem to have more to do with being responsive to wind and water than controlling them. "The boat responded / Gaily," Eliot wrote. This connects in my mind to the dolphin imagery in Part II, "A Game of Chess," and the "sad light" in which "a carved dolphin swam." Also connected, of course to Yeats's "Byzantium," "That dolphin-torn, that gong-tormented sea." And of course the various myth traditions in which dolphins escort the souls of the dead to Paradise. There are a whole bunch of gatherings here. The extent to which they are there in this text or not, I don't know. I'm interested in finding his conversation with the other poems in this tradition. So it really doesn't matter how conscious are these echoes. (And it's not pedantic to notice them. This business of transmission is not pedantic.) What matters to the poem is whether and in what way we're moved by this gorgeousness. And at what level we can assent to it all the way up and all the way down as a philosophical proposition. Here an argument has begun to be made, but it's still essentially gorgeousness, I think. Snyder at least means to gather up the boat theme, the travel by water theme, and the animal theme that's been introduced through "Jackrabbit." And perhaps also the dreamtime theme. To say "We are led by dolphins toward morning" is another matter than seizing the tiller of the planet to the man chipping paint on an old tanker while the boat of a million years floats by.

We've about come to the end of the first movement of the long poem. And you can see what I would do here. We've watched Snyder gathering all this stuff going back to that period of 1968, so that now he can place a poem in which, in earnest, next to the play and high spirits of "Night Highway 99" and "Bubbs Creek Haircut" he can set down in earnest (maybe too Poundian an earnest for some tastes, but not for mine) his first full scale introjection of Buddhist and Hindu lore and transplant it into the last section of the first movement of *Mountains and Rivers* as a kind of healing spell and evocation of the power and beauty of Buddhist thought (M&R 40):

> "Eastward from here
> beyond Buddha-worlds ten times as
> numerous as the sands of the Ganges
> there is a world called
> PURE AS LAPIS LAZULI"

It's a way of summing up the state of his learning and of his consciousness as he set out on the path of this poem in 1968.

Well, what then? To read the rest of the poem in this spirit, try to pay attention again to what gets made through thematic rhymes and the implicit biographical arc of the poem. Try to make an account of it in these terms and whatever other terms grow up in the course of reading. (One has to do with the deepening theme of spirit possession and shamanism.) But enough! The rain has let up, it's starting to get dark, and you're probably ready to eat, whether food exists objectively or not.

NOTE

1. "Tārā is not another version of the Earth Mother. She's not the mother of all beings. She's the mother of the Buddhas. She's the mother of the beings who see *beyond* being. . . . She's a different kind of mother. She's the mother of Wisdom, the mother of Wisdom and Compassion. She's not giving birth to beings. She's not even the mother of God, like Mary. She is also the same as Prajnā. The goddess Prajnā is represented exactly the same in the iconography. . . . I'd say she is the mother of non-dual insight, beyond birth and death. So she can [be a mother and] look like a virgin if she wants. It doesn't matter. Actually she's just portrayed as a very young woman in the iconography" (Gary Snyder in *Nobody Home: Writing, Buddhism, and Living in Places, Gary Snyder in Conversation with Julia Martin* [San Antonio, TX: Trinity University Press, 2014], 63–64).

9

Thoughts on *Mountains and Rivers Without End*

MICHAEL McCLURE

FIRST THOUGHT

I'm speaking from some fairly detailed notes, and what I say presupposes you have read the poem.

I wrote some preliminary notes called "First Thoughts." I wrote here about the aesthetics of deep nature. "Macaques in the Sky." Remember that section? The macaques swing through and in the trees while Gary and his friends walk and look at them.

I wrote, "Deep nature of Sesshu" (Japanese painter). And then I wrote, "As deep and shallow as zazen." I have some questions about the spiritual value of nature as being another way of missing what nature really is. I hear a lot about the spiritual value of nature. I wonder what that means. Or if it means anything.

This poem touches nature, which I feel is important.

"Walking the New York Bedrock": I feel as though this poem in one or several ways solves the antinomy of the duality of city and nature as in John Ashbery's "A Wave," if you happen to know that poem. It's a very, very, very different poem, but they share this melding, almost the way that Zen harmonizes activity and quiescence. "A Wave" harmonizes our deep mammal nature with the city. And I must confess to you that I am not an Ashbery fan. But "A Wave" is a poem I like very much.

I would compare "A Wave".... This is a preliminary note, I'm not taking you aside. I did not even stop to reread Ashbery, I continued to read Gary's poem. But the understructure of the city in the mammal's muscles and imagination is characteristic in very different ways in "A Wave" and Gary's *Mountains and Rivers Without End.*

All of John Ashbery's poems after his first few books are composed almost entirely of figures of speech. This flow of figures of speech speaks, eventually, for the class that Ashbery represents. This becomes the speech of that class, which becomes the experience of nature they are having in their bodies in the city. Ashbery's mammal experience of the city is ugly and plain and vital and vocal and it is not just cocktail chatter, as Allen Ginsberg says. That is the end of the first thought, before I started taking notes.

SECOND THOUGHT

Here is the second thought before taking notes: *Mountains and Rivers Without End* may be a new model, versus other models like Pound's *Cantos* and Kerouac's *Mexico City Blues*. Pound's *Cantos* being cantos and *Mexico City Blues* being fascicles, Snyder has made an organismic bundle in each fascicle, and this results in his whole poem being a kind of medicine bundle in the American Indian sense of putting together spirit objects to make a greater spirit power that one carries with one, whether in the heart, or in a pouch, or wrapped in an otter's skin and painted green (as in the Field Museum of Natural History in Chicago).

This is a medicine bundle in the guise of autobiography, with the whole thing being a wisdom book like the *Tao Te Ching*.

I find myself writing at the end of the first section, "What spectacular delicacy!" From the hand-carved shapes of real memory things in Seattle and Portland, for instance, to dreams recounted and revisited, to this tiny eagle dropping into the blue at the end of the first larger bundle.

Rereading "The Blue Sky" at the end of section one of *Mountains and Rivers*, the eagle flies away and falls flying "tinily" (if there is such a word) out of sight. I think of the heroic smallness of many of the pictures in *Paradise Lost* and that ongoing, everflowing iambic pentameter of Milton's.

I'll read that ending to remind you of what I am speaking of here (M&R 44):

> Thinking on Amitabha in the setting sun,
>   his *western* paradise —
>   impurities flow out away, to west,
>   behind us, *rolling,*

planet ball forward turns into the "east"
light-years beyond,
Great Medicine Master;
land of blue.
The blue sky

the blue sky

The Blue Sky

is the land of

OLD MAN MEDICINE BUDDHA
where the eagle that flies out of sight
flies.

BIG MIND

I think the realms — and I'm using that word in the Buddhist sense of the
Flower Garland Sūtra — are permeated with the stuff in the basement of the
Goodwill. I've been there and felt the griminess and coldness of the Good-
will in the 1950s. If I was going to make a long aside here, I would talk about
what the '50s were. If you weren't in the '50s, there's no way to know about
it unless you are a real historian.

It was not the good old days.

It was a grimy, cold, psychically distressed, overwrought time follow-
ing World War II. A time of great conformity and, being an outlaw in those
days was, honest to God . . . to be an outlaw. I mean, to say you were a poet
was tantamount to saying "hit me on the jaw or beat me up, or hang me on
the flagpole, I'm a fairy." That is what it meant. In 1954, there were about a
dozen people in the Bay Area who would say they are poets.

(Sorry, got kind of grim there, didn't I?)

Where I'm going, though, is that the Goodwill was a different place. I go
by Goodwills today and they are all on one floor. They look great. There's a
lot of them. Doesn't look like anything very interesting is in them.

In the 1950s, there was one, huge Goodwill in downtown San Francisco with a big basement just the way Gary Snyder describes it. It was filled with the ghosts and the ghosts of the ghosts of of dead old things. And then there was another area for things, that were, like, beyond repair, do you want one of these?

There was a different ethos in those days. When I moved into the house of a friend of Robert Duncan's who went with him to Majorca in 1954, Jas gave me their paintings and Robert gave me their furniture. The guy who had the flat before moved out and left his furniture in there. We threw it out in the street or gave it to somebody else. What we didn't want we gave to somebody else and somebody else gave us theirs. When you needed a car, somebody gave you their old car and charged you $50 for it. It rarely ran. You had to tie the door shut with a piece of rope so you could drive over to Mill Valley and see Jack Kerouac in his shack up on the hill that Gary was using as a zendo. You were really poor. You didn't *think* you were poor: you really were poor. If you were going to have dinner, you didn't go out to a slick restaurant. Maybe you had to scrimp for it a little bit, but you scrimped and saved and maybe fixed the first bouillabaise you had ever fixed in your life. It was very different.

And this poem comes out of that. It doesn't show those pictures. But that is the substrate. The feel of the griminess and coldness of the basement of the Goodwill is evoked directly and indirectly. These are different from the "The Elwha River" dream and the octopoid shapes and sidebars of dream consciousness it authentically shows. The "Bubbs Creek Haircut" becomes a haircut containing the dream of real life that one wakes up to to go out into the world where the stuff of dreams then happens. In the real world, there is a jackrabbit. Just a jackrabbit being a fascicle in the overall medicine bundle of the poem. The rabbit — actually it is a hare — is huge and real, breaking all proportion by being only a tiny set of verses, but given the weight of a canto. And it knows more about us than we could know about it. That's what Gary says.

I could be anthropomorphic and say that the quantum world knows more about us, is us, I suppose, than we under any circumstances could know about it.

In those days, there were small forests inside of Seattle. And the edges of the city were small forests, surrounded by more forests, with crusty old folks living in cabins, and raising chickens, and pigeons, and pheasants. The world recounted, whether it is Gary painting it with a fine-tipped brush, or me remembering my childhood is gone, gone, gone to the other bank, all the way gone, *bodhi svāhā*!

Ah, but here it is palpable, and only a fool could deny it. Wait a minute! This is consciousness. And it is very large. It is so large that it has no scale. That which has no scale is without proportion. That which is without proportion is both as monumental as a behemoth or leviathan by Blake or a macaque by Sesshu. And as tiny as an image in a sonnet by Keats or a line by Milton in *Paradise Lost*.

To experience that which is proportionlessness makes all things immune to comparison. All things are equally the center of the universe, the center of the Dharma.

In this flurry from realm to realm, dream to remembered dream, to hitchhiking, to jackrabbit, to dreamer getting a haircut, to a mountaintop, to the Sung Dynasty, from great to tiny.... Each receives equal attention as a notion of proportionlessness.

So Shunryu Suzuki-rōshi's rule of thumb: Big mind should not be hunted for. Big mind should be used. Big mind is being used in this poem.

In *Mountains and Rivers*, the Zen of big mind opens up. The physics of *śūnyatā* allows time diving, like a dolphin diving, in waves around a sunlit rusty tanker in the Persian Gulf. Everything is emptiness. The expressions of dream, psyche, history, memory, do not need to be separated in the practical planes of daily life, because they are all, whether a piece of lapis lazuli or the experience of a toothache, comprised of the same emptiness as big mind.

"MACAQUES IN THE SKY"

Of all the poems in the book, the one I would have wanted to have written myself is "Macaques in the Sky" (M&R 114–15):

Walking the trail with Wang Ch'ing-hua, Red Pine, Lo Ch'ing,
and Carole from Nanren Lake, we see a clear spot in the jungle
canopy of leaves — a high point arch of heavy limbs, a lookout on
the forest slope —

A mother monkey sits and nurses,

A couple perching side by side,

A face peeks from another leaf screen, pink cheeks,
shining eyes,

An old male, silver belly, furrowed face,
laid back in a crotch

harsh little cough-calls echo

faces among the leaves,
    being ears and eyes of trees
soft hands and haunches pressed on boughs and vines

Then — *wha!* — she leaps out in the air
the baby dangling from her belly,

they float there,

— she fetches up along another limb —
    and settles in.

Her
arching like the Milky Way,
mother of the heavens,
    crossing realm to realm
    full of stars

as we hang on beneath with all we have

enjoy her flight
Drink her light.

Rhesus macaque.

I always call this poem "Starlight." I think it is a perfect poem, inherently whole and beautiful with delicacy and canniness of observation. In addition, it does not hide that it is a poem, which makes it a great poem. It does not try to pass itself off by loveliness. Each perception hangs separate from the others, like petroglyphs on a canyon wall, or maybe on a subway car. Finally, it is truly emphatic that it is not a lovely poem, but is experience recounted — not trying to mime the experience, or be the experience. And it is pure condition.

~

No mere gathering of 39 individual poems, Snyder's epic work is a carefully constructed interweaving of sound, image, and sense, the result of both intuition and conscious intention. Each complete reading of the poem is a circumambulation of this magnificent landscape, yet in order to "open" the resonant energies of Snyder's poem, a reader must integrate an attentive step-by-step passage along these spiraling verbal pathways with an inspired consciousness of what lies off, or beyond, its virtual trails. Nor should we forget, as a mountain has a way of just "being mountain" regardless how many times one walks around it, so *Mountains and Rivers Without End* ultimately has a way of just "being poem," always awaiting another reading, another critical circumambulation. Despite the fixity of words and images on the page, Snyder's virtual streams and mountains, like their counterparts in our "real" world, "never stay the same" and each reader's attentive "walking" of this poetic landscape will produce new interconnections, new inspirations, new insights. It is the allure of the poem's constantly shifting web of associations that remains an invitation to transformation for those who attend to the interweavings of its tapestry.

— Anthony Hunt, adapted from his *Genesis, Structure, and Meaning in Gary Snyder's* Mountains and Rivers Without End (2004)

ENGAGING BUDDHIST PERSPECTIVES

~

The mercy of the West has been social revolution; the mercy of the East
has been individual insight into the basic self/void. We need both. They
are both contained in the traditional three aspects of the Dharma path:
wisdom (prajña), meditation (dhyāna), and morality (śīla). Wisdom is
intuitive knowledge of the mind of love and clarity that lies beneath one's
ego-driven anxieties and aggressions. Meditation is going into this mind
to see this for yourself — over and over again, until it becomes the mind
you live in. Morality is bringing it back out in the way you live, through
personal example and responsible action, ultimately toward the true com-
munity (sangha) of "all beings."

— Gary Snyder, "Buddhism and the Coming Revolution" (1961)

10

Buddhism in *Mountains and Rivers Without End*

CARL BIELEFELDT

INTRODUCTION

My job here is to give you a lecture on the Buddhism in *Mountains and Rivers Without End*.[1] I'm not going to take you through the book itself looking for signs of the religion in particular poems or passages. I may do a little of that along the way, but mostly I want to focus on one specific Buddhist text and use it to reflect a bit on the kinds of Buddhism you might look for in the poems when you have time. As I trust you realize, there are many different kinds of Buddhism. They often think about the same topics from different angles and use the same vocabulary in quite different ways. So, if we're looking for Buddhist influence (whatever that means) in Gary's poems, it's not enough just to recognize the vocabulary or plug in some generic account of what Buddhists believe; we also have to think more broadly about the range of Buddhist approaches and how they may (or may not) fit into Gary's work.

The text I've chosen to look at, the *Mountains and Waters Sūtra* by the Japanese Zen master Dōgen, deals especially, as you might guess from its title, with Buddhist views of the natural world. If you've had a chance to look at it, I think you'll agree it's a rich and difficult work, and I can't claim myself to have figured it all out. But I want to claim that woven through the work we can find three different strands of thinking about the natural world around us. One of these, the best known from textbooks on Buddhism, is what we can call the "metaphysical" strand — i.e., abstract analysis of what's really going on in the world. Alongside this kind of analysis, we'll also find a second type of Buddhist talk — what we might call the "mystical" or "cosmological" — that emphasizes the symbolic significance of the natural world.

And finally, we'll find a "mythological" strand, in which the landscape is read through the narratives of a community. I think these three approaches can be found not only in Dōgen's text but in Buddhism more broadly, and I encourage you to keep them in mind as you look for the religion in Gary's poems.

I've chosen Dōgen's *Mountains and Waters Sūtra* not only because it's an interesting work in its own right, well worth a lecture or two, but more importantly for us because it seems to have been particularly influential in Gary's thinking about his book. When he did his reading at Stanford last autumn, he mentioned that his encounter with this sūtra in the early seventies set back his progress on *Mountains and Rivers* by ten years, as he tried to figure out what it was all about. Of course, Gary was also busy elsewhere during this time, writing other things and getting set up at his place in the Sierras; but it is a fact that, if you look at the dating of the individual poems in *Mountains and Rivers*, you'll find almost none from the early seventies till the early eighties.

The story of Gary's encounter with the *Mountains and Waters Sūtra* raises a broader issue we need to bear in mind when we think about the Buddhism in *Mountains and Rivers*. The poems in this book were written over the space of some forty years — years that saw an extraordinary transformation in our knowledge of Buddhism. Nowadays, it seems as if Buddhism is all over the place in America: in groups of every persuasion from every Asian Buddhist culture, in the media, new age pop psycho-religion, the peace and ecology movements, and in an academic industry of Buddhist studies putting out a regular flow of articles and translations. In such a scene, knowledge of Buddhism comes cheaply, and it may be hard for us now to imagine what it was like for someone like Gary to piece together that knowledge bit by bit when Buddhism was still an arcane subject and every new book a revelation. There may be a Zen master or Tibetan lama on every corner now, but when Gary first went looking for real Buddhists in Berkeley in the early fifties, all he could find was the old Japanese-American Jōdo Shin mission. There may be Zen and the art of the internet now, but when Gary started work on *Mountains and Rivers*, American Zen was still an exotic vision in the books of people like D. T. Suzuki, R. H. Blythe, and Alan Watts.

In effect, then, Gary's poem grew up with the growth of American Buddhism. Of course Gary himself didn't just sit around waiting for American

Buddhism to grow up: he learned Chinese at Berkeley, took off for Japan, and spent many years studying the religion there. But the fact remains that his Buddhism was not a given, not a system simply plugged into a poem but something growing as the poem grew. So, if we're seriously thinking about the Buddhist influences on his work, we need to think not just about Buddhism in the abstract but about the history of Gary's encounter with the religion, the various kinds of Buddhist environments in which he's actually lived, and how they figure in the work.

THE MOUNTAINS AND WATERS SŪTRA

Our text tonight, the *Mountains and Waters Sūtra*, is a good example of how Gary's Buddhist environment shifted as he worked. The text is part of a large and very rich collection of Dōgen's writings called the *Shōbōgenzō*, which can be translated as something like "The Treasury of the Eye of the True Dharma" (i.e., the essence of the Buddhist teachings). In our day, Dōgen has become one of the icons of American Buddhism. His collection is celebrated as a classic of Zen literature, has been translated in whole or in part several times, and has become the subject of a number of books. Throughout the 1950s and '60s, however, Dōgen and his *Shōbōgenzō* were almost unknown in the West. Thus, when Gary came upon the *Mountains and Waters Sūtra*, he must have been stunned by what he'd been missing. And when he quoted another chapter of the *Shōbōgenzō* as the epigraph for *Mountains and Rivers* to help us understand what he'd been up to for forty years, he was explaining himself with a text that he himself almost certainly didn't know till years after he started the work. This obviously raises the broader question of how Gary's understanding of what he was up to evolved over the decades and was influenced by changes in his environment, both Buddhist and otherwise.

I'll leave that question to the Snyder scholars and go back to my Buddhism. Before I get into specifics, however, I want to pose one other general question, in order to clear a space for our text. Like Gary's book, Dōgen's *Mountains and Waters Sūtra* is in some sense a work about nature. But in what sense? Nowadays, we often tend to think of Buddhism as ecologically-minded, a religion that doesn't think of the natural world as something created for humans to play with, but rather sees the human as but one node in an interrelated whole. Gary's own mix of Buddhist practice and environmental activism thus seems like a natural expression of such a religion. But, historically speaking, the vision of the natural world as an ecological system is more a product of Western science than of Asian wisdom, and the ethic of environmental activism probably has more to do with Western notions of human stewardship over the earth than with Buddhist ideals of the compassionate bodhisattva working for the salvation of all beings.

Our author, Dōgen, was no environmentalist ahead of his time; he was a traditional Buddhist cleric, more interested in what nature can do for humans than what humans can do for nature. Of course, as a Zen Buddhist cleric, he had a particular regard for the spiritual meaning of the natural world and what it can do for us. Among Buddhists, Zen masters are famous for their love of nature. They built their monasteries in the mountains and walked the ranges, traveling from monastery to monastery. These mountain monasteries became retreats not only for monks but for the lay literati, who sought them out to escape from the hustle and bustle of the big city. The monks and the literati hung out together, wrote poetry about the landscape, and painted pictures of the mountains with Zen hermitages tucked in the corners. It's not that other kinds of Buddhists didn't live in nature, but Zen turned it into an art form.

Zen has often advertised itself as a "natural" religion, a religion that celebrates both the world of nature and what is natural within us, our pre-reflective, pre-cultural experience as living beings. Zen masters like to play the old Taoist role of the simple, unlettered, rustic type, in contrast to the learned, sophisticated, citified Confucian gentleman. I think you'll agree that this traditional image of Zen plays well in America. It plays to a certain American sense of the value of nature in the raw, to a certain romanticism we have about the land and about ourselves as somehow more "earthy," more authentic than the cultured, effete Europeans. It probably plays especially well in the western United States, with its storied past of mountain men wandering the wilderness. When Gary Snyder works as a logger or lives as a solitary fire watchman in the Cascades or wanders out into the Great Basin, it's easy to see him as at once the mountain man and the man of Zen.

But let's go slowly here. The Great Basin can serve as a handy reminder not to collapse Zen nature onto ours. China has its own great basin — the wilds of the Tarim Basin in the far west along the old Silk Road — but Zen masters don't go there. Zen masters tend to stick to the outskirts of the city, where they can get good books and hang out with the literati, talking about nature. Zen masters may be famous for their wanderings, but they aren't backpackers, striking out into the wilderness. Take Dōgen, for example. He may have had to walk from place to place during his four-year pilgrimage to the Zen monasteries of China, but you'd never know it from his own reports. All he seems to remember about his experience went on once he was safely inside the monasteries. He often talks about this, but he never even mentions the countryside in between, let alone lingers over the beauty of a wayside flower. Back in Japan, Dōgen did eventually build his own Zen monastery in the mountains, but he seems to have remained throughout his life the consummate "indoorsman" — an aristocratic, intellectual ecclesiastic, at home in the church, surrounded by the nature of manicured gardens and landscape paintings.

In thinking about these "indoor" and "outdoor" views of nature, I'm reminded of two notions I talked about in my presentation to the Mountains & Rivers Workshop last fall. One is that nature is a cultural construct. Nature in the abstract, nature independent of culture, is a category we've carved out of our experience. In fact, it's not just one category but many. "Nature," as we use it, sometimes refers to a scientific object, the bits and pieces of the subatomic world or galaxies thrown off by the big bang. Other times, it's the wilderness or the law of the jungle. Or it's the pastoral landscapes in paintings or poetry. And, of course, increasingly in our day, it's an ecosystem or biosphere. All quite distinct, perhaps, but all readings of some obscure text, maps of some mysterious territory we find ourselves in.

The other point is a little more difficult: that the territory includes the maps, or that culture is part of the natural landscape. There are two ways of thinking about this. One is that culture is everywhere: there just ain't no nature in the raw out there to which we can escape from the hustle and bustle of the city; we always take our city with us when we go and litter the landscape with its stuff. We can't, in other words, really perceive nature apart from our cultural representations of it. The other way of thinking is that nature is everywhere: we can't hide indoors with the windows shut and keep the natural world outside: it always seeps through the cracks and into all the stuff we own. Insofar as we're natural beings, even our culture is part of the natural landscape. Both these ways of thinking are in Dōgen's Zen and in Gary's poetry. The mountains are in Dōgen's monastery as much as his monastery is in the mountains; the trail to Bubbs Creek runs through the basement of the old Goodwill store on Howard Street and down the highway littered with the carcasses of old tires.

In short, then, our two texts are not just about nature but about the intricate intertwining of nature and culture. For his part, Gary goes out of his way to frame his vision of mountains and rivers with a Chinese landscape painting, a representation of nature. Thus the reader is twice removed from "nature itself" — through the cultural layers of poem and painting. Indeed, in the first poem of the book, he pushes us back still further, by objectifying the painting as an historical artifact hung on the wall of the Cleveland Museum. From this distance, he takes us down into the art and walks us slowly through the imagined landscape of the artist. Then once we are lost in this world, he suddenly looks up, reminds us that the museum is on a rise overlooking Lake Erie, and steps outdoors. "Low gray clouds over the lake — chill March breeze." There's a double shock of recognition here: that the art has had an outdoors all around it, and that even Cleveland is an artistic landscape. Gary warned us in his epigraph for the book to be ready for this kind of shock, when he quoted the mysterious remark in Dōgen's essay, "Painting of a Rice Cake," that the entire universe is "nothing but a painting."

THE LANDSCAPE SŪTRA

Dōgen's remark could also serve as a warning about his own *Mountains and Waters Sūtra*. At first glance, this may look like it's going to be a Buddhist sūtra about nature, or perhaps a Chinese classic about interesting things in the landscape, like the ancient *Classic of Mountains and Seas*.[2] But the very first sentence of the text puts us straight: "These present mountains and waters are the expression of the ancient buddhas." The landscape, then, is not just the subject of the sūtra; it is the sūtra — that is, the text of a sermon by the buddha. Apparently, in Dōgen's world the natural landscape is somehow preaching to us. Or, to put it back in terms of the passage Gary quoted in his epigraph, the entire universe is "nothing but talk." Not just any talk, mind you, but good talk, of the sort a buddha gives, good old talk of the ancients going on all around us right now. No wonder a talker like Gary was interested in this text.

To say that the landscape is an "expression" of the buddhas is actually a translator's cop-out covering up an important ambiguity. The term Dōgen uses, *dō genjō*, can mean either "expression of the speech" or "expression of the way." The word *dō* is more familiar to us in its Chinese pronunciation, *tao*, as in "Taoism." Usually we translate this word as "way." The Chinese Buddhists used it for the "way of the buddha"—i.e., what we would call "Buddhism," understood as a spiritual way of life or a path of spiritual practice. But *tao* also means "to speak," "to say something," and in fact Dōgen regularly uses the word in this sense. Dōgen can drive a translator crazy by playing with these two meanings, as we see him doing here. As "expressions of the ancient buddhas," the mountains and waters are at once speaking to us, telling us about Buddhism, and at the same time themselves somehow putting Buddhism into practice and living the Buddhist life. The landscape, it seems, is not just all talk but also action.

When Dōgen sat down to write about the landscape as a sūtra, he probably had in mind a poem by the famous Buddhist layman, Su Tung-p'o, on which he had just written another essay a few months before. Gary put the poem and Dōgen's comment into *Mountains and Rivers* in the poem "We Wash Our Bowls in This Water." Here's my homemade version:

> The sound of the stream is His long, broad tongue;
> The mountain form, His body.
> This evening's 84,000 verses —
> How will I tell them tomorrow?

The pious poet sees the mountain scene as the Buddha's body and hears the rushing water as the Buddha's voice. In Dōgen's work, sight and sound collapse into a single text of mountains and waters. This expression, "mountains and waters," translates the Japanese term *sansui*, commonly used for what we would call "landscape," as in "landscape painting." But Dōgen wants to take the binome apart and play with the contrasts between its two elements. This is an old Chinese literary tradition, which uses "mountain and waters" to set off such polarities as "yang" and "yin," "male" and "female," "hard" and "soft," "solid" and "fluid," and so on. Dōgen himself is particularly interested here in the contrast between "permanent" and "changing": what is ancient and always so, like the teaching of the buddha; and what is ever presently going on, like the practice of the buddha. Since, according to the buddha's teaching, what is always so is that things are ever-changing, the contrast is built right into the Buddhist landscape.

IMPERMANENCE

The notion that things are ever-changing introduces what I'm calling the "metaphysical" strand of our text. Change is, of course, a kind of baseline of the Buddhist teachings, their famous doctrine of impermanence. Gary picks up on this baseline in a haunting refrain that runs through *Mountains and Rivers*: "Walking on walking / under foot earth turns." The unnerving image of the solid earth walking under our feet reminds us of the opening section of Dōgen's *Mountains and Waters Sūtra*, in which he comments on a Zen saying, "The blue mountains are constantly walking." (Gary himself did a commentary on Dōgen's commentary called "Blue Mountains Constantly Walking," one of his essays in *The Practice of the Wild*.[3]) Zen masters love this kind of unnerving image, making a mockery of our sense of permanence and a mush of our solids — like the master who said, "the bridge is flowing and the river isn't." Or Dōgen, who says it's the mountain that's flowing, not the water.

Such sayings may be unnerving, but they're not so strange if we think about things in terms of scales. One scale is what we might call the "geological." When Gary meets up with the Mountain Spirit near the end of *Mountains and Rivers*, she repeats the refrain, "Walking on walking / under foot earth turns." Then she says to the poet, "What do you know of minerals and stone./ For a creature to speak of all that scale of time — what for?" The creature who lives on the human scale can't know the life span of stones, the "ceaseless wheel of lives" of "red sandstone and white dolomite." The creature can't feel the earth turning underfoot, "Erosion always wearing down;/ shearing, thrusting, deep plates crumpling." The pace of the mountain is just too slow, its gait too long for us to see it walking. We find this geological scale of change in Zen sometimes, often mixed together with Taoist notions of the great cyclical fluctuations of the *tao* and even greater scales of Indian Buddhist cosmic aeons.

But, like the Indian Buddhist philosophers, Zen plays especially at the opposite end of the scale, with the microscopic changes of the moment. Here, we can't see the mountain walk because it's happening too quickly, like the buzz and flash of subatomic particles. Though they didn't have electron microscopes, the Buddhist philosophers saw things in their mind's eye not as things but as series of momentary events, each event replacing the next with nothing in between — everything in the world, and people too, just one damn little thing after another; the entire landscape nothing but swarms of very small happenings. And nothing in between: no substance, no essence, no soul, no self. Hence, the mountain doesn't endure as a mountain, under-going glacial change through the ages; on the microscopic scale, it recreates itself as a new array of mountain events in every moment. But, on the human scale, we don't notice what's going on.

Of course, things are also changing on the human scale. We live in a landscape not only of seemingly timeless peaks but also of obviously rushing water. Nowadays, we may like to think of change as progress and celebrate all the new stuff it brings, but for most Buddhist believers, like most people throughout history, change is mostly sadness and loss: everything's imper-manent; nothing's safe; there's no security; sickness, old age, and death will come to us all. Hence, the call to escape this life of change, into the time-less state of nirvana. Some Buddhists, interestingly enough, try to get out of change by getting further in, by speeding up their lives, so to speak, till they catch up with all its momentary fluctuations, or slowing down their minds till they come to rest in the present moment (these two amounting to the same business). The classic mental exercise for this is usually called "mindfulness," a standard practice of Zen Buddhists that Gary did for years in Kyoto and still does up in the Sierras. When you do it right, they say, the mind becomes like a mirror, just reflecting whatever comes in front of it in each moment — a quality of detached attention that seems to run through much of Gary's poetic use of pure description.

This traditional way of dealing with change has its psycho-Zen cousin in our pop virtues of "going with the flow" or being in the "here and now."

In the fifties, when Gary started writing *Mountains and Rivers*, there was a more muscular, more frenetic version in the hip ideal of "getting up" — of going full speed all day and all night like a rocket shot across the landscape. This is the Zen of Kerouac's *On the Road* and *The Dharma Bums*, and I think there's a little of its flavor left in a road poem like Gary's "Night Highway 99," with its sense of the world as a series of snapshots and snippets of talk picked up on a trip somewhere else. A little of the flavor's left, perhaps, but Gary's a lot less absorbed with the excitement of his own trip and more respectful of the folks he meets along the way. It's a nice combination of engagement and detachment, maybe more in the spirit of Bashō's *Narrow Road* than Kerouac's *On the Road*.

EMPTINESS

"Getting up" in the fifties might be seen as a jazz riff on the old Zen style of "crazy wisdom," practiced by the masters who liked to act up and act out their presence in the moment through spontaneous performance. They were acting crazy not just because they were stoned on the moment (or because they wanted to tease the stuffy Confucians) but because they saw in the moment — in the Buddhist doctrine of momentariness — a freedom from the rules of the world. This idea goes back to the famous old theory of the Mahayana Buddhist philosophers in India, who held that a radically impermanent world couldn't be real. A world that was really nothing but change was "empty," they said, of any real nature. It wasn't that it didn't exist at all, but its status was weird: like a magic show, they said, like a mirage, like a dream. We might think of the Zen masters' crazy wisdom, then, as a kind of lucid dreaming, with its own crazy dream logic.

The "Logicians of Emptiness," as Gary calls them in one of our poems, had a crazy argument something like this: because everything is changing, everything is still. Why? Because, if the changing things aren't really real, they don't really occur; they don't really come into and go out of existence. Therefore, the whole world of change is perfectly calm. Dōgen puts it this way in his *Mountains and Waters Sūtra*: because the blue mountains are constantly walking, they're constant. The mountains turn out to be constant and unchanging after all — not because they are as we see them but precisely because they aren't as we see them. They're constant to the eye of what the Buddhists call the "perfection of wisdom": the eye that sees all things as empty and unarisen. Gary invokes this perfection of wisdom in the final poem of *Mountains and Rivers*:

> Sound swallowed away,
> no waters, no mountains, no
> bush no grass and
>   because no grass
> no shade but your shadow.
> No flatness because no not-flatness.
> No loss, no gain. So —
> nothing in the way!

The title of the poem is "Finding the Space in the Heart," partly a pun on the famous *Heart Sūtra*, whose long list of "noes" lies behind these lines. In fact, when Gary read from his book last autumn, he put a recitation of the *Heart Sūtra* into his performance. The sūtra tells how the bodhisattva Avalokiteśvara, through cultivating the perfection of wisdom, saw that all things are empty and thus was freed from all obstacles and fear. The sūtra's list of "noes" clears away the obstacles, leaving nothing in the way; it empties the landscape of mountains and rivers, clearing a space, as Gary says, where "the ground is the sky / the sky is the ground, / no place between." This empty space then becomes the place where hearts and bodies meet, "leg hard-twined to leg," and the world begins again.

In this logic of emptiness, then, the Buddhist world is a mysterious mix of two sharply contrasting images: it's at once a restless, hard-driving world, pressing on in moment after moment, and at the same time (and for the same reason) it's a world completely at ease, stretched leisurely out beyond all horizon, with nothing really going on. Such contrasts of time and space, motion and rest, would seem to be perfect for a poet. But while the doctrine of emptiness was in one sense an invitation to play with language — and in fact certainly influenced Chinese poetics — in another sense it was a warning against taking language too seriously. If all things are empty, the philosophers said, then our words have no real referents. Our words and categories, they said, are merely "conventional": they just work to make sense of our world but don't really get at what's really the case. What's really the case can only be got at by the direct experience of the perfection of wisdom. As the Zen masters liked to say, "We don't depend on words; we just point directly at the person's heart." As Su Tung-p'o says, "How will I tell them tomorrow?"

Zen masters say they like the real thing—the "real dragon," as Dōgen says in our text, not just a picture of one. There's a lot of talk in Zen about transcending language and the "constructs" of dualistic reason. There's a lot of sarcastic remarks about people who "chase after words and phrases," people who try to warm up by saying "fire," or try to fill up on a painted rice cake. Part of this suspicion of the representations of language and art probably comes from the felt need for distance from the city, the celebration of nature over culture; part of it comes from the philosophers' critique of conceptual thought and the conventional distinctions of the discriminating mind. But the Zen masters kept a sense of irony about their own distinctions between the real thing and the picture of it and about their cultural constructs of nature and culture. They recognized that, in the weird world of emptiness, where rice cakes themselves weren't real in themselves but only representations, pictures of rice cakes were about as real as rice cakes.

In his *Mountains and Waters Sūtra* and elsewhere, Dōgen is quite strong on this point, dismissing as fools those Zen types who cling to the claim that language is false and argue that authentic Zen sayings are not descriptive of anything real but just nonsense remarks made, as they say, to "cut off words and extinguish thought." Don't these fools notice, Dōgen counters, that, if their argument were true, their own claim would be false? Such types are just dumb, he says, "dumber than beasts"; they're "naturalists," hung up on the notion of a prelinguistic world, who don't know that "words are free from thought"—by which I take him to mean that language has a life of its own, no less real than the other things in the world. Then, as if to rub the beasts' noses in the power of language, Dōgen launches into a purple passage on the landscape, during which the waters "dance beneath the mountains' feet," and the mountains "mount the clouds and stride through the heavens."

It might be easy to read this type of passage as mere poetic metaphor: the mountains tower above us, seeming to "mount the clouds"; their peaks range off into the distance, almost as if "striding through the heavens."

Alternatively, it might be tempting for philosophers to reduce the mountain's heavenly travels to literary codes for the metaphysical doctrines of impermanence and emptiness: all things are changing, "walking," so to speak; they're really empty, like fleeting "clouds" in the sky. Of course, these may be valid and valuable ways of reading, but they run the risk of reading out the living Buddhism actually embedded in Dōgen's landscape. Remember what he told us back at the beginning: mountains and waters are themselves practicing the way of the buddha. The mountains, he goes on to say, have their own spiritual life: they travel about practicing the art of walking, studying themselves as they walk. Through this study of themselves, they themselves become buddhas and Zen patriarchs; indeed, all the buddhas and patriarchs emerge precisely from the mountains' walk.

Whatever exactly we may make of such strange claims, I think it's fair to say that the notion that the natural landscape has a spiritual life of its own was not mere anthropomorphic metaphor in Dōgen's Buddhist world. Dōgen's peripatetic landscape wasn't our world of dead matter, merely blind stuff all around us, meaning nothing in itself. It wasn't the world of modern Zen theory, safely sanitized as pure philosophy and privatized as personal psychology. We won't understand Dōgen's Buddhism if we try to locate it in such worlds, and we certainly won't understand Gary's Buddhism if we try to read it as a philosophical doctrine of impermanence and emptiness in poetic drag. We have to take the mountain walk more seriously. We have to ask how Dōgen can say that "mountains and waters become wise men and sages," how Gary can say, in "The Mountain Spirit," "Mountains will be Buddhas then." This brings me to what I'm calling the "cosmological" strand in Buddhism.

DŌGEN'S COSMOLOGY

Dōgen lived in a Buddhist cosmos, where spirit and meaning were embedded in the landscape. In such a cosmos, the way of the buddha was not just the private affair of human beings in the world but the way the world itself behaved. The structure of the cosmos was drawn by medieval Japanese Mikkyō, or "esoteric teaching" — the style of Buddhism that we often call "Tantra." This style taught a mystical cosmology, in which all things found their place in a sacred order, often called the "realm of dharma." The order was typically personified as the "dharma body" of Vairocana, the Great Sun Buddha; and the spiritual properties of this buddha body, its myriad virtues and powers, were then further personified as a kind of pantheon, or spiritual court, of buddhas and bodhisattvas that surrounded the buddha in his cosmic palace. You can see something of what this sacred order looked like from the Buddhist mandalas, or mystic diagrams, best known to us today in Tibetan tanka paintings.

The masters of Mikkyō worked out elaborate mystical correspondences, or homologies, between this hidden macrocosmic realm of dharma and the microcosm of our apparent world. Everything here was somehow an expression of something there — every finger of the hand embodied a force or realm of the other world; every sound of the alphabet invoked a power or principle of the buddha's teaching; every thought had its correlate in the buddha's omniscient consciousness. Such correspondences held not just in our human practices of body, speech, and thought; they were spread throughout the world around us, mapped onto the landscape: every direction, every time, every physical element, every color and shape belonged to a particular buddha and had a mystic meaning in the sacred structure of the whole.

When Dōgen's mountains reach the heavens, then, they're not just seeming to scrape the sky; they're communicating with the *deva-loka*, the hidden realm of the gods beyond our world of nature. And when Dōgen's water rises up, as he says, it's not just evaporating into the atmosphere but climbing into other worlds. Water, he says, flows everywhere throughout the entire realm of dharma, from the highest heavens to the deepest hells; it flows into worlds ruled by other buddhas than our own. In fact, water is everywhere that buddhas appear, and every drop of water contains within itself countless buddha lands. In effect, I suppose, if we looked closely enough at a drop of water through a mystical microscope, we could see it as itself a tiny mandala. If water flows into rice cakes, it's no wonder Dōgen said that rice cakes are paintings.

So, the flowing of water, like the walking of mountains, is not just a symbol of constant change, one damn thing after another, in the physical world; it's an expression of a much larger, richer landscape, in which the symbol and the symbolized, the physical and the spiritual, the natural and cultural orders, are fused in a single scheme. Motion in such a landscape isn't just random relocation but progression through Buddhist abodes; change in such a landscape, even a shard flaked loose from a cliff face, is a kind of practice, through which mountains and waters cultivate the way and become wise men and sages. For humans in such a landscape, going with the flow of water isn't simply detached mindfulness of each passing moment; it's plugging yourself into the mandala and getting into motion, visualizing the sacred realms, embodying the sacred beings, speaking the sacred sounds of the buddhas — enacting, in other words, through ritual performance the spiritual life of the cosmic buddha body.

This kind of formal ritual performance is what you might call the "indoor" version of Mikkyō practice, through which the esoteric masters in their monasteries sought to invoke the other world by contemplative exercise, mystic rite, and magical spell. But there was also an "outdoor" version, which used the natural landscape itself to communicate with the other world. Since the land was the mandala made manifest, every spot on the land could be spiritually significant. The Japanese landscape was in fact littered with sacred sites — peaks belonging to particular buddhas, ranges incarnating buddha lands, passes protected by bodhisattvas, caves leading into the underworlds, dark groves of local gods, deep pools of dragon spirits making the water, as Dōgen says, into their palaces and pavilions. To walk the land, then, was itself to put yourself into the mandala, and pilgrimage to sacred sites was itself to follow the way of the buddha. In his essay "Blue Mountains Constantly Walking," Gary talks about joining such pilgrimages, still going on amidst the industrial sprawl of modern Japan; in his poem "The Circumambulation of Mt. Tamalpais," he even gives us an account of the ten stages through which we can ritually pursue the ten spiritual stages of the bodhisattva path by walking around in Marin County.

Gary does a lot more walking around to the sacred sites on Turtle Island than Dōgen seems to have done in Japan. Dōgen's one big trip was to China to seek out the Zen patriarchs and come home with the Zen lineage. He did this when he was in his twenties, and the rest of his life he spent remembering the masters, going all the way back to the first master, the Buddha Shakyamuni. Dōgen was a time traveler, wandering through the records of the past, from the Western Heavens, as he called the ancient land of Shakyamuni, to the Eastern Earth, the land to which Bodhidharma brought Zen from the west. For Dōgen, what made the landscape sacred was probably less the buddhas of the Japanese Mikkyō pantheon standing behind it than the Chinese patriarchs of the Zen history running through it. He was, to put it in the terms I'm using here, probably more interested in the "mythological" than the "cosmological" reading of the landscape.

MYTHOLOGY

The Chinese also had their sacred sites and hidden buddhas behind them, but the Zen monks Dōgen met in China weren't really into the sort of systematic Tantra that made a mandala of Japan. Their landscape was less symmetrical, less neatly mapped on the geometric patterns and hierarchical structures of the buddha's spiritual court. They self-consciously ruled themselves out of court, preferring to live apart in the funkier, more romantic geography of the landscape artists and poets. But their land was no less enchanted for that. Their mountains were hallowed as the haunts of great sages of the past — the places where the First Patriarch sat gazing at a wall for nine years, where the Sixth Patriarch received the robe of Bodhidharma, where Huang-po hit Lin-chi with his stick and Lin-chi roared at him.

The Zen monks Dōgen met and the Zen books Dōgen read in China were into sacred time: the myths and legends of the lineage, the traditions of the golden age, when mighty masters walked the earth. Of course, Buddhists of all persuasions have always used the past to locate themselves in the landscape. The axis mundi of the Japanese Buddhist world was not only Mount Sumeru, the central mountain of the cosmological geography; it was also the mythic Vulture Peak, where Shakyamuni had once revealed the *Lotus Sūtra* for our age. The mountain ranges of Japan were sacred not only as embodiments of buddha fields; they were also the places where the legendary Mikkyō master Kōbō Daishi had once walked. But the Zen monks had a special love of history: they claimed their past was a "special transmission outside of scripture," handed down from "mind to mind" through the generations since the time of the founder, Shakyamuni. They had an elaborate cult of their ancestors, worshipping them in special halls, painting their portraits, copying out their spiritual genealogies, writing up their hagiographies, collecting their sayings and meditating, lecturing, and composing commentaries on them. Dōgen's *Shōbōgenzō* was such a commentary, inspired by — though in fact very different from — a famous Zen book he had read in China.

The landscape of the *Mountains and Waters Sūtra* is enchanted by the ancients. Particularly in the final section of the text, Dōgen peoples his mountains and rivers with spiritual practitioners: sage kings of China enter the mountains for instruction from Taoist wizards; Shakyamuni leaves his palace to pursue austerities in the mountains; the Zen master Te-ch'eng fishes for himself on the Hua-t'ing River. Te-ch'eng, they say, got so into water that he dove in the river one day and disappeared. He wasn't the only one to lose himself in the landscape: Dōgen says that, although wise men and sages always enter the mountains, you can never meet one there; not even a trace of them remains. They seem to merge with the place, making the mountains, as Dōgen says, "their own bodies and minds." If the mountains and waters can themselves become wise men and sages, I guess we shouldn't be surprised when the sages become mountains.

The mountains seem to love it when the sages merge with them. In the sexiest section of the *Mountains and Waters Sūtra*, Dōgen describes a love affair between the wise men and their alpine resort. The mountains belong to the wise who love them and love their masters in return. Drawn by their love, the wise men enter the mountains and dwell in them. Infused with the wise men's spiritual powers, the mountains take delight, and their trees and rocks, birds and beasts flourish and abound. Unlike the Zen master Ikkyū, Dōgen isn't known for erotic verse, but it seems he could get worked up about mountains. Notice, incidentally, that the mountains here have suddenly gone passive on us: they're no longer the yang member of the old mountains and waters contrast; we're closer here to the sort of male spirit, female earth affair familiar in much nature romanticism, East and West.

As the resort of the past masters, the natural landscape sustains the patriarchal lineage. It offers itself as the place where the lore of the lineage resides, a kind of sacred text spread out around us recording the traditions of the forefathers. This is the sort of landscape Gary obviously loves and longs for — places haunted by the past, storied places sacred to the memory of ancient peoples. He's on a kind of mission to re-enchant the land for us, turn it back into Turtle Island. His "Hump-backed Flute Player" in

Mountains and Rivers is in part a paean to such myth-rich places, from the Canyon de Chelly in the Great Basin, where Kokop'ele used to play his flute, to the Pamir range that Hsüan Tsang passed bringing sūtras back to China. Dōgen says that sacred places like this don't belong to king or country but to the people who love them, and in this poem, Gary gives us a kind of Ghost Dance chant, returning the land to its owners. Some people say that Gary himself is Hsüan Tsang and Kokop'ele, carrying the lore of the Buddhist ancients around in his backpack and sacralizing the land with his songs. I don't know about that — only time will tell if Gary's songs will sink into the landscape — but it is the case that, in the landscape of modern Japan, Dōgen's monastery in the mountains is now a major tourist site.

DISCUSSION

QUESTION: In Buddhism, what's the relationship between emptiness and everythingness?

CARL BIELEFELDT: They're like the flip side of the same thing. The Sanskrit word for "emptiness," *śūnyatā*, means "void," "absence," "hollowness," and certainly has a negative connotation. In this negative sense, it's used to deconstruct the world of our ordinary experience — all that stuff is "empty" of the reality we give it, not what we think it is. But the same word is also used to point out what's really there, the same stuff as it really is, what Buddhists like to call "suchness" — which I guess you could call "everythingness" if you wanted to.

COMMENT: You were talking a little bit at the end about historical narratives and the idea of Turtle Island, but there seems to be so much more Buddhist and Japanese influence in the poem than Native American.

MARK GONNERMAN: For Native American influences, you might look at "Arctic Midnight Twilight," look at "Haida Gwai North Coast, Naikoon Beach," look at "The Bear Mother," look at "Old Woodrat's Stinky House," look at "Raven's Beak River" — all those poems are informed by Native American myths and tales.

BIELEFELDT: And "The Hump-backed Flute Player" I mentioned at end. I think the question of Buddhist or Native American in this poem is a good one, because the Native American trickster figure Kokop'ele gets identified here with Hsüan Tsang, the great Chinese pilgrim, who went from China to India in the seventh century and brought back Buddhist sūtras. Like Kokop'ele, he was the carrier of culture in his pack on his back.

GONNERMAN: Related to this point on the mixing of cultural traditions, on page 146 in "The Mountain Spirit," there's a passage that I think well exemplifies the way that different teachings come together in Gary's work:

> Ghosts of lost landscapes
>
>> herds and flocks,
>>> towns and clans,
>> great teachers from all lands
>> tucked in Wovoka's empty hat,
>>> stored in Baby Krishna's mouth,
>>> kneeling for tea
>> in Vimalakīrti's one small room.

BIELEFELDT: Yeah, this is a perfect one for thinking about the notion of Gary's mythic landscape, filled with all sorts of ghosts. Gary gives a note, I think, about the famous Buddhist story of Vimalakīrti's one small room. Even though it's small, everybody can fit into it. Maybe like Gary's landscape itself? The story might also take us back to the first question, about emptiness and fullness. When the people get to Vimalakīrti's house, it looks like there's no place to sit; but then, boom! Vimalakīrti just magically creates enormous chairs reaching miles into the sky and says, "Have a seat, gentlemen."

COMMENT: A story like this brings up something I'm wondering about: whether we really have to be interested in Buddhism to read the poem intelligently and relate to all its imagery. I think readers can find their own patterns of mythology in it, and that's why it stands up as art.

BIELEFELDT: Gary can sometimes be a difficult poet, like Pound or Eliot, bringing in stuff from all over. And of course the Buddhist and Native American stuff doesn't come so naturally to most of us. But think about Gary's situation: he's struggling to create a place for us, for himself, where the local resources have kind of gone dead. So he has to think in global terms, bringing in resources from all over, creating a legend, or a narrative, for the whole watershed, as he calls it, the whole planet.

QUESTION: Along those lines, I was struck by your comments about human products as part of the natural landscape. I expected Snyder to be more political. Is there irony in these poems? He seems so matter-of-fact. Freeways to me are just totally anti-nature. I realize that Snyder may not want a dualism of nature versus anti-nature, but I feel that somehow there has to be political movement that I don't quite see.

BIELEFELDT: Other people have talked about the disparity between some of Snyder's essays on the one hand, where he's trying to change our consciousness and save the planet, and his poetry, which seems so non-judgmental (you call it "matter-of-fact"). It's true, I think, his poems tend to be non-judgmental, forgiving, open, a celebration almost of everything on equal terms. This is what I meant by his simply mirroring things, whatever comes before him. Except he's a kind of warped mirror: he doesn't just see it without judgment, but he loves it and embraces it.

COMMENT: It seems to me that the politics of this is the praxis — the praxis reflected in his writing the poetry, and the praxis required of us in order to engage the poetry. What I admire about him as a person is the integrity of his praxis. I know these are sort of out of favor at the moment, but it's like a Socialist or Communist sort of politics or praxis.

BIELEFELDT: Well, I've known a lot of unforgiving Socialists. There may be an additional element here that we haven't really talked about. I think I said that ecological politics may have more to do with Western ideals than with Buddhist, but in his politics Snyder may also have something of the bodhisattva ideal of compassion for people, and a program of long-term, patient demonstration of truths and values — just putting it out there to let people see how beautiful it could be without haranguing them too much.

COMMENT: This is what was so shocking to me in the *Mountains and Waters Sūtra*. It seems that Dōgen has a very elitist, superior tone — calls his opponents "worthless little fools" and so on. This tone is completely missing in Gary Snyder. So, if Dōgen is a major influence on Snyder, that's part of Dōgen that Snyder just didn't take.

BIELEFELDT: Yes. We may be dealing here with quite different personalities. And also maybe with class styles. Gary's a proletariat type and proud of it. Dōgen was upper class, from the northern branch of the Fujiwara family, the most powerful family in all of Japan. So alongside his elegant talk, he has a certain upper class way of putting people down. He's a very interesting, complicated guy.

COMMENT: But this absence of judgment should come from the vision of the whole world as a sacred organism.

COMMENT: Or from a different angle, I would think Gary might say that judgment is a form of blindness. You put a wall between yourself and the object, and so you blind yourself to what is.

BIELEFELDT: Any kind of judgment?

COMMENT: Well, obviously, he isn't totally immune to it in his essays, but I think that's part of the message of the poems.

BIELEFELDT: Now we're touching on one of the great mysteries for all Zen students. Zen talks about non-discrimination — no judging — just take things, whatever comes, as they are. And yet the world has to be full of judgments of all sorts. The artist has to make a judgment if he wants to make something beautiful, not something ugly. Your mention of judgments as walls reminds me of the time the Zen master down at Tassajara was building a rock wall and had all of us get rocks for him out of Tassajara Creek. He'd hold one up and say, "This rock goes to hell!" and throw it back in the river. Even though all those rocks were supposed to be "empty," he was making very clear judgments about them: "This ugly rock!" And, of course, the students were all trying to figure out what was going on.

QUESTION: Was he throwing out your attachment to the rock?

BIELEFELDT: Whoa! I wish you'd been there! I thought he was just throwing away my rocks!

QUESTION: There seems to be a lot of walking meditation in Snyder's work, and I was wondering how that worked into walking versus sitting meditation.

BIELEFELDT: In the Zen monastic routine, there's a rhythm of sitting and walking, in a kind of passive/active relationship. Gary has done years of this routine. But there's also the kind of "outdoor" walking I talked about in my lecture — the tradition of pilgrimage and circumambulation of mountains that's built into some forms of Buddhist practice. One of the things that separates Gary from a lot of pop American Zen is that he's lived in a Buddhist culture, in which all the rich stuff, like the mythology and the cosmology I was talking about, is in play. His Zen, like Dōgen's own Zen, is filled with all this stuff, including walking outdoors across a very spiritually articulated landscape, a historical, narrative landscape.

CHARLES JUNKERMAN: I think what you just said, Carl, about Gary Snyder having lived with Buddhists and drawing on their spirit, is very important. One of the things that struck me in reading through his poem this year is how completely authentic he is and it is. There's never any place where you can say "Oh, come on, you're just doing that for the book." It rings true. And this leads me to another point that came up earlier. It seems to me the Native American references are very sparse, even in the list of poems Mark gave us. Tim Dean made reference, in his lecture for our seminar, to the Native American novelist Leslie Marmon Silko, a great talent, who accused Gary of "white shamanism" for appropriating Native American ways of thinking and culture. It seems to me that he doesn't do that. I think he's extraordinarily careful not to be a wannabe Native American. I think, as a whole and as a teaching text, the poem is profoundly Buddhist with almost no Native American teaching.

GONNERMAN: There's a very interesting point in Snyder's biography, when, in college, he realized that Native American traditions and practices really weren't available to him the same way Buddhist traditions were. I think a lot of the Native American influence, especially in the poems I mentioned, has to do with a sense of the place for each of those poems and a sense of the native stories connected to the places he's visiting. He uses the native stories as a way of framing or drawing up a certain kind of language for those particular poems.

JUNKERMAN: It's interesting how very careful he is.

QUESTION: Scott Momaday wrote something about how essential it is to really get to know one piece of land. It seems to me that's what really makes the poem American: the way he speaks for the land — his experiences living on it, listening, watching, sensing it — saying, if the land could speak, these are its stories. We all travel so much these days, but how many places do we really get to know well? Really know the sounds and the smells and the animals?

BIELEFELDT: One of the things that I got out of this book was an extraordinary sense of place. Of my own place. I began to look around me, where I live and work on the Stanford campus — the place I share with those raccoons that come out at night. I never thought much of this place: it was just a good job in a high-rent district. But I started thinking about it as a place with a long story, going back to the days when it was a horse farm, and beyond that before anyone owned it. I think this sense of place is one of the remarkable things about Gary, not only in his poetry but in his own story: he came back from Japan and said, "I'm settling down in this place and am going to be an inhabitant."

NOTES

1. A much revised version of this talk was given to the International Conference on Korean Son Buddhism, Paekyangsa, 1998, and subsequently published as "The Mountain Spirit: Dōgen, Gary Snyder, and Critical Buddhism," *Zen Quarterly* 11:1 (Tokyo, 1999): 18–24.
2. See Anne Birrell, trans., *The Classic of Mountains and Seas* (New York: Penguin Classics, 1999).
3. See "Blue Mountains Constantly Walking," in *The Practice of the Wild* (San Francisco: North Point Press, 1990), 97–115.

~

In Buddhist metaphor, a "stream-enterer" is one who has irreversibly embarked on the way of liberation. In *Mountains and Rivers*, the speaker is continually entering and floating on streams and rivers: real rivers, real kayaks which at the same time signify metaphorically the wider stream. "Afloat" (M&R 130–32) describes floating among mountains in a twin kayak. Free and light, the boat is "like a cricket husk — / like an empty spider egg case . . . like froth on the lip of the wave." Rippling and rocking in the river, the autonomous "self" exists nowhere, yet here we are: "there is no place we are / but maybe here." Instead of demanding a choice between essentialist/absolutist essence and postmodern/nihilist constructedness, Buddhist practice discovers an awareness that bypasses this dualism. As Anne Klein puts it in *Meeting the Great Bliss Queen: Buddhists, Feminists, and the Art of the Self* (1995), mindfulness provides "a visceral sense of personal continuity in the midst of clearly observed flux" (p. 66). In this space, sky and water are "stitched together" and the little boat paddles in a liminal place "where land meets water meets the sky." Distinct, yet trembling in the ripples of the stream in which it travels, the boat's membrane evokes the frail lightness of our skin-bound identity. After a fifty-nine line "sentence" describing what sounds like an actual excursion, the poem ends by pointing in one line to the realisation it offers: "The tiny skin boat." This, here.

> —Julia Martin in "Seeing a Corner of the Sky" (paper sent to the Mountains & Rivers Workshop, May 1998)

II.

Heart to Heart

Instructions in Nonduality

STEPHANIE KAZA

In these reflections on Gary Snyder's signature work, I take up the question, How is this work a piece of instruction? What is the content and what is the instructional method? How exactly does Gary Snyder instruct us in this cycle of poems? I draw here on my life practice as a Sōtō Zen student and my efforts as a scholar and teacher to investigate Buddhist principles and practices that relate to environmental concerns.

My investigation begins with one of Snyder's key sources, the *Mountains and Waters Sūtra* by the thirteenth-century Zen master, Eihei Dōgen. Let us start with Dōgen's words:

> Mountains and waters right now are the actualization of the
> ancient buddha way, each abiding in its phenomenal expression
> realizes completeness. Because mountains and waters have been
> active since before the Empty Eon, they are alive at this moment.
> Because they have been the self since before form arose they are
> emancipation-realization.[1]

What does he mean by "actualization of the ancient buddha way?" This is the great teaching, the way to liberation from suffering, the fundamental work, that which informs all other work on the path. But, how does one accomplish or follow this path? What do you actually do? To read Dōgen's words, this might seem to be a mysterious, paradoxical, difficult process, not easily described or transmitted. I will attempt to lay out the specific Zen pedagogical methods for the kind of radical learning I believe Snyder embodies in this piece. This will serve as a fresh contrast to what David Abram has offered us, demonstrating how we can bring distinctive minds to a shared learning field and reflect what we see through our own conditioned views.

In *Mountains and Rivers Without End*, Gary Snyder has laid out both method and content, presenting his instruction as direct pointing to the Way. For Snyder, actualization of the Buddha way is not an end in itself, a spiritual goal to be accomplished for the salvation of the individual. Rather it is a way of liberation for all beings, spoken of as the "bodhisattva vow": "Beings are numberless, I vow to save them. . . ." From an ecological perspective, what could be more appropriate than saving all sentient beings?

As Snyder declared in his classic piece, "Four Changes" (1969/1995), "Humanity has become a locust-like blight on the planet" (APIS 39). At that time the impacts of greed, pollution, and population growth were already alarmingly evident. Those of us feeling attuned to this but quite isolated wondered, "What is this going to look like in thirty or fifty years?" Snyder put forth the vision that, "If humans are to remain on earth, they must transform the five millennia-long urbanizing civilization tradition into a new ecologically-sensitive, harmony-oriented, wild-minded, scientific, spiritual culture" (APIS 41). In this, I see him standing not so much on his Zen ancestors as on the shoulders of Henry David Thoreau, John Muir, and Aldo Leopold, all of whom were saying similar things. He received their transmission and passed it along to us in another form. As he noted in his 1995 postscript, the apprehension we felt earlier has not abated. In fact, things have generally gotten much worse. Now we not only fear loss of irreplaceable species, but the collapse of whole systems through global warming, ocean death, soil and groundwater poisoning. So this is certainly an auspicious time for awakening! With great perspective and equanimity, Snyder spares us a debilitating harangue, refusing the cheap drug of anxiety. Instead, with the long view of age and many lived stories, he lays out a path marking the way for those who choose to follow.

INSTRUCTIONS

What, then, is Snyder offering to teach us, and what is this method of realization? I suggest he is giving us three fundamental instructions. The first is about where we are; the second is about how to behave (the ethical instruction); and the third is about the true nature of reality — what is this world, really? That is quite a big task for one little book to undertake! However, I believe it is Snyder's sense that if we as humans have a proper understanding of where we are in place and time, we will then be motivated to behave in a more harmonious and respectful way with all beings. Thus he sets the poem cycle in the Big Scale of time and place, first invoking the storytellers themselves, "Old ghost ranges, sunken rivers, come again / stand by the wall and tell their tale" (M&R 9) — and then the story: "What we ate — who ate what — / how we all prevailed" (M&R 10). This is for all beings, not just human, animal, tree beings but mountain ranges, watersheds, and glaciers.

The Big Story explains the Big Scale setting of *where we are*. It is not some distant, abstract, cosmic revelation reified by religious consecration. Instead Snyder shows us how the Big Story is made up of many smaller stories, each a history of specific moments and places. "Night Highway 99" (M&R 11–24) demonstrates just this, and begins the teaching of "where we are." Snyder journeys past shingle mills and stump farms, fifty weary Indians, the sheriff's posse and the naked Wobblies, "woodsmoke in my brain." This poem lays out the first *songline* on the land — Highway 99 from Ferndale, Bellingham, just below the border with Canada, on down to San Francisco. I began my review of this poem by mapping out Snyder's route; I was drawing the songline — where does Highway 99 go? It forms the north-south songline, with all the hitchhiking points along the way — Mount Vernon, Everett, Seattle, Tacoma, Olympia. This is how I heard it, like the voice over the loudspeaker I remember as a child in the Portland Greyhound Station: "TaCOma, OLYMpia, CenTRAlia, ToLEdo, CASTLE ROCK, PORTland."

For Snyder, where we are in the big sense of place begins by tracing the songlines of the ground beneath our feet. As David Abram said earlier, this is the original way of the human, of the indigenous people. This is the way to understand the *iworu*, or force fields through the body, arrow points meeting, direct contact. In Dōgen's words, "You should study the green mountains, using numerous worlds as your standards. You should clearly examine the green mountains' walking and your own walking."[2] In "Bubbs Creek Haircut," Snyder adds the east-west songline out to the Sierra: King's

River Canyon, Upper Kern River County. The songlines continue in Part II, extending the southern connector to Los Angeles, traveling down the Central Valley on Highway 99, "blossoming almond orchard acres . . . culvert after culvert far as you can see . . . yards of tractors . . . frizzy lonely palm tree" (M&R 65).

Snyder has spoken of the land as a mandala, refering to Buddhist depictions of complex worlds. These songlines provide a way to trace the structural lines of the physical Earth mandala. One follows the routes across high peaks and broad valleys, adding the Great Basin and Canyon de Chelly along the east-west line, and Baja, Alaska, and Haida Gwai to the north-south songline. Then Snyder invites the walker to reach out across oceans and continents to Japan, Tibet, and even to Europe, to the old bones in Moravia. These songlines are like magnetic ley lines, tracing energy flow around the whole globe. Each story is a piece of the journey, each journey a piece of the songline. The instruction is: if you want to know where you are — if you want to locate yourself in the Earth mandala — walk the songlines.

This is how Snyder teaches his readers to be grounded in place. But "where we are" is also about where we are in *time*. For this lesson, Snyder turns to the mountains and rivers themselves. In "The Flowing" (M&R 68–72) we are invited into geologic time: "Sierra Nevada . . . fault block uplift / thrust of westward slipping crust . . . Rivermouth . . . the vast loosing / of all that was found, sucked, held, born, drowned, sunk sleepily in / to the sea." From the early people near the Morava River twenty-six thousand years ago, he gives us a distant taste of "burnt reindeer-pelvis bone bits in her mouth" (M&R 96). Even our animal lineage speaks of ancient time in "New Moon Tongue": "a million years of sniffs, licks, lip and reaching tongue" (M&R 105). The big picture of time that's been hinted at throughout the volume comes together in "Old Woodrat's Stinky House" (M&R 119–21) where Snyder asks us to consider the incomprehensible: "Us critters hanging out together / something like three billion years." This is a Zen kōan of unfathomable dimensions. I confess I really don't know how to think about that. Maybe I can imagine a family woodrat house that's been in use for eight thousand years. When you see such a nest in the brush — stacks of twigs three to five feet high, many layers, many chambers — you see they are built to last. But still, what is eight thousand years, really? Big Time, Big Place, this is the first teaching. The point is not to have mistaken views about the significance of human life in the scale of things. Don't get that mixed up.

The second teaching is about how to behave. In Snyder's view, proper behavior derives from one's understanding of the Big Story. It is based less on *who* we are as unique individuals and more on *where* we are, which determines what is necessary for low-impact dwelling in a particular place. Snyder believes the land "will welcome whoever chooses to observe the etiquette, express the gratitude, grasp the tools and learn the songs that it takes to live there" (APIS 234). The specific forms of etiquette and gratitude express the ethics and values a culture holds in relation to the land. Thus good manners are the embodiment of good ethics. This is not an impossible task; people can reinhabit a place if they simply learn proper manners.

Snyder offers his readers a range of spiritual practice forms in "The Circumambulation of Mt. Tamalpais" (M&R 85–89): walking, bowing, chanting, reciting the sūtras, making offerings, and walking meditation. These are all good behavioral and ethical forms. They refer directly to the time-honored Zen teaching method: hold to the forms of right behavior and the rest will follow. That is why there is such tremendous emphasis in Zen training on sitting posture and practice forms — how you bow, how you offer incense, how you greet the teacher, how you get up on the *tan*, how you handle your *ōryōki* bowls, how you *contain* yourself.

Though Snyder seldom points directly to zazen, it is obvious that sitting underlies the entire poem cycle. It would be clumsy and self-reverential to announce one's practice overtly. Instead, Snyder shows us how to be still and *listen* — listen for the voices of others, listen for the mountain voices, listen for the river voices. This is his second significant instruction in how to behave. A first hint comes from Jackrabbit, who appears in both Parts I and II, showing Snyder "bell chilled blue jewel sky banners" (M&R 73). Later, Snyder listens to Raven, Bear Mother, Artemisia, Bristlecone. Listening directly, what does Raven have to say? At Haida Gwai, "wheeling birds make comment:/ on gray skies, big swells, storms,/ the end of summer, the fall run — " (M&R 103). Listening to Artemisia, powerful medicine plant — "she's always there . . . emptiness far as the mind can see" (M&R 126). As for Bristlecone, I urge you to make the long mountain pilgrimage to meet Bristlecone yourself; you will never really be the same again.

Snyder invites us to listen as well to the voices of the ancestors. This is very difficult in our present-time-oriented culture. "Ghost bison, ghost bears, ghost bighorns, ghost lynx swirling, gathering, sweeping down" (M&R 80). It is difficult to listen to these voices because they evoke tremendous "eco-karma" for us, to use my colleague Ken Kraft's term.[3] Why are there so many ghosts? How were they killed? What was the intent behind the killing? What cruelty and grief lies behind those ancestral voices? They are very painful for us to listen to. This kind of deep listening, deep remembering, can point the way to behaving well.

Zen practice, if it is anything, is practice in being present and paying attention. Mindfulness tends to promote good behavior. The entire poem cycle is one invitation after another to pay attention, to be engaged with the mountains themselves, not our ideas of mountains or our metaphors of mountains, but "all things abiding in their own phenomenal expression," as Dōgen says.[4] In *A Place in Space*, Snyder writes that there are two modes of learning: direct experience and hearsay, and that most of what we know today comes through hearsay (94). The Internet is one big gossip circuit, isn't it? Chat groups, websites — it is almost all hearsay, all secondary information about the world. Hearsay knowledge is secondhand, indirect, someone else's story. For Snyder and the long Buddhist lineage before him, paying attention is the path to direct experience. This is the power of Snyder's words. They are not secondhand, they tell the stories he has seen and heard. Beneath the lines in the poems is the message: Go and find the stories that are happening to you. Let this listening teach you how to behave.

The third lesson is about the nature of reality. This is spelled out quite clearly: all forms of reality are impermanent. The poem starts and ends with this: "Streams and mountains never stay the same" (M&R 9, 152). If you want to try an experiment in meditation, sit still for ten minutes every day and say that line over and over again for a year; your entire perspective on the world will be changed. Snyder shows us how the whole Big Story is one complicated swirl of streaming energy, changing continuously from one form to another: "the mountain slides, the moon slides,/ the waters churn together" (M&R 130). The world is a mandala painting in which colored sand grains pile up into beautiful forms and are then swirled and brushed away, always changing.

In an earlier essay, Snyder writes, "The true source of compassion and ethical behavior is paradoxically none other than one's own realization of the insubstantial and ephemeral nature of everything" (APIS 246). We, too, can taste this impermanence because we are also ever-shifting and will fly "off alone" in the passing of a lifetime. "Walking on walking,/ under foot earth turns." Buddhist death meditations address this quite directly in the most intimate context possible: the loss of our own precious lives. Snyder reveals this teaching through the land as a study in the nature of reality, seeing that all of it will pass away. Snyder invites us to enjoy mountains and rivers passing away and taste how this truth extends to our own ephemeral bodies.

Yet he does not sink into the trap of nihilism: if it is all impermanent, why bother to change our ways? Sometimes people will say this sort of thing and then throw their beer cans out the window. This interpretation is quite mistaken. Grasping impermanence awakens us to the very fleeting moments that make up this lifetime, and then we see how extremely short this one life is. Why would anyone want to waste one minute of it?

THE METHOD

Where we are, how to behave, and the nature of reality — these are the main lessons or teachings of the poem as I see it. How then does the instructor instruct? What is Snyder's method for revealing these teachings? Here I am not speaking about Gary Snyder as a skilled poet but rather as a teacher, one who has followed the Path and can point the way to others. Coming back to Dōgen's *Mountains and Waters Sūtra*: "An ancient Buddha said 'Mountains are mountains, waters are waters.' These words do not mean mountains are mountains; they mean mountains are mountains."[5] Now what is one supposed to make of this?

I believe this passage points to the progression of learning suggested in *Mountains and Rivers Without End*. Let me explain what I believe Dōgen identifies as three stages in learning or awakening. First, you see the mountains just as they are, naively, straight up: "Oh look, there's Mount Shasta. Isn't it beautiful?" Hitchhiking down Highway 99, mountains are just as they are. This is very clear in Part I. You're just traveling by on your way to somewhere, and you take the mountains for granted. This naive view is a dualistic view. The mountains are out there and I am here; in order to get there, I'll have to hitch or drive or walk or something, but clearly the mountains and this human existence are separate.

In the second stage of realization or learning, you begin to see that the mountains are not really mountains the way you are used to perceiving them. You explore the foothills, the high slopes, the icefields, and you start to see, "Oh, there's Dall sheep. Oh, there's Bear Mother talking. On the other side where the mountains drop off, there's Artemisia." You sense the mountains and waters swirling and in that stage of sensing the swirl, it can get rather scary because you see *nothing* is permanent; it's all moving and changing. You wonder, where am I? What happened to the big "I" that I used to identify with? Oh, no! It is dissolving right before my very eyes. This is the struggle and resistance phase. You get a glimpse of what reality is but you prefer to hang on to the dualistic view because it is more familiar and you are convinced you can survive better if you identify with that small ego "I." Such seesawing generates quite a bit of tension, because you have seen the truth and find it doesn't really quite work to hold on to your small self "I." This is when the Zen masters can really break through your illusions: the crack is open and they will whop, whop, whop, when they see the "I" appear. They make sure you notice it every time, and you can feel quite naked in front of your teachers.

The third phase is when, as Dōgen says, "mountains are mountains [again]." But this is distinct from the first "mountains are mountains." In the pivotal breakthrough to a nondualistic view, you see that you, too, are swirling and changing and it is all one big impermanent brew.

How does Snyder lead us through this progression, inviting us to taste the experience of this profound shift of consciousness, the Big Learning? I believe these stages correspond pretty closely to the work's four major divisions. Let us begin with Part I. Here our main figure is engaged in seeking, asking the questions, going on the journey, going traveling. The opening poem can be taken as pure description, independent of the thoughtful symbolism that Robert Hass has given us. "Hills beyond rivers, willows in a swamp, / a gentle valley reaching far inland" (M&R 6). Snyder shows us the mountains as mountains, just as he finds them. This continues in "Three

Worlds, Three Realms, Six Roads" (M&R 25–30) and "Things to Do Around a Lookout": "paint pictures of the mountains ... bake coffee cake ... go climbing all alone" (M&R 26–27). The scenes and stories are very straightforward; "a half-iced-over lake ... filled with leaping trout ... bare sunlight on the spaces / empty sky" (M&R 35). It is noteworthy that in "Night Highway 99" the "I" is quite present, appearing much more frequently than later in the book. This is typical of a dualistic orientation to the world, marking the separation between observer and observed.

In Part II, however, things begin to come apart as our guide meets the complexities of reality. The marketplace, which at first looks pretty interesting and entertaining in Seattle and San Francisco, becomes quite disturbing by the end of the poem. The market in Varanasi is not the sort of place you'd necessarily want to go:

> They eat feces
> in the dark
> on stone floors
> one-legged monkeys, hopping cows
> limping dogs   blind cats
> crunching garbage in the market
> broken fingers
> cabbage
> head on the ground.   (M&R 51)

What is this suffering? How is one to respond? Snyder evokes the story of Siddhartha who left the palace and was confronted with suffering. In "Night Song of the Los Angeles Basin" (M&R 62–64) the traveler runs into the pretty people: "godlings ride by in Rolls Royce," the suffering of Hollywood, "slash of calligraphy of freeways of cars." Then down the great Central Valley, he finds the suffering of "us and our stuff just covering the ground." "Yards of tractors, combines lined up ... quarter-acre stacks of wornout car tires" and in particular, the suffering of loss. The closing reference to John Muir in "Covers the Ground" points to what once filled the spectacular valley before the piles of human stuff.

"The Great Central Plain of California
was one smooth bed of honey-bloom
          400 miles, your foot would press
a hundred flowers at every step
it seemed one sheet of plant gold;

all the ground was covered
with radiant corollas ankle-deep:
bahia, madia, madaria, burielia,
chrysopsis, grindelia,
          wherever a bee might fly — "   (M&R 66–67)

These complexities also appear in some of the dream pieces, for exam-
ple, the glimpse of the journey ahead when Kō-san takes Snyder to the edge.

          I asked him — what's that up there,
      then — meaning the further mountains.
      "That's the world after death." I thought it looked
      just like the land we'd been traveling, and couldn't
      see why we should have to die.   (M&R 55)

This is the "I" saying, "No, really, I'd kind of like to stick around." But the
"I" gets pulled off the cliff. "I hit and I was dead. I saw my body for awhile
and then it was gone" (M&R 55–56). In Part II, then, our instructor reveals
the complexity of suffering that begins to generate compassion. This is a very
specific method; it is not so mysterious. You have to go right toward the suf-
fering in order to feel compassion awaken. Also, in this section, it is inter-
esting to note that in "The Flowing" and "The Hump-backed Flute Player,"
mountains and rivers are addressed independently, not as a single universe.
The seeker's questions continue: "what am I carrying? What's this load? . . .
/ what world today?" (M&R 81) And the answers begin to echo back from
the teachers: "it was whispered to me / by the oldest of trees" (M&R 82).
    In Part III, the journey is well on its way. The traveler has met with suf-
fering and glimpsed the impermanent nature of reality. What is the next
stage of learning or awakening? It is not uncommon for students of the

Way to hit a plateau: you can't go back, and you're not quite ready to go forward. So you just practice for awhile, mark the spot, consecrate by chanting, keep walking, stay present, and take the ride. Some of you in Zen practice know that years can go by while you are just marking the spot and practicing steadily. All that time something is wearing down under the slow dripping of water on stone and getting ready for breakthrough.

Part III opens with "The Circumambulation of Mt. Tamalpais," a chronicle of this kind of walking and settling in place, chanting the "Dhāranī for Removing Disasters" at almost every stop. In this poem and throughout the section, we are helped by our guide, Snyder the teacher, to see mountains and rivers through other beings. The Dall sheep come speaking to us — "sheep impermanence, sheep practice,/ sheep shapeshifting," bringing the riddle or Zen kōan, "who am I?" (M&R 93, 95). The canyon wren sings above the roar [of the mind] to "purify our ears" — "ti ti ti ti tee tee tee" (M&R 90–91). Even city people in New York City wander through mountains and rivers that have taken form as skyscrapers, sewage channels, subways, and condominiums. The teacher invites us to hear the animals and trees who keep talking to us, coming around, encouraging the dropping of the "I." "Squawk, squork, crork / over the dark, tall spruce" (M&R 103).

The turning point in this part is "An Offering for Tārā" (M&R 106–12). Here the guide shows us not just mountains, not just rivers, but the connections between them: "water from the icefields ... wanders on the terraces ... alluvium carried up the slope / shaped into gompas, temples." The vast worlds of high and low places come together, and we see the glaciers, the Indus River,

> Rock stuff always folding
> turned back in again, re-folded,
> wrapping, twisting in and out like dough.   (M&R 109)

Shifting maps of visionary worlds, flowing sand mandalas, crumbling rock temples — everything is moveable; the teacher serves as witness to the magnitude of "mountains are mountains." Cause and effect begin to interweave, nothing is separate. But almost as a postscript, the "I" returns in the challenging voice of Bear Mother: "'What do you know of my ways?'" (M&R

113). This is Māra talking to the Buddha in the very last hours of his night watches: "What right do you have to sit there, you little dumb guy? What do you think you're going to find out?" To counter Māra and all the temptations of delusions, confusion, and doubt, the Buddha touches the earth, becoming grounded in time and place and freed of mental distractions.

In Part IV, Snyder takes the Zen instructional method to completion, the mountains revealing the full interdependent nature of being mountains. The opening poem, "Old Woodrat's Stinky House," shows us this inter-braiding as we look at millions of years and ice ages coming and going, language, lifespans — all one continuous reality. Then in "Raven's Beak River" stable nouns are replaced by shifting, fluid verbs.

> Looking north
> > up the dancing river
> Where it turns into a glacier
> > under stairsteps of ice falls
> Green streaks of alder
> > climb the mountain knuckles
> Interlaced with snowfields
> > foamy water falling
> Salmon weaving river
> > bear flower blue sky singer   (M&R 123)

The teacher shows the reader: this is mind-consciousness, not something happening "out there." It is all happening within the mind as well; the "I" has disappeared.

> Skin of sunlight
> > skin of chilly gravel
> Mind in the mountains, mind of tumbling water,
> > mind running rivers,
> Mind of sifting
> > flowers in the gravels   (M&R 123)

In "Afloat" mountains and rivers slide together even more: "Green mountains turn to clouds / and slip slow by . . . glaciers shift and murmur like the tides" (M&R 130, 131). In "Cross-Legg'd," human love itself is "mixed with / rocks and streams, / a heartbeat, a breath, a gaze // makes place in the dizzy eddy" (M&R 128). The weaving and braiding has opened up the fullness of mountains, and the instruction is almost complete.

But first, Snyder the teacher grants us a celebration, a dance, the great dance of nonself told through Japanese tales of Big Time opening. What a grand show, this birthing of nondual mind! And then we wash our bowls and get completely soaked in nonduality:

> upwellings, sideswirls, backswirls
> curl-overs, outripples, eddies, chops and swells
> wash-overs, shallows confluence turbulence wash-seam
> wavelets, riffles   (M&R 137)

Bouncing along in the raft of the teachings, the traveler is permeated with the waters of nonduality. All that is left is to offer it up as a realization and bow before the offering.

> *We wash our bowls in this water*
> *It has the flavor of ambrosial dew —*
> . . . .
> *We offer it to all demons and spirits*
> *May all be filled and satisfied.*
> *Om makula sai svaha!*   (M&R 137, 138)

This is the traditional blessing chanted at the end of morning and noon meals during a Zen meditation retreat, offering up the teachings to all beings. But Snyder goes one step further, paraphrasing Dōgen's teaching in the *Keisei Sanshoku*, "The Sounds of the Valley Streams, the Forms of the Mountains," a talk given several months before he wrote the *Mountains and Waters Sūtra*:

"Billions of beings see the morning star
and all become Buddhas!
If *you*, who are valley streams and looming
mountains,
can't throw some light on the nature of ridges and rivers,

who can?"   (M&R 139)[6]

The instruction is not over yet. In "The Mountain Spirit" (M&R 140–47) the author receives one last test to see if he is attached to fame. "You had a bit of fame once in the city / for poems of mountains, / here it's real." The test is loaded with questions of meaning: "For a creature to speak of all that scale of time — what for?" (M&R 141). What is the meaning in this? These are the kinds of questions that haunt us all the time — what's my life for? what's this world for? And we must return to others for guidance. This poem is, I believe, a return to the teacher, in this case, Bristlecone Pine. From my reading, Bristlecone is the strongest teacher in the entire poem cycle because it is the oldest being and the only one who speaks so sternly with Snyder. The seeker completes the instruction by returning to the teacher for the seal of transmission. Bristlecone Pine is certainly no Zen teacher, but bristlecone pines were around long before Zen. So if you want the original seal, go back further to the earliest ancestors, and then dance with your teacher — one mind, one nondual mind, no gap.

But this book could not end after the final testing for the gift would not have been passed on. The transmission is part of the receiving; it is all one act. The last poem, "Finding the Space in the Heart," transmits the teachings of nonduality in a desert paraphrase of the *Heart Sūtra*:

no waters, no mountains, no
bush, no grass, and
          because no grass
no shade but your shadow.
No flatness because no not-flatness.
No loss, no gain. So —

nothing in the way!
— the ground is the sky
the sky is the ground,
no place between, just

wind-whip breeze,
tent-mouth leeward,
time being here.
We meet heart to heart   (M&R 151)

This is the emptiness of nonduality: that the mountains we thought were mountains turned out to be much more than mountains and are actually empty of any absolute meaning. We cannot assign anything absolute to them because we are made of the same stuff as well. So the teacher gives the last instruction to pass the song along.

Gary Snyder once said, "A poem, like a life, is a brief presentation, a uniqueness in the oneness, a complete expression and a gift" (APIS 115). So today I feel very much like one of the young ones eating those grasshoppers (I still don't know why—what were they doing out there?). The challenge now seems to be to receive these teachings and be brave enough to walk through to the final stage of mountains being mountains and let that teaching completely transform me and all of us, and then find a way to pass it along.

DISCUSSION

KAZ TANAHASHI: We talked about the instruction of the poem, and I'd like to ask, Do you see any kind of instruction for environmental protection? It seems activist actions are somewhere behind the scenes, and I wonder how you feel about that.

STEPHANIE KAZA: I think the instruction lies in *how* to do the action, not which actions to take or which are most important. The greater question is, What will you be called by? What demands your response? This is what I try to teach my students. In our introductory Environmental Studies courses, the students are exposed to all the environmental problems of the world in two semesters. They sometimes call this "Gloom and Doom 101 and 102," so we offer support groups so they won't just give up in despair and be useless to society. We talk about "finding your calling." Yes, you need to be eco-literate about the shape of the world and know about problems with big dams, endangered species, and climate change. You should be able to understand what economic and political forces are driving these problems. But when you feel called by something in your heart, you need to follow that, because it has the strong energy of passion and motivation behind it. If you try to *think* too hard about the arena in which you're working, you will become discouraged and it will become too hard. Something else has to feed your energy.

Mountains and Rivers demonstrates that kind of calling without saying it overtly: "And then I was called to Artemisia, and then I founded the Yuba Watershed Institute." It's perhaps more Japanese than that. You wouldn't tell somebody what to do. You would just lightly indicate a possibility. There is very clearly a non-dual way to take up action, but it is very hard to actually achieve. As a teacher I encourage students to go toward that instead of the traditional Western adversarial approach. My hope would be that a Buddhist environmentalism would be based more on non-dualistic collaboration and even dancing with people who have different perspectives. They may appear to be your enemies, but if you do lovingkindness practice with them, then you cannot think of them as separate from you. This non-dualistic teaching from the Zen tradition offers a profound alternative for environmental activism, one based less in frustration and enemy-ism and more in hopeful working together across difference.

NOTES

1. Dōgen, "Mountains and Waters Sūtra" in *Moon in a Dewdrop*, trans. Arthur Koestler and Kazuaki Tanahashi (San Francisco: North Point Press, 1985), 97.
2. Dōgen, "Mountains and Waters Sūtra," 98.
3. Kenneth Kraft, "Nuclear Ecology and Engaged Buddhism" in *Buddhism and Ecology: The Interconnection of Dharma and Deeds*, ed. Mary Evelyn Tucker and Duncan Ryūken Williams (Cambridge, MA: Harvard University Press, 1998), 277–80.

4. Dōgen, "Mountains and Waters Sūtra," 102.

5. Dōgen, "Mountains and Waters Sūtra," 107.

6. See Dōgen, "The Sounds of the Valley Streams, the Forms of the Mountains" [*Keisei Sanshoku*] in *How to Raise an Ox*, trans. Francis Cook (Los Angeles: Zen Center of Los Angeles, 1978), 97–107.

~

CAROLE KODA SAID,

An Orange-Crowned Warbler sang in the Black Oak yesterday. Every repeat was full and strong. No "the world is too full of warblers anyway." No "why keep this up, no mate is coming or ever will."

GARY SNYDER SAID,

This is Zen. To give a hundred percent and know it does not matter.

— Sometime in 1990, at Kitkitdizze,
From David Robertson, *Real Matter* (1997)

INTERVIEW

~

JAMES MCKENZIE: Does what you said about *Mountains and Rivers Without End* mean that you don't see it as endless cantos?

GARY SNYDER: Oh, no. Not at all. No, I don't like that idea about endless things.

MCKENZIE: But you say, without end.

SNYDER: That's the name; the name comes from the Chinese scrolls. That's what they title them themselves, but only endless inasfar as they become cyclical finally. After that you can see where they go so you don't have to keep on doing it; no need to, you know, state the thing ad infinitum. Let the universe be endless, works of art don't have to. In fact, you know, craft-wise, I have perhaps an excessive sense of structure.

MCKENZIE: Yeah, I would certainly agree with that.

SNYDER: And bringing things through to a close.

— Gary Snyder with James McKenzie, from "Moving the World a Millionth of an Inch: Gary Snyder" (1974)

12.
———

"The Space Goes On"

A Conversation about *Mountains and Rivers Without End*

GARY SNYDER WITH ERIC TODD SMITH

Kitkitdizze, May 1998

W hen I arrived at his home in the Sierra Nevada foothills in May of
1998, Gary Snyder was covered with ants. He was on the roof of a
shed, straddling solar panels and pulling out insulation that a colony of car-
penter ants had claimed as its own. A few minutes later, he was showing
me around his tool shed and the old barn that houses his office, occasion-
ally slapping at stray ants crawling in his hair. We talked about how to use
the old crosscut saw and logging cables hanging from the walls, about local
birds and trees, and eventually wound our way into poetry, Buddhist phi-
losophy, and natural resource management. Such simultaneous immersion
in concrete tasks and abstract ideas is normal for Snyder, who has lived with
his family at Kitkitdizze, the house he built himself, since the early 1970s.
His long poem, *Mountains and Rivers Without End,* testifies to his convic-
tion that the quotidian and the cosmic are inseparable. For Snyder, poetry,
like all of life, is a collaboration with "the great commons of the world." This
idea of collaboration derives equally from Snyder's Buddhist practice and his
interest in ecology. In this interview, we explore how these influences merge
in *Mountains and Rivers Without End*.

ERIC SMITH: During the recent symposium at Stanford, "Ethics and Aes-
thetics at the Turn of the Fiftieth Millenium," which focused on *Mountains
and Rivers Without End*, your friend Jim Dodge used the Jungian model
of four centers of perception to talk about the dimensions of the poem.
These four centers — which are really ways of experiencing the world — are
the physical, the intellectual, the emotional, and the intuitional. Dodge

suggested that the emotional dimension of *Mountains and Rivers* is perhaps the least developed, even though, as he put it, the book as a whole "moves toward emotion" in the final section. What do you think of that assessment?

GARY SNYDER: Jim is such a trickster. I don't think he cares that much about those four Jungian positions. He's trying to tease me out. This reflects back on conversations we've had and games we've played on each other for years. I would prefer not to take a position in regard to that. First, because to do so would require a lot of definitions as to what we mean about emotion, and then we'd have to focus in further on what people call emotion in the post-Romantic, late-twentieth-century era of indulgent self-disclosure. Whatever the quality of emotion in *Mountains and Rivers* is, it does not belong to the late twentieth century. [*laughter*]

SMITH: Dodge joked that your next book of poems will be all confessional poetry. Maybe he's humorously driving at these different ways of assessing emotion . . .

SNYDER: That is just Dodge's wicked humor. He knows I don't need that, [*laughter*] although it's kind of a charming thought in a way. But as a Buddhist — and not just in the Buddhist tradition, except in very specific cases — personal histories are boring. [*laughter*]

SMITH: There are many voices in *Mountains and Rivers*: quotations from many different sources, found poems, and voices that do not belong to what you could call a traditional lyric "I." You have said yourself that you "like to think of *Mountains and Rivers* as a collaborative poem." And in many places you have explained that you think of the poet's role as shamanic. A shaman's words, strictly speaking, aren't his own, because he is trying to put into language a realm of experience with *other* beings that does not exist primarily in human language. You've also said that Zen first attracted you because of the way it encourages us to "empty the self." All this notwithstanding, it is possible to read *Mountains and Rivers* as autobiographical. Robert Hass, for instance, in his talk at Stanford earlier this year, suggested that was one way into the poem. *Mountains and Rivers* draws upon journeys you've made, experiences you've had, realizations you've had. So, I wonder what kind of poetic self you see in *Mountains and Rivers*. Is there a "Gary Snyder" in control? Are there many "Gary Snyders" in the poem?

SNYDER: First of all, when I say it's collaborative I'm thinking of two kinds of collaboration. One is the collaboration with various living persons and comrades from the past. The insights and the voices of those from whom I have learned, or, actually, those with whom I have engaged in the imagination — in some sense they are some of the contributing voices. In particular, of course, there's a collaboration of sorts with my teachers — my living, actual teachers both in painting and calligraphy and also in poetry and poetics. And in other realms, as well: working in the engine room on the *Sappa Creek* under the first engineer, learning how to be a caregiver to machinery. So those all become part of a collaboration if one is able to free oneself from the notion that art is self-expression to begin with — or, like, "which self"?

So, when I mention "which self," that brings us to the other aspect of collaboration, which is the collaboration of your various selves in producing a poem, or in producing a work of art. Since we are not just a single self — we are a number of selves, some of which come forward more than others — but an array of possible faces, possible angles, possible takes on the world. This is what neo-Jungians like James Hillman, who practices what he calls "archetypal psychology," are good at. But the acknowledgement that we reflect a number of selves, all of which, of course, are illusory anyway, and which resolve into a non-self — which is another way of speaking of the totally collaborative quality of any individual entity, namely that we are an intersection of influences in the present and in the past, from the present and from the past. That is, the self is a moving target. That's the non-self. Hillman speaks of the daimon, or genius, which drives some people's lives. Like the Muse, it is a force from "outside." A gift.

SMITH: From *Mountains and Rivers* you get a sense of wholeness and of community, rather than of fragmentation, especially by the end. One could say that this is because this notion of the self as the intersection of different influences and beings creates that wholeness. But recent Western attempts to say there is no coherent self have often been cast in terms of a crisis. Lacan, for instance, spent a long time arguing that there is no "real" ego, and that this leaves people in a fundamentally anxious state.

SNYDER: There's no need for people to be in an anxious state about that. It's simply that he and others of his ilk argued those things in the context

of Occidental individualism, substantialism, and arrogance. And an unwill-
ingness to let go. You could turn it around the other direction and say, "Oh,
thank god! No self, no ego; at last I'm free, and now I can begin to enjoy the
universe!" [*laughter*] You don't have to be locked into this narrow perspec-
tive that is self-imposed, anyway. Don't have to carry these old tapes around
that obsess about what mommy or daddy did, you know? [*laughter*]

SMITH: You have said in an interview that you think quite consciously of
your poetry as an attempt at communication. On the face of it, this seems
to differ from the idea of poetry as "self-expression" that we could perhaps
trace back to the Romantic tradition.

SNYDER: I don't know anybody who's serious as a writer who says poetry is
self-expression. Of course, there's a few apprentices who might think that,
but I don't know any serious, engaged, knowledgeable poet who thinks that
for a minute.

SMITH: Why do you think that is? What about the poetic process would,
say, disabuse a junior poet of that notion?

SNYDER: You can't. They have to find it for themselves. But when you get a
real poem coming in, you know that you didn't invent it. It's not you that's
writing it. That's a metaphoric way of saying it comes from perhaps a deeper
place in yourself, a powerful, creative current of insight that you cannot in
some ego-personal sense take credit for. And that's what we mean by poetry
not being self-expression. It's *expression* expressing itself, if you like. It's the
world expressing itself. It's some deeper insight or angle, or even simply self-
less perception of the world at this moment. Look at every single haiku.
Each haiku is a selfless poem. The only way a haiku can exist is by a momen-
tary act of such selfless clarity that there is no way for the ego to mess it up.

SMITH: So, if you're thinking about poetry as communication, that implies
a kind of responsibility to the expression you just mentioned.

SNYDER: Absolutely.

SMITH: It seems significant to me that communication, community, com-
munion, and the commons all come from the same root. Perhaps this relates
to the shamanic aspect of poetry you have talked about — the poet commu-
nicates the commons?

SNYDER: The commons is a very productive conceptual territory, and is of course, as you point out, related to all those etymologies of coming together, coming as one. But in this case, commons means, usefully and specifically, those parts of the world which we cannot privatize, which cannot be seized as the territory of any self, or any company, or any corporation, or even ultimately any government. So, originally "commons" meant forest and pastureland which was larger and more useful as seen in its natural and possibly semi-wild state, to be shared by all users fairly and equally, rather than divided up into private holdings. So everyone can go into the commons — into the commonly-held forest to get a little firewood or a little lumber. Everyone can put some cattle or sheep out to graze in the commonly-held pasture. Mushrooms, berries, and so forth. Berry picking. That's the old European idea of the commons, and it was found in China and Japan, as well: managed by the village. And not *mis*managed up until very recent centuries and the pressure of the money economy. So, Garret Hardin's essay, "The Tragedy of the Commons" [*Science* (December 1968): 1243–48] simply reflects a very narrow spectrum of behavior and problems created in the last three centuries in western Europe, particularly England, because of the money economy and all kinds of social tensions.

An extension of the commons as commonly held land is what we call "common-pool resources." There are some very technical and interesting books on the subject of common-pool resources. Water cannot be privatized. Air cannot be privatized. There are people who would try to do it, but it won't work. Game cannot be privatized. Deer run through your pasture, run through your yard, but you don't say, "They are now mine." They come and go. They belong to all of us. We manage them as a society with hunting season. So they are the commons. But beyond that, the oceans are the world's major commons, really, with the stock of fish and marine life in the oceans as something that we all have almost equal access to. But there are efforts to privatize the ocean right now, and to privatize the fisheries in the oceans. It's very dangerous. Even admitting, as I say that, that the question of how to peaceably manage and share in those resources is very difficult, it's also our only hope, to be able to do that.

SMITH: You mentioned Hardin's essay. He said that the "tragedy of the commons" was essentially that everyone is only out for themselves. So this conception of "no-self" that we've been talking about would seem to be an interesting potential development in ways to think about the commons.

SNYDER: Well, prior to the rise of competitive and individualistic capitalism, the no-self that was functioning in those terms was the agreement to cooperate with each other in terms of the welfare of the whole population of the village. So a person would have felt socially inappropriate to take more than their share. Everyone would see they were doing that. People had a sense of civic responsibility to the whole. Hardin, having grown up in a bourgeois, capitalist-individualistic society, assumes that there is no civic conscience at work, as so many people now do, forgetting that even a few decades ago the idea of a civic conscience was common in the United States and was one of the things that stood against the competitive and greedy side of capitalism.

So, to carry on where the idea of the commons and common-pool resources goes — those areas that possibly cannot, hopefully cannot, and in any case, *should* not be privatized, but should only be seen as, in a sense, gifts from the natural world that we share: the gene pool. Genetics is a vast commons of organic life itself.

SMITH: What do you think of the Human Genome Project?

SNYDER: That follows from this. That the gene pool should be seen as the commons, and nothing should be done to impinge on the gene pool in any individualistic or privatizing way, or in any patenting way, so that we are enabled as a world society to participate in these sensitive management decisions and bring the full weight of conscience to bear on it.

Language is a commons that cannot be privatized by schoolteachers, the French Academy, or any other institution that thinks it can seize on, frame, and determine what is correct or incorrect. Usages, slang usages, escape from any control. Always.

SMITH: This is the "wildness" of language . . .

SNYDER: It's one of the aspects of the wildness of language. It is a great shared resource that eludes management almost entirely. So, those are two other territories.

And then you could say that the imagination is the great commons of the world. It certainly is the great commons of the literary and artistic world, into which we all tap. One of the ways I'd say there is no way I can claim *Mountains and Rivers* purely for my own, quote, "self," is how much of the commons of the imagination I have drawn on, that I have played with, gone into. Now, there are foolish people who would like to privatize the commons of the imagination, and they raise the bugaboo of cultural appropriation, which is for the most part self-serving, and sounds like a grant application to me.

SMITH: A related issue here is intellectual property rights.

SNYDER: I'm arguing that there should be very few intellectual property rights, that ideas are not to be patented; they're to be shared.

SMITH: What about copyright?

SNYDER: Copyright is not a big problem, because there is a time limit on it. It benefits whoever put in some work on it — and I can go along with that — for a span of years, and then it benefits the heirs of that person for another span of years, then it's in the public domain. All the folk songs are in the public domain. Walt Whitman is in the public domain. Emily Dickinson. Shakespeare's in the public domain. That's fine. That's the way it should be.

SMITH: Picking up that idea of the commons of the imagination, I wonder how that might relate to the actual performance of poetry. You've said many times that you think of poetry primarily as an oral art. What difference do different audiences make? For instance, what difference would it make if you read it to your local community of neighbors, as opposed to an audience in New York City?

SNYDER: Oh, yeah, I would read it differently. One of the things performance enables us to do is respond to a given situation and make it work for that situation a little better. Things that you highlight, things that you leave in, and things that you leave out are part of that. Just as when I'm in a part of the world where there's part of *Mountains and Rivers*, like in the Pacific Northwest, say, or wherever it is, I'll be sure to read those poems. If I'm not going to read them all, I'll certainly hit on areas there, and talk about it a little bit.

SMITH: Let's move into *Mountains and Rivers* itself; we've been kind of talking around it. You have spoken of meditation as "composting" — of consciousness, of ideas, myths, images, and experiences. Meditative composting allows relationships between seemingly disparate things to come forth. It would seem that *Mountains and Rivers* is the result of a long period of composting; you let all these materials ripen and combine for forty years, turning it over the whole time! I wonder if you could comment on how meditation factored into the shape the poem took.

SNYDER: Well, some of the portions of *Mountains and Rivers* were more or less settled early on, and some are quite recent. So the whole process becomes, in some sense, progressively richer as time goes on, because the reflections I am having on the work-in-progress become increasingly more complex; there's more material involved.

SMITH: Over the years, you've described it as "intractable material."

SNYDER: Well, you know, sometimes it felt intractable. So, patience, patience is the key. Reflection, meditation enables things to break down, lose their rigidities, release their metabolic energies, so that separations between things begin to fall apart, or connections between things begin to come clear. In that sense, I had to give the poem whatever time it took for me to realize what it was I was trying to do. I wasn't even sure what I was doing, and it kept on instructing me in that way. Some of the poems that came to me were like further instructions on the whole poem. Having been created in the light of reflections on the whole poem, new poems come along as gifts that also reflect the thought of the whole poem. Consequently, I'm able to end it. [*laughter*]

SMITH: Which is the biggest gift of all, maybe?

SNYDER: Really, yeah. I'm able to end it without feeling I just chopped it off and said, "This far is enough. Let's quit here," but to feel like it's made its little journey, made its little walkabout.

SMITH: I recall your saying once that you wrote "Finding the Space in the Heart," the final poem in *Mountains and Rivers*, some time before you finished the whole book. Did you always know that was going to be the last poem of the book?

SNYDER: Yeah, as soon as I wrote that I said, "Oh, now I know how it ends!" But then that opens up the territory that you still have to take care of before it ends, and throws light on that. To get from here to there — I mean I know where there is now, but I'm still here, so now I know that there are still some things missing that take me from here to there.

SMITH: Part of the way you got from "here" to "there" was by thinking about Japanese Nō drama. During the ten years you lived in Japan, you saw many Nō plays performed. In your essay, "The Making of *Mountains and Rivers*," you state that you "began to envision *Mountains and Rivers* through the dramatic strategies of Nō." In an aesthetic sense, what was important about Nō as you were working on *Mountains and Rivers*?

SNYDER: You know, that's like asking me, "What is it about Greek tragedy that is important to you?" Even for a contemporary reader, you'd have to stop and give a lecture on Greek tragedy to then say, "These are the elements I thought I could reflect on and use." Nō is one of the world's great, complex, amazing, artistic, dramatic traditions. It bears a lot of study, so all I can say is very sketchy in that regard.

No is a remarkable mix of dance, song and recitation, very specialized musical background, a very specialized set and established body of conventions for everything, and a more or less set body of plays that share certain characteristics and certain plot structures. Out of all that, a couple of things are important to *Mountains and Rivers*. One of the things is the *michiyuki*, the "journey-going song." In many Nō plays, the play takes place within the context of a pilgrim's journey and is a stopping point at some historical or mythological moment to review the drama of this event, its place in history, and the unresolved karma of those who played in it. That's where it becomes a Buddhist moment, in that the traveler is frequently a Buddhist monk on pilgrimage, and the resolution of the karma is frequently, in a sense, no more than the ghost who's still bearing a painful story from the past being allowed to tell this story one more time and be freed — in a Buddhist way — and then be able to go on. This is a very powerful quality of Nō that is one of the levels, certainly, that inspired me as I was working on *Mountains and Rivers*. And that's one of the places where, for me, and for the poem, the East Asian horizontal landscape scroll and the plays overlap. There is a traveler in the scroll, even though you don't see him, and there is a traveler in the Nō play.

SMITH: I recall you or possibly someone else speaking of East Asian landscape painting as being somewhat like a mandala, as an exercise for working out one's karma or realization.

SNYDER: Well, I'm the only person I know of who says that. Art critics, including the Chinese and Japanese art critics, don't exactly say that, so that's one of my quirky interpretations of it all. But I think there is a powerful spiritual component, which is very much like the spiritual component in the Nō play, that runs through the landscape paintings, without, however, any clear invocation of a particular node or knot from mythology and history. (Except for genre paintings, which do do that. There are East Asian genre paintings that will bring forward a known sage or a known poet, things like that. But that's not quite what I'm talking about, either.) So that's one level that we can talk about.

The musicality of Nō fascinates me. I've always felt that Nō offers probably the most inspiring territory for bringing together music and poetry, and that if there is the possibility for poetic drama that Nō is one of the ways we can think about it, still. Of course, that's what inspired Yeats, who saw some Nō performances with a troupe that came to England in the 1920s, and then wrote his short plays, like *At the Hawk's Well,* modeled after Nō plays he had seen, and he did a very good job with it. Nō drama, of course, is in a sense outside of time, and it's outside of any wimpy, weepy individual egos.

SMITH: How would the musicality of Nō differ from that of say, Wagnerian opera?

SNYDER: It's dry. It's percussive. There is passion in Nō, there's profound passion, profound suffering, profound sorrow. It's a bit understated, though. [*laughter*] But you know, those who watch Nō are deeply moved by it.

SMITH: You first read Dōgen's *Mountains and Waters Sūtra* in the mid-1970s, is that right?

SNYDER: Yeah, when Carl Bielefeldt's MA thesis first came out.

SMITH: How did reading Dōgen influence the way you thought about *Mountains and Rivers,* and how did it influence your thinking generally?

SNYDER: Well, as anyone who looks at that text knows, it sends you back to the drawing board with how you view these things. It uses mountains and rivers as a metaphor for the universe, also for the psyche, and also for the human body. It's a wonderful multi-leveled text. I realized that if I'm calling this poem *Mountains and Rivers Without End,* then these are the territories and the depths I'm involved with — which I had sort of guessed at, but Dōgen put it right in front of me. So, I said I've got to go to work on this, and being a Zen student already, I knew the path into it.

SMITH: When I read the *Mountains and Waters Sūtra* the first time, I was impressed by the way it seems to harmonize a sort of metaphorical understanding of mountains and rivers with what seems to be presented in scientific circles as fact. For instance, we hear from geologists that mountains move around — very slowly, to our perception, of course — and Dōgen says, "mountains walk" and "mountains flow."

SNYDER: Well, those guys — Dōgen and his time and place — as I said in my essay, "Blue Mountains Constantly Walking," really did walk mountains. If they used the metaphors of mountains, it's because it's very real to them. They went on very long walks. That is the world. The up and down of the landscape is the world, as experienced before the age of airplanes and automobiles, with the body. You go uphill and then you go downhill; you *walk.* And so Dōgen takes a wonderful Asian reality (the hilly landscape of China and Japan) and uses it as such a creative metaphor for the life of the mind.

SMITH: Since you mentioned your essay, "Blue Mountains Constantly Walking," from *The Practice of the Wild,* I'd like to ask you something about that. In that essay, you reflect on Dōgen's statement: "If you doubt mountains walking you do not know your own walking," which plays off the Zen master Furong's cryptic claim: "The blue mountains are always walking." As a commentary on these statements you write: "Dōgen is not concerned with 'sacred mountains' — or pilgrimages, or spirit allies, or wilderness as some special quality. His mountains and streams are the processes of the earth, all of existence, process, essence, action, absence; they roll being and nonbeing together. They are what we are, we are what they are. For those who would see directly into essential nature, the idea of the sacred is a delusion and an obstruction: it diverts us from seeing what is before our eyes: plain thusness." Now, many environmentalists in the late twentieth century argue that unless we see nature as sacred, we will never act responsibly toward it. Could you explain how "the idea of the sacred is a delusion and an obstruction"?

SNYDER: I think those environmental thinkers are a bit off, although their intention is excellent. And as a matter of fact, the tide has already shifted in that regard. The language about pristine nature, pristine wilderness, and wilderness thereby as "sacred" has come to be realized as not productive in terms of protecting or saving nature. First of all, nature is not a virgin; if it was a she, it would be a tough old lady. She can take a lot of hits. Let's not fool ourselves — she can take a *lot* of hits. However, it's our obligation not to do too many bad hits within our own sphere of time on an earth that will outlive us. In the long run, as I was saying down at Stanford, that stuff will all take care of itself. So, our job is not to do too much harm within our own ten-thousand-year time frame. We've got 10,000 more years that we'll clearly be operating in. Beyond that, there'll be more things going on, but we can take the next 10,000 years as our responsibility for now.

We can't fool ourselves that we don't use lumber, or don't drink water, or don't eat the fish out of the sea, that we aren't thoroughly involved in everything that goes on. And that wilderness, and beauty, and self — like, the wilderness areas are only there because they're useless. The high elevation glaciers, rocks, and ice that we love so much — if they were full of minerals, they would have been all torn up for mining. The western senators and the big corporations would have seen to that. So in a sense, we get what we think of as lovely, beautiful, pristine wilderness by default.

Biologically speaking, we should have a huge section (or at least a respectable section) of the Sacramento Valley set aside in its pristine form, so we can observe it, study it, and appreciate it. And so it can provide habitat for millions of waterfowl and all kinds of other creatures and plants that were originally there. But what we have is a few fragmentary acres here and there. Of course, a lot of people are working hard to get some of that acreage back, but my point is we don't take a great big fertile valley and declare it a sacred wilderness and save it, although we *should*. So there's a certain sense of realism and clarity that comes through admitting our engagement with all the aspects of the natural world that then translates, in my thinking, not to a condition that permits us to extract resources even more recklessly, but to a condition that admits that we are going to continue drawing on resources, but we have to become more respectful, mannerly, tender, careful, and *truly* scientific — not just using science as a fake language for justifying what we want to get. So, I'm kind of jumping ahead to that by arguing that.

The other point is a spiritual point. The universe is not to be divided up into the sacred and the secular, into the beautiful and the less beautiful. Everything is equally real. [*laughter*]

SMITH: It's significant, then, that "mountains and rivers," in Chinese, is a way of referring to all of nature.

SNYDER: Landscape. Landscape, which includes cities. Toxic waste dumps are in the landscape. You know, during the Maoist regime in China (I'm trying to figure out which period this was flourishing; I wish I had bought some of them) there was a period probably during the seventies, maybe earlier, in which Chinese painters were painting quite expert landscape scrolls and hanging scrolls that included little dams, and little power transmission lines, and little trucks — you know, showing that Chinese industry was still working. But the landscape was like the old beautiful landscape. By now I'm sure they're all destroyed or burned — they're not fashionable anymore. But it was such an interesting way of dealing with it.

SMITH: Some environmentalists might say, "Isn't that bad? Doesn't it show acquiescence to industrialism?"

SNYDER: You know, that's not the question. The question is: how do we live with it? How do we get some control of it? Suppose you've got a crazy, wild horse bucking and running around, doing a lot of damage, and you can't shoot it. You've got two choices: one is to run away from it and try to go someplace else, the other is to come up to it, try to manage it, hold it down, calm it down, try to get a halter on it, and learn how to ride it, how to train it. Now, we have an economy and an international set of governments that are all out of control. A lot of people want to walk away from it. But you know, poets are foolish. [*laughter*] Artists and writers and intellectuals are foolish; they'll still try to figure out a way to make a halter for it.

And in terms of what's going to transpire with the natural world, we can't just say, "Let's leave industrial society and technology behind." I mean, you *can*, and you can go off and have a neat little commune somewhere in western Australia or something, and you may live out your life with your friends in a condition of peace and beauty and harmony and sort of over-look all the stuff that's going on in the rest of the world. You can do that. But if you're thinking of your children and your grandchildren and you're thinking of the world and of nature as a whole, then we're all brought to the point of trying to figure out what the heck we can do.

SMITH: I'm guessing that's where poems like "Walking the New York Bed-rock" and "Night Song of the Los Angeles Basin" in *Mountains and Rivers* come from. That's an attempt at —

SNYDER: — at trying to find a language to get into it with. Especially the "New York Bedrock" poem. At the time I wrote that the whole internet thing was not so big then, was not such a big topic, and I wasn't even think-ing that much of the "information economy," but of the whole totally inter-connected realm of human information that we all are in. But that line, "Alive, in the Sea of Information" becomes more and more pregnant with implications as we get into the twenty-first century.

SMITH: This past March, you received in Tokyo the Numata Foundation's 1998 Cultural Award for furthering the appreciation and understanding of Buddhism. This award was especially significant because it was given to an American, a Westerner. Do you think you have contributed to cer-tain changes or developments to Buddhism by practicing and promoting it in North America, specifically, as opposed to, say, Japan? Has the West changed Buddhism?

SNYDER: I think it's too early to say. I think it's fair to say that the way I have thought and taught in regard to Buddhism certainly reflects my own North American experience, and some of the desperate concerns of our own time. I have made a push toward bringing ecological concerns toward the front in Buddhism. They're already in there, but they're not foregrounded, his-torically. And so my effort has been, in a sense, to push to make Buddhism play the role it could by asserting the rights of all beings, rather than a nar-row ethic that applies only to human beings. Who can say whether or not that makes any difference in the long run to Buddhism, at this point? Or whether or not that even makes any long-run difference or shape for Amer-ican Buddhism, because we're talking about a huge cultural phenomenon.

It took Buddhism seven or eight hundred years to work its way into China. It probably won't take that long to go to the rest of the world now because of all the media stuff we have, but it will still be a long process of assimilation and reflection and consideration. I'm just making one little contribution to it. Although if my poetry stands up, it will in any case be regarded as a poetry which was affected by, and made its own interpretation of, in some ways, the Buddhist practices.

The Numata Foundation people and others over there have recognized that — I think this is a fair thing to say — that the way I go about Buddhism nowadays and for the last twenty years has been increasingly non-sectarian, increasingly broad-based, and in a certain sense, increasingly orthodox. That is to say, *really* orthodox: I appreciate peasant Buddhism. I appreciate the mix of folk religion and sophisticated philosophy that is found in the living Buddhist traditions. I'm not so charmed by sort of rationalized, elite, intellectualized American versions of Buddhism in which they think that they've got the pure version now, without the superstition, or something. They miss that archetypal stew that makes it rich when they do that. They'll find out, though. [*laughter*]

SMITH: You said once in an interview that it wasn't until you went to Japan that you discovered you were "an American pragmatist." In your concluding remarks at the Stanford symposium last weekend, you were quoting from C. S. Pierce to explain the relationship between ethics and aesthetics. What about American pragmatism — I'm thinking here of people like Pierce, William James, John Dewey — do you find useful or appealing?

SNYDER: Well, I'm not an intense reader of those writings, although I grew up with it. It's part of the air you breathe, especially at mid-century in America. You were breathing a mixture of Thomas Jefferson, John Dewey, and Marx, whether you knew it or not, in the mid century. That Deweyan and '30s socialism, a sort of '30s Marxist curiosity, was part of the world we grew up in. But when I say I see myself as an American pragmatist, that's more based on my working habits and my use of tools. I found myself trying to instruct the monks and the head monks in what I felt would be some more efficient ways of doing things, [*laughter*] or telling them that they ought to get certain tools that were better for certain jobs. They finally told me,

"Look we don't want to be more efficient or faster here. The work we do (out in the little woods they had, and in the vegetable garden, and in the pickle shed, firewood splitting, and so forth) is not being done to get it *done*. It's part of our practice, and this is the right speed to do it at." I was supposed to know that. [*laughter*] So we have to learn that the approach to life that Buddhist practice implies is an approach which truly would transform our sense of what is useful in technology, and our sense of what is called for in the matter of production.

Wendell Berry has said for years that part of the problem with American agriculture is that it overproduces. The same can be said of a lot of other things in our capitalist economies. And also, people spend too much time working — overproducing and overworking. There have been moves afoot several times in this century to shorten the length of the work week (as they're trying to do in France now), to diversify the workplace and give people different roles to play. These are wonderful ideas. But the overriding thrust of our mass-culture, capitalist society is such that everybody wants to make more money, period. Nobody wants more time. Nobody wants more leisure. Nobody wants more time with their family. They want purely and simply more money. Until we break the stranglehold of that on the consciousness of the culture — now it's gone all the way through the society — we're going to be nuts. We *are* nuts.

SMITH: That leads me to another connection. You talked about work as practice. In a seminar at UC Davis a few years ago, you explained a general difference between Eastern and Western religions by saying that in the West basic questions are, "What do you believe?" and "What is your faith?" while in the East a basic question is "What is your practice?" Could you elaborate on this difference? What kind of orientation in the world does "practice" imply?

SNYDER: The Abrahamic religions of the West — Islam, Judaism, Christianity — are all religions of creed, articles of faith. In most cases, to be an actively good member in one of those religions is to express deep faith. Not learning, not meditation, not contemplation, not even prayer.

SMITH: Calvinism says you can't be saved by "works."

SNYDER: Right. And in the Occident we take that so much for granted that the Occidental world has a hard time understanding some of these alternative streams of spiritual and religious feeling where a doctrine or a set of articles are not important except in a very broad and general way. And so, Buddhism is one of those. What people share in Buddhism is the intent of enlightenment. The intent of finding the way. That is shared by Taoists, and by Hinduism, too.

Another way of distinguishing those Eastern religions from the West is: religions of faith as against religions of wisdom. They are, in essence, gnostic; they seek *gnosis*, rather than a relationship with a deity established by faith and trust. They seek to know the deity, or the truth of things, not to believe in the deity. There's a very special distinction there. There have been people like that in Christianity, and they are generally in trouble, historically.

SMITH: Interestingly, that reminds me of American pragmatism, in a way. I know you weren't talking about the philosophical strain of William James specifically, but his "radical empiricism" runs along these lines.

SNYDER: Yes, I should have mentioned James. I read more James than Dewey. *The Varieties of Religious Experience* is a very instructive text. So anyway, what interests people in religious life in East Asia is assuming that we all share an intention of enlightenment. Then it's not a question of what you believe; the intention is shared. The question is: what do you *do*? "What practice do you follow?" They might be, in some cases, scholarship and research; some are practices of meditation via ritualized magic and chanting; some are meditation using devices of form; there are meditations of the formless variety; there is pilgrimage; solitude and retreat; copying texts — some people do that for their whole lives; beneficent social work; and art — painting, drama, dance are also considered possible religious practices.

But the main practices are varieties of meditation. When someone says, "What practice do you follow?" you name your teacher, and your tradition. When I was in India in the early '60s, I visited one of the more impressive gurus, Swami Shivananda, up at Hardwar, where the Ganges comes out of the Himalayas. When I approached his seat, he said, "What is your path?" I said, "I'm a Zen Buddhist." "Oh," he said, "then you are a *Shunyatavādin*." The term *vādin* means rider of the vehicle, traveler. So, there are Theravādins, following the "vehicle of the elders," and there are Mantravādins, following the path of chanting mantras. *Shunyatavādin*, then, meaning follower of the path of emptiness, which is held in very high regard in East Asia. That's the way we talk about things. The Dalai Lama, years back when we visited him, wanted to know who were our teachers. Allen Ginsberg said, "My teacher is William Blake." And the Dalai Lama said, "Oh, tell me about William Blake." [*laughter*] We're interested in the question, "What does your teacher have you do?"

SMITH: I'd like to talk a bit about how two rather large ideas intersect in *Mountains and Rivers* and in your thinking generally. These ideas are *place* and *impermanence*. Specific places have always been important to you, from your childhood on a stump-farm in Washington up to your present, ongoing project of reinhabiting San Juan Ridge here in the Sierra Nevada. You have said that one of the most revolutionary (and ecological) things one can do in American society is to "not move," but instead stay in a place and put down some roots.

On the other hand, a basic tenet of Buddhist thought is the impermanence of all things. As you said in your concluding remarks at the Stanford symposium, "All phenomena are non-substantial because they are all contingent and impermanent." I think many Americans would be confused by the coexistence of these ideas in your thinking. Some might argue that the impermanence and disposability of American culture is what makes Americans move around so much — that what Americans really need is a sense of permanence. Could you explain how rootedness in a specific place is reconcilable with an understanding of the world as impermanent and changing?

SNYDER: There is truly an element of paradox in that, I cheerfully admit. [*laughter*] It is, in a funny way, a paradox in Buddhism itself, which resolves it in part by arguing that if you give up any thought of clinging to the ideas of the self and of permanence, then you've found your place. [*laughter*] Then you are centered. And so there's a metaphorical center, which is T. S. Eliot's "still point of the turning world," that is implied. And that metaphorical center is a metaphorical place, which is nowhere, but also everywhere, or it's right where you are. So that's one way of looking at it. And that's why the Buddhas are all seated, you know. Those figures are so stable, so calm.

They are somewhere. [*laughter*] Where are they in this realm of imperma-
nence? They look very settled. How did they manage to settle down like
that? [*laughter*]

But let's go into this a little more deeply. To grasp the common-sense
truth of impermanence is to realize your physical limitations. Each of us, in
our brief life, can only be in one place at a time, and no matter how much we
might move about, it's finally not many places. We are born some-specific-
where and die somewhere, and in truth live in specific places all our life.
So this, as Dōgen says, is where practice begins. Knowing one's limits, to
explore the sphere given us (this mind-body, this neighborhood, this valley
and ridge) well. Then, to grasp the somewhat less common-sense truth of
no-self, is to realize that the boundaries between inside and outside, yourself
and the surroundings, is permeable, and that the air and water of this neigh-
borhood, this valley, is also inextricably part of your being.

Applying that, as you raised the question, to life in twentieth-century
America: our society is full of stress and anxiety, in part, because it is torn
by a metaphysic that seeks permanence and substance, and which clings to
innumerable ideas of objects in the face of inevitable impermanence. And
then connect that with the emphasis that has been put on individualism and
individual personality in a society in which the most elemental social orga-
nization — the family itself — is up in the air in everybody's minds, and you
get a quick take on the problem.

People don't know whether family's important or not important to
them, and in any case, larger, more extended families and relatives and sup-
port people are not common. When I look at the pain brought into our
society by the combination of all these things, plus the materialism, and the
competition, and the envy — one thinks, how can we rectify this?

There are a number of avenues. One of the most simple is to become
literally more settled. Maybe then you can have more of a neighborhood, a
community of known people and non-human neighbors too. This isn't say-
ing we should all become "peasants."

It's more like saying we should get into the truths of our own lives. Get-
ting to know a city is very rewarding. Well, the same thing is true of a water-
shed or an ecosystem. And so we are learning a few details here on San Juan
Ridge. For instance, that pileated [pointing at a woodpecker that has been

in the nearby trees throughout our interview] has been coming back right here every day for several weeks now. I know where its nest-cavity is, and I've seen its young stick their heads out of the hole. It's hunting for food for them right now.

SMITH: How does the orientation implied by "practice" relate to the kind of rootedness you're talking about?

SNYDER: Practice at root is meditation. Meditation is a matter of deepening your relationship with your mind and body. To carry that on out to the surroundings, which in a way are of a piece with the mind-body, becomes a further meditation — (hear that woodpecker's cry?) — that is, in a way, obvious. We and our world are impermanent together; we meditate together. Whether we know it or not, we're all involved in this practice. [*laughter*] Not knowing it doesn't mean you're not in it. The pileated and I bang our heads together.

And then, Hua-yen, or, Avataṃsaka, philosophy says the whole phenomenal world is the community. The place. The Sangha. Inorganic, organic — it doesn't matter. Hua-yen argues that to have a deep perception of this interconnectedness is of itself liberating. What many people seem to fear about death is losing their own particular body of information, their own unique story. Yet what's lost? Some non-unique information. [*shrugs*] Their own story is in a sense what people cling to. But, in a way, practically everybody's story is basically the same. So the metaphor is not that every human being is a different song, it's that every human is the same song but with a slightly different arrangement. [*laughter*] A very slightly different arrangement. This extends to the rest of life. The size of the place of "rootedness" is fluid. It's the engagement with the Way that counts.

SMITH: So then you're back into collaboration, like with your poetry.

SNYDER: Yes, and you're back into enjoying what's happening, that it is happening everywhere and will continue on regardless of whether any specific individual entity is here. And so, as they used to say in China when somebody dies, "She rejoined the mountains and rivers."

SMITH: To me that calls up one of the last lines of *Mountains and Rivers*: "The space goes on." This line comes directly after a vision of community — of friends and family gathered in the desert of the Great Basin — which contrasts with some of the visions of solitary journeying that come earlier in the poem. To say, "the space goes on," seems like a way of saying that the sangha, the community, the commons — this grand "happening" — will continue beyond any individual, or any act of writing, and that this is reason to rejoice.

Maha Prajñā Pāramitā Hṛdaya Sūtra
Heart of the "Gone-Beyond-Wisdom Sūtra"

Avalokiteshvara Bodhisattva practicing deep prajñā pāramitā,
clearly saw that all five skandhas are empty
transforming all suffering and distress. Saying, "Shāriputra,
form is no other than emptiness emptiness no other than form
form is exactly emptiness emptiness exactly form;
sensation, thought, impulse, consciousness are also like this.

Shāriputra, all things are marked by emptiness:
not born, not destroyed not stained, not pure
without gain, without loss.
Therefore in emptiness there is no form,
no sensation, thought, impulse, consciousness
no eye, ear, nose, tongue, body, mind;
no color, sound, smell, taste, touch, object of thought;
no realm of sight to no realm of thought;
no ignorance and also no ending of ignorance
to, no old age and death and also no ending of old age and death;
no suffering, also no source of suffering,
no annihilation, no path; no wisdom, also no attainment.
Having nothing to attain,
Bodhisattvas live prajñā pāramitā
with no hindrance in the mind. No hindrance, thus no fear.
Far beyond delusive thinking, they attain complete Nirvana.
All Buddhas past, present, and future live prajñā pāramitā
and thus attain anuttara samyak saṃbodhi,
highest perfect enlightenment.
Therefore, know the prajñā pāramitā is
the great mantra, the wisdom mantra,

the unsurpassed mantra, the supreme mantra,
which completely removes all suffering.
This is truth, not deception.
Therefore, set forth the prajñā pāramitā mantra,
set forth this mantra and say:
'Gate, gate, pāragate, pārasaṃgate, bodhi svāhā!'
Gone, gone, gone beyond, gone beyond beyond, bodhi svāhā."

GREAT WISDOM SŪTRA

— Ring of Bone Zendo Translation

For commentary, see Red Pine, *The Heart Sutra: The Womb of Buddhas* (Washington, DC: Shoemaker & Hoard, 2004).

Mountains and Rivers Without End
Notes for Some of the Poems

GARY SNYDER

9 October 1997

This is a poem-sequence that reaches toward an imagining, a visualizing, of the whole planet as one watershed, one great place. Like an old time Buddhist pilgrim, it tries to move through the world in the spirit of Compassion and Insight / Emptiness / Transparency.

The structure of the sequence is inspired, in part, by the East Asian sumi-ink paintings of landscapes (particularly the horizontal scrolls or "handscrolls"); the dramatic strategies and aesthetic insights of Japanese Nō drama; and twentieth-century open-form long poem traditions. It moves between lyric, dramatic, and narrative modes, and is best experienced as performance.

It was begun in the spring of 1956, and at the rate of about one poem per year, finished in 1996.

The opening quotations are from Dōgen Zenji's *Gabyō* — "Painted Rice Cake."

ENDLESS STREAMS AND MOUNTAINS A handscroll by this name showed up in Shansi province, central China, in the thirteenth century. Even then the painter was unknown. Now it's in North America. You unroll the scroll to the left, a section at a time, as you let the right side roll back in. Place by place unfurls. The East Asian landscape painting tradition invites poetic commentary. In a sense the painting is not fully realized until several centuries of poems by subsequent owners and viewers, and their seals, have been added.

OLD BONES Takes us back to the upper paleolithic life of hunting and gathering peoples.

BUBBS CREEK HAIRCUT Bubbs Creek is in the southern Sierra Nevada range. Shiva, the "Destroyer" of the Hindu trinity, is always practicing in the mountains. His lover and yogic partner is Parvati.

BOAT OF A MILLION YEARS was written working on a ship in the Red Sea. Its imagery is drawn in part from the *Egyptian Book of the Dead*. The philosopher Teilhard de Chardin suggested that human beings should take charge of all of nature. It is very charitable to say he is just joking. That the universe governs itself is a great gift.

THE BLUE SKY This section is an exploration of some of the lore of healing as found in Mahayana Buddhism and in Native North America. Bhaiṣajyaguru (Sanskrit) — the "Medicine Buddha" — is known in Japan as Yakushi Nyorai. He holds a tiny medicine bottle in the palm of one hand. Eons ago he made a vow to work for the welfare and healing of all sentient beings.

Another element is the ancient lore of the protective and healing powers of the color blue and of certain blue stones. The character *k'ung,* used for the Buddhist term *shunyata* or "emptiness" in Chinese, also means "sky." I was once told by a Native California elder that the diagnostic and healing hand of a "trembling-hand healer's hand" was guided by an eagle so high up in the sky as to be out of sight.

MĀ This was a found poem. I found a letter on the floor of a long-abandoned logger's cabin in the Yuba River country. It was from "Ma." Names and places have been changed. Mā, with the long mark over the *a,* is the Sanskrit name of the Earth Goddess.

"FALLS" from THE FLOWING is a poem for Yosemite Falls, in the Sierra. A Puget Sound Salish friend once said that some cedar trees dreamed of becoming canoes and going to sea even while still young trees.

THE HUMP-BACKED FLUTE PLAYER Ancient rock art, petroglyphs, of a walking flute-playing figure, sometimes with a hump on his back, are found widely in the Southwest and into Mexico. They are several thousand years old. There is a Hopi secret society that takes the Flute-player as its emblem. Some of the figures have an erect penis, and some have feelers on their heads that look like insect antennae.

It has been suggested that the hump is possibly a pack, and that the figure may represent Aztec or Toltec wandering traders, who once came up into the Southwest with trade items. In Peru even today you can see young men with a sort of sling-pack on their backs, carrying a load and playing the flute while walking.

Hsüan Tsang, the Buddhist scholar-pilgrim, brought the famed "Heart Sūtra" back to China from India — the one-page condensation of the whole philosophy of transcendent wisdom — in his pack. Once he had translated it into Chinese it was set in moveable type — the first text in the world to be printed this way, it is said.

Note: "White man" here is not a racial designation, but a name for a certain set of mind. When we all become born-again natives of Turtle Island, then the "'white man' will be gone."

THE HEART SŪTRA (CHANT)

THE CIRCUMAMBULATION OF MT. TAMALPAIS Walking meditation, circumambulation, *pradakshina*, is one of the most ancient human spiritual exercises. On such walks one stops at notable spots to sing a song, or to chant invocations and praises, such as mantras or little sūtras.

THE CANYON WREN The Stanislaus River comes out of the central Sierra. The twists and turns of the river, the layering, swirling stone cliffs of the gorges, are cut in nine-million-year-old latites. We ran the river to see its face once more before it went under the rising water of the New Melones Dam. The song of the Canyon Wren stayed with us the whole time.

ARCTIC MIDNIGHT TWILIGHT This poem is from the landscape of the Brooks Range, which divides the Arctic Ocean from the Yukon River basin of Alaska. Dibée is the Koyukon name for Mountain Sheep. If you listen close you will hear echoes of Shelley's great poem "The Cloud."

UNDER THE HILLS NEAR THE MORAVA RIVER Excavations by Bohuslav Klima at the Dolní Věstonice site in the Pavlovské Kopce hills of southern Moravia (Czechoslovakia).

HAIDA GWAI NORTH COAST, NAIKOON BEACH Haida Gwai is the old/new name for the colonially named "Queen Charlotte Islands."

NEW MOON TONGUE celebrates the antiquity of romancing, even in the world of animals, and a quality of elegance that precedes human beings.

AN OFFERING FOR TĀRĀ Out of the upper Indus River watershed, on the

Western Tibetan Plateau, around Ladakh and its main town of Leh. Tārā, "She Who Brings Across," is a Buddha of both Compassion and Wisdom. She is one of the most revered figures in Buddhism, especially in Tibet, Mongolia, and Nepal.

THE DAIHISHIN DHĀRANĪ, SPELL OF GREAT COMPASSION (CHANT)

OLD WOODRAT'S STINKY HOUSE Coyote food from: Classification of 5,086 coyote droppings gathered in Yellowstone National Park.

Human food from: Classification of 6000 dried human droppings found in the Lovelock Cave north of Fallon, Nevada.

Prehistory of woodrat nests in the Great Basin, see: Julio Betancourt, Thomas Van Devender & Paul Martin, eds., *Packrat Middens* (Tucson: University of Arizona, 1990).

Cottontail boys and woodrat: from the Maidu (Northern Sierra) myth-cycle as told by Hanc'ibyjim.

RAVEN'S BEAK RIVER is also called the Tatshenshini. One of the wildest rivers in North America, it cuts through massive ice fields to empty into the Gulf of Alaska. Strictly speaking the world is not yet out of the Ice Age. In that part of the world this is clear to see. Human beings are "Ice Age babies." This is our time in the world.

EARRINGS DANGLING AND MILES OF DESERT This is a celebration of Great Basin Sagebrush. It is also in spirit a "Hymn to Artemis" as per the Homeric hymns. The formulaic ending echoes the traditional envoi starting with the Greek word *chaire* or *chaírete* — a salute and farewell, invoking, hailing, rejoicing, in the deity, all in one.

THE DANCE The story of Ame-no-Uzume, and the rowdy dance she performed to lure the Sun Goddess back out of her cave, is a pivotal narrative node in the Japanese creation mythology. Her dance is seen as the founding performance of Shinto sacred dances, and the dance that underlies Nō drama.

WE WASH OUR BOWLS IN THIS WATER This poem incorporates a Zen Training Hall meal verse. Su Shih (Su Tung-p'o) was the great eleventh century Chinese poet and Zen adept. This was his "enlightenment poem." The translation is my own. Dōgen gave a lecture on it to his students, some two centuries later.

THE MOUNTAIN SPIRIT This poem follows to some degree the structure of a Japanese Nō drama, and the styles of chanting and speaking. It retells the story of the Nō play *Yamamba*, in North American terms. The North American way to tell the story goes thus:

Throughout western North America there are tales of the Mountain Spirits — sometimes fierce and jagged as lightning, sometimes smooth and sweet as a rainbow, sometimes seen as an old ragged woman. Some years back, in San Francisco, there was a poet who made his reputation largely on the basis of a poem he had written about the Mountain Spirit, even though he had not actually visited the mountains very much himself.

One year he decided to pay a visit to the unique groves of ancient bristlecone pine — the oldest living beings in the world — that are located in the remote upper elevations of the White-Inyo mountains of eastern California. After considerable travel he made his way into the White Mountains and set up camp as it was getting dark. As it happened it was the time of the annual Perseid meteor showers, which he also hoped to enjoy. While looking over the dusk landscape, a voice out of the dark challenged him, and asked that he read aloud his famous poem on the Mountain Spirit for her. He promised to do so at midnight, and then tried to put this strange encounter out of his mind. At midnight however he was awakened, and he saw that his visitor was indeed the legendary Mountain Spirit. As the meteors streaked through the sky, he read his poem to this mysterious personage, and then the two of them danced the dance of the bristlecone pine. The spirit suddenly slipped away, and the poet fell back to sleep.

There are stands of bristlecone pine, *Pinus longaeva*, in the mountains at the western edge of the Great Basin that contain individual trees that are dated well over four thousand years old. Those growing on the bone-white outcroppings of dolomite from ancient seabeds live to be oldest. They are thought to be the most ancient of living beings.

Wovoka was the visionary founder of the Ghost Dance religion. He had a big hat that he sometimes let his followers peek inside of: they said it contained all the wildlife and native homelands of the pre-White world.

Lord Krishna, when a baby, sometimes ate dirt. Once when his Mother tried to take a lump of dirt off his tongue, he playfully let her see the whole universe with its stars and planets, all in his mouth.

Vimalakīrti was an enlightened Buddhist layman from North India who fell sick. In the sūtra named for him an incredible number of beings of all categories from all over the various universes come at the same time to pay him a sick call. No matter how many keep arriving, they all fit into his one small room "ten feet square."

EARTH VERSE was written in the incredibly lonely Musgrave mountains of the central Australian desert.

FINDING THE SPACE IN THE HEART At various times during the present ice age there has been a vast inland sea covering much of the Great Basin. At the moment it is almost entirely dry. Paleogeographers call it Lake Lahontan.

APPENDIX 3

Fieldwork: Gary Snyder, Libraries, and Book Learning

MARK GONNERMAN

I once took a summer job cataloging images of Japanese prints for the slide library of the Museum of Fine Arts, Boston. In the morning, I walked to Harvard Square from my Shaler Lane apartment, caught a shuttle to Harvard Medical School, and walked another ten minutes to the museum. At day's end, I meandered on foot through Boston and along the Charles River back to Cambridge. Prompted by Ezra Pound's observation that "artists are the antennae of the race," my reading turned to interviews with contemporary artists.[1] Before long, the Widener Library copy of Gary Snyder's *The Real Work: Interviews & Talks, 1964–1979* was in my backpack and on my mind as I made my way.[2]

These interviews brought me into Snyder's world. I was struck by the keen awareness of this rural, American, Buddhist intellectual who wears prodigious learning lightly and brings it to bear on a range of historical, political, philosophical, and literary concerns. Before long, *Riprap and Cold Mountain Poems*, *Myths & Texts*, *Earth House Hold*, *The Back Country*, and *Turtle Island* were making the rounds with me as well.

When I arrived in California to study for my doctorate, I hoped to meet this estimable teacher, and I did as the Mountains & Rivers Workshop got underway in the fall of 1997. Gary occasionally traveled to Stanford for our seminar meetings. One November morning at breakfast he asked, "Would you like to read through the fire-safe copies of my personal journals?" I was careful not to choke on my toast and replied, "Sure. That would be great!" A few weeks later, Eric Todd Smith showed up at my door with forty-five bound volumes, Snyder's personal record of life and learning from 1947–95.

With this generous loan in my possession, I became curious about ways the anthropological tradition of Franz Boas (1858–1942) — the intellectually

291

adventurous German-Jewish émigré who fostered the field of cultural anthropology in and of North America — informed Snyder's work as an artist, culture-change agent, and pioneering Zen Buddhist.[3] My dissertation, "'On the Path, Off the Trail': Gary Snyder's Education and the Makings of American Zen," was submitted to Stanford's Department of Religious Studies in 2004.[4]

I was interested in approaching Snyder's intellectual biography through attention to his books and reading on the model of Robert Sattelmeyer's *Thoreau's Reading: A Study in Intellectual History with Bibliographical Catalogue.*[5] For this, I spent five weeks at Kitkitdizze during the summer of 1998, perusing the stacks and cataloguing parts of Snyder's library. I was also able to browse neat files of 3" × 5" index cards — mostly notes from Snyder's reading and research in college and graduate school — that remain in his collection. From this, I got a good, though by no means complete, sense of Snyder's lifelong learning from texts.

YOUTH AND REED COLLEGE

> Remember once (1949–50) plotting how to spend a whole day reading without serious interruption even while cooking & eating--when all you need for any day is a good dig of anything, even for a minute, the heart freed the mind sincer'd.
>
> — Gary Snyder (19 January 1956 GSJ)

Snyder discovered a love for books and reading in the wake of a crippling accident that happened when he was just seven years old. At age two (1932), he and his parents moved from San Francisco to Lake City near Seattle to live on a small dairy farm. The farmland had been clearcut in 1905, and Snyder remembers his father, Harold (d. 1968), "dynamiting stumps and pulling the shards out with a team. . . . Some of the stumps were ten feet high and eight or ten feet in diameter at the ground" (PW 116–17).[6] In June of 1937, while his father was burning brush and parts of stumps, the boy ran barefoot through a fifteen-foot diameter mound of ash, presuming it was cold. However, hot coals glowed at the center, and Gary burned both feet so badly he was unable to walk for four months: "At the beginning of that period I could barely read. At the end of that period I was reading books. I was drinking them up. And so that was my little slip into an understanding and appreciation of what you could learn from reading a lot, and I never stopped."[7]

His mother, Lois (b. 1906), took Gary on weekly trips from Lake City to the University District Goodwill and Seattle Public Library branch, keeping him connected to the world of books.[8] In boyhood, his reading mostly concerned North American history, Indians, and animals, and he found all these themes in the work of the Canadian nature writer, Ernest Thompson Seton (1860–1946). Snyder came to see Seton as a revolutionary who worked to change "'the myth of the white man' because he was 'on the side of nature, on the side of the Indians, on the side of the unconscious, on the side of the primitive.'"[9] An ability to imagine and appreciate different perspectives was one enduring outcome of Snyder's youthful appetite for knowledge through books.

When Snyder speaks of his formal education, he emphasizes library skills: "I went to Reed College in Oregon, I had some marvelous teachers, I learned how to use a library" (TRW 64). Snyder refers to libraries as "shrines" where one must "learn the rituals to approach layers of knowledge. . . . I suppose nine-tenths of your university education is finished when you learn how to use the bibliographies and the card catalogues."[10] When he moved to Kyoto to study Zen, Snyder eventually chose not to live in a monastery because "in a monastery you have no access to texts or dictionaries. . . . As an outsider-novice-foreigner, you are continually wrestling with problems of translation and terminology — you have to look things up" (TRW 100). Contrary to what may be a popular misunderstanding of Zen Buddhist life, Snyder enjoys extraordinary book knowledge and knows how to use it: "I'm a rural intellectual, I'm a shamanist Buddhist intellectual, but I'm still an intellectual. Ideas and language are the sharpest tools in my tool kit. So I use my tool kit to the best of its advantage."[11]

WARM SPRINGS AND THE CUL-DE-SAC OF INDIANA

> SNYDER: [Reed] was an intense enough education that I perceived that I would have to de-educate myself later. An education is only valuable if you're willing to give as much time to de-educating

yourself as you gave to educating yourself. So, you go to college for four years, you have to figure you're going to do four years coming off it, too.

GENESON: When you say "de-educate yourself," you mean what?

SNYDER: I mean get back in touch with people, with ordinary things: with your body, with the dirt, with the dust, with anything you like, you know — the streets. The streets or the farm, whatever it is. Get away from books and from the elite sense of being bearers of Western culture. . . . But, also, ultimately, into your mind, into *original mind* before any books were put into it, or before any language was invented.

— Gary Snyder, "The Real Work" (1977)

With his Class of 1951 BA degree from Reed College tucked away, Snyder took a summer job as a timber scaler with the U.S. Indian Service on the Warm Springs Reservation just east of the Cascade Range in north central Oregon.[12] As he looked back on that experience at the end of the year, he noted a frustration:

> Last summer I failed again, brought into contact with Warm Springs, the loggers, Indians, pine trees; I simply couldn't digest them. The Greek alphabet, Li Po, the I Ching, Thompson's motif-index, and that inexpressibly real countryside wouldn't fuse. It was maddening, and I ended up simply reading all the time.   (30 December 1951 GSJ)

This tension between book learning and other life experience would not soon go away, and Snyder's default position was to take refuge in myths and texts such as Stith Thompson's *Motif-Index of Folk-Literature.*[13]

Between the mid-August end of his Warm Springs work and his September departure for Indiana, Snyder took a trip to "the Olympics with Hoodlatch [Bob Allen], Cameron Creek & out — county fair, & ferryboat to Victoria, then back down the Sound & bus to Portland in the night, hitched off to SF Coast Hwy 101 — full of linguistics & graduate school plans" (20 August 1964 GSJ). The trip down 101 took " 4 rides" (29–30 August 1951 GSJ), and Snyder left San Francisco on 7 September after a visit with Philip Whalen (1923–2002). He arrived in Bloomington three days later.

In "On the Road with D. T. Suzuki," Snyder recounts a life-changing reading experience as he went east:

> I was standing by the roadside in the vast desert of eastern Nevada hitchhiking the old Route 40.... I was on my way to enter graduate school in Indiana, and here by the highway in the long wait for another ride I opened my new book. The size of the space and the paucity of cars gave me much time to read *Essays in Zen*, First Series. It catapulted me into an even larger space.[14]

In the introduction to Suzuki's first published collection of papers on Zen, Snyder read: "Zen in its essence is the art of seeing into the nature of one's own being, and it points the way from bondage to freedom."[15] Five pages later, Suzuki addresses one of Snyder's main concerns at the time by saying, "Zen proposes its solution by directly appealing to the facts of personal experience and not to book knowledge."[16] Soon Snyder would find that graduate school was pointing from freedom to bondage.

If Snyder was heading toward a scholarly career in anthropology and linguistics, Indiana was an excellent place to go. Dell Hymes (1927–2009), a comrade at Reed, was already there, and the two scholars shared "an apartment above a little Chinese restaurant on Kirkwood Avenue."[17] Soon after school started, Snyder paid his bills by teaching Turkish as a graduate assistant in the Army Airforce Language Program and assisting Professor Charles ("Carl") Voegelin with a course on American Indian languages, staying one step ahead of the other students as the course proceeded.[18]

Carl Voegelin (1906–1986), Snyder's academic advisor, was hired by Stith Thompson (1885–1976) in 1941 to develop the study of American Indian languages and cultures, and, in 1946, he founded the Department of Anthropology along Boasian lines.[19] Snyder also studied with semiotician Thomas Sebeok (1920–2001) and philosopher David Bidney (1908–1987).[20] Bidney's course in Western philosophy was especially valuable to Snyder; his notes from Bidney's lectures on philosophical idealism indicate he used this opportunity to articulate and hone by way of comparison his knowledge of East Asian thought.[21] Here he also began the Chinese language studies he would resume at Berkeley in 1953: "Of all things, morning; and a Chinese test in two hours" (26? November 1951 GSJ).

Snyder was ambivalent about this graduate school adventure from the start. The semester at Indiana in what he called "this cul-de-sac of Bloomington" confirmed he would not become a PhD anthropologist (30 December 1951 GSJ). On the day he arrived in Bloomington, he writes: "I am not interested in the scientific or objective aims of anthropology. I do concern myself with those areas of human experience which are not available to scientific study; and may be seen in religion, art, language. Anthropology has facts and a few methods; but not concepts capable of dealing with these" (10 September 1951 GSJ). By the end of October, Snyder knew he was not going to find what he was looking for in academia and decided he would stay "at least until the end of the semester" (30 October 1951 GSJ). On 16 January, he "dropped the boom" on his advisor who "was certainly gracious, understanding & sympathetic. . . . So I feel clear & good now that it's off my chest & by grace of god, Voegelin, & conscience, am no longer an anthropologist" (16 January 1952 GSJ).

A question of vocation was at the heart of Snyder's deliberations, for he continually measured academic life against a dawning realization that he might in fact be a poet. He put it this way at that time: "For vocation, however, I must admit it is poetry. As scholar one must keep his reputation continually going; writing papers, attending conventions, in short fitting into a managerial society. . . . The financial security that it represents means nothing to me" (26? November 1951 GSJ). A month later, in a conversation with Dell Hymes, he clarified his intentions:

> Poetry to bridge the experiences and the reality; including all of nature in this realm by extension (nature not as a stage, but as a direct part of humanity & human experience, or rather human experience as a part of it) using a technique of mythical reference, particularly to the animal-transformer & trickster myths of Amerinds, and factual material based on historical & anthropological studies. The key thing will be concrete objects & relationships, but seen through image & metaphor to their infinite extensions. And in doing this to forge a language that is colloquial, direct, and rich & precise, all in one time by use of symbols,

paradoxical and ambiguous juxtapositions, to charge the collo-
quial with greater & new meaning (29 December 1951 GSJ).

These convictions were further clarified by Snyder's reading at the time,
especially in D. T. Suzuki (1870–1966), R. H. Blyth (1898–1964), Alan
Watts (1915–1973), and Kenneth Rexroth (1905–1982). In fact, Snyder cred-
its his discovery of the Indiana-born Rexroth — whose work he first found in
the Indiana University library — as a major impetus behind his decision to
return to California: "His evocation of California landscape and the unique
combination of a classical and biological sensibility helped give me courage
to make the break from the academy, return to the West coast, and launch
myself into a life as worker/scholar."[22]

In planning for his return to the West Coast, Snyder resolved to "aim
at reading & practicing Zen, studying a general body of poetry . . . studying
poetic craft . . . and practic[ing] the forms & background reading in Orien-
tal cultures. . . . BUT always with one aim: Purifying my own vision & insight
into the object, the act — and increasing my skill in the manipulation of sym-
bols to the end of clarifying and communicating the perceived" (16 January
1952 GSJ). In this way he would hone his mind.

In the summers of 1952 and 1953, Snyder took work as a mountain look-
out in the Skagit District of Mt. Baker Forest.[23] In November 1954, he pub-
lished a notice in *Zen Notes*, the First Zen Institute of America newsletter,
entitled "Anyone with *Yama-Bushi* Tendencies: A Message from a California
member of special interest to those seeking jobs which leave time for study
and zazen."[24] While the job requires "physical and mental toughness" it also
allows "vast leisure": "The hardest work is chopping and packing firewood
(alpine trees are tough to split) from timberline to the station. . . . I found an
excellent period for zazen between sunrise 4:30 a.m. and the radio check-
in at 8 a.m. One must be able to pack a 50-lb. load and walk 10–15 miles a
day for this work, for you may be expected to go out and fight a fire. But as
a rule you can schedule 8 hours of study a day. . . . (They do hire women as
lookouts rarely)." Here one might strike an ideal balance between books and
other ways of knowing.

In the years between Reed and Kyoto (1952–56), Snyder read voraciously and had difficulty regaining the equilibrium he enjoyed as a lookout. As his journal entries indicate, this imbalance remained a matter of concern: "It is no good, this reading books, this learning to manipulate more & more symbols. Multiplications of unrealities by visionary means; illusion piled upon illusion" (17 November 1953 GSJ). Two months later, he strikes the same tone: "It is time I consider seriously the limitations of time & the idiocy of most printed matter & start a serious self-curtailment in reading activity.... Learn instead to rely on the oral tradition? It wd be interesting to try to do without books altogether — practice memorizing a few key poems and stories & one or two Buddhist sutras, & then recite them at proper times, & also pay attention, great attention, to the styles & devices of all people talking" (15 Jan 1954 GSJ). Yet the allure of book learning persisted, and after another two months we read, "I regret my intellectual failures, stand appalled at the books yet to be read, wait for the stew to get hot, hope for better poetry, curse my insincere heart (*ch'eng hsin*), & try to remember: there is no striving in the Tao" (14 March 1954).

Snyder's concern about his enmeshment in text-based culture is understandable, for his anthropological studies made him well-aware of "preliterate" civilizations and the fact that cultures with writing are an aberration from the world-historical norm.[25] Secondly, Buddhist traditions seemed to offer access to that norm, and, in Snyder's reading of Suzuki especially, these traditions appeared suspicious of books. Furthermore, Snyder's life as a working man called into question the value of his identity as an intellectual and scholar. Soon after arriving in Kyoto (and just days before becoming an official *deshi* of his teacher, Miura Rōshi), he writes: "I am a free man: in no fancy Buddhist sense perhaps, but in the old American individual sense--& I learned it not out of books but from the old guys who have been working hard & been broke all their lives, Ed McCullough, Roy Raymond, Blackie Burns, & many" (5 July 1956 GSJ). Snyder dedicates *Riprap and Cold Mountain Poems* (1959) to these and other men "*In the woods & at sea.*"

KYOTO AND THE LIBRARY AT RYOSEN-AN

Atop the mountain, another mountain.

— Zen saying

Snyder's interest in Asian religions began in the late 1940s, but it was not until the mid-1950s — when he was studying Asian languages at the University of California, Berkeley — that plans were set in motion for a voyage to Japan. In April 1955, Alan Watts (1915–1973) introduced Snyder to his former mother-in-law, Ruth Fuller Sasaki (1892–1967), at the Fairmont Hotel in San Francisco. This began the process of creating a place for Snyder at the First Zen Institute of America in Japan, her Kyoto research center at Ryosen-an, a branch temple of Daitoku-ji. There she built a library to support scholarly English translations of Rinzai texts.[26]

On 5 May 1956 (three days before his twenty-sixth birthday), Snyder sailed for Japan on the *Anita Maru* freighter, arrived in Kobe sixteen days later, and was met by "Ruth Sasaki & Washino-san at the pier" (21 May 1956 GSJ). Soon after Snyder took up residence at Rinko-in of Shōkoku-ji in Kyoto, he knew he would not become a resident monk. He writes: "With considerable relief I suddenly realize, this morning, that I should in no case become an *unsui*. The undeterminable coyote-nature of poetry & working-man life would make it a foolish thing. I have a karma of intransigence & city-&-mountain wandering that won't be put down. But I can't make it as a householder either — just a *vagrante*, a strolling vagrant, a dharma bum, I guess" (29 August 1956 GSJ). Since he felt unsuited to full-time monastic life, and conventional householder life did not seem quite right, he found a happy compromise that would allow peregrination between the monastery, Kyoto hills and streets, and the Ryosen-an library, where he could pursue life as a scholar-poet.[27]

Sasaki's Zen Institute provided an excellent setting for Snyder to find once more a balance between books and other approaches to learning. Sasaki's intentions are evident in the following statement from the opening chapter of her *Rinzai Zen Study for Foreigners in Japan*:

> I believe — unorthodoxly, no doubt — that the basic principles of Mahayana Buddhism as they are interpreted in Zen can be put

into words. To present these principles accurately, the first and most important thing is realization of them through practice, then clear intellectual understanding of what has been realized, and lastly ability to express this understanding simply and straightforwardly in words and terms that are as exact as possible.... When this has been successfully accomplished and when the basic Zen texts have been made available through translations of those who have prepared themselves for their work by Zen practice as well as linguistic studies, I feel sure that such westerners as have a natural relationship with Buddhism and with Zen will find they have been provided an unparalleled foundation for abstract thinking and a guide for daily life as well. Please do not mistake what I have said. These westerners will not gain through reading that realization which is the pivot of Zen today, as in the past. But perhaps through the expedient of words, the import of which they can grasp, they may achieve a clearer view of the depth and breadth of Zen teaching, and from there be led on to undertake such of the practices as their way of life permits.[28]

Sasaki hoped her endeavor would produce literate Zen Buddhists: practitioners who know their way around the tradition's texts, teachers, and temples. The Kyoto institute was largely based on this notion that "clear intellectual understanding of what has been realized" would enhance Zen practice and vice versa. She aimed to create a setting whereby Western students might enter the hermeneutic circle of religious life through active, open-ended engagement with the tools and techniques of Rinzai Zen.[29]

In Rinzai tradition, monks work mainly with kōans, questions posed by the teacher to better enable meditation practice.[30] A kōan is literally a "public case" or verbal expression that sets a standard whereby an awakened mind is both encouraged and confirmed by a teacher. Questions such as "Two hands clap and there is a sound, what is the sound of one hand clapping?" or "All things return to the One; where does the One return?" are posed to help the monk move toward an experience of *kenshō*, which means "seeing things as they are." Typically, *kenshō* is thought to mean "things as they are without conceptualization," though Victor Hori points out this could also mean "'without attachment' or 'without value judgment.'"[31] In fact, Hori argues against the idea that kōan practice is intended to take the student into a realm of prelinguistic consciousness and for the notion that this is a way to understand emptiness (*śūnyatā*) by wielding the sharp tool of language. Rather than a hindrance to liberation, language may be the vehicle that brings it about!

As Hori says, "The entire monastery kōan curriculum operates on the assumption that beginning monks start with a slight insight which further training systematically deepens and makes intelligible."[32] As soon as a monk passes a kōan, the master gives the apprentice yet another. Working full time, a monk can expect to work through the entire kōan curriculum in fifteen years. While there are many ways in which a monk might demonstrate his comprehension, the following report from Michel Mohr is very telling: "In a sermon given on December 4, 1994, Daigu Sōkō (Morinaga 1925–1995) Rōshi commented on the expression 'true understanding' (*cheng chien-chieh*, J. *shinshō no kenge*) that appears in *The Sayings of Lin-chi*. He confessed, 'What I am eagerly waiting for in the consultation room is for someone to come in possessed by an irrepressible joy [*osaerarenai hodo no yorokobi*]; I am not looking for an answer to the kōan."[158] To realize a kōan — to make it real — is itself an experience and expression of aliveness.

A monk may take from six months to several years to pass the first kōan (*shokan*). While early stages of this highly structured curriculum bring about and deepen awareness, more advanced stages are meant to undercut the monk's attachment to a sense of accomplishment by posing ever-more difficult challenges. Hori quotes Asahina Sōgen Rōshi on this point:

> Once a person feels he has attained some degree of satori, he
> becomes satisfied with the Dharma joy of this new world and
> thus it is hard for him to make any further advance. In the
> history of Zen, there are many who at this stage have sat down in
> self-satisfaction and stopped here. Such people think themselves
> fine as they are and therefore have no ability to help other
> people. Indeed on closer reflection [we see that] they have not
> even saved themselves. The Nantō [advanced-stage kōans] are a
> painful stick to the one who undertakes them. They make one

know what it means to say, 'Atop the mountain, another
mountain.'[34]

This process of letting go of any notion of self—even of a self that has awak-
ened—is concomitant with the work of arousing compassion for others.
Though one rarely hears this said with regard to Rinzai Zen (which has a
reputation for toughness), compassionate service to others is the endless
end (*telos*) of kōan work. As Hori says, "*Kenshō* is not the self's withdrawal
from the conventional world, but rather the selfless self breaking back into
the conventional world."[35]

Snyder's formal kōan practice commenced in 1959 with Oda Sessō Rōshi
(1901–1966), his teacher and the abbot of Daitoku-ji.[36] His most explicit
description of his engagement with this practice is in a letter to Katsunori
Yamazato (27 July 1987):

> I started formal Zen study with Oda Sesso Roshi at the begin-
> ning of the Rainy Season Sesshin (Nyusei Sesshin) 1959. He
> assigned me the "first koan" called "sound of one hand" or in
> Japanese "*sekishu onjo.*" I lived in the monastery for all the sesshin
> that year, but worked off days at the Zen Institute, Ryosen-an, a
> temple with a research wing and a small library that was just
> across the lane from the Daitoku-ji monastery. Morning and
> evening for over a year I went into the Roshi's room with nothing
> to share. Then I was fortunate enough to fully experience the
> import of this koan on June 11, 1960. I was shelving books in the
> stacks of the Ryosen-an library, and while pushing a book into its
> place suddenly and totally saw myself together with all the other
> entities of the universe each totally 'in place' and beautifully so,
> all fitting together in all directions, each full of wisdom, each
> transparent. That evening I ran to the monastery for the evening
> sanzen. Roshi took my answers and excitement with a charming
> nod, and started me on the 'checking koans' that help one deepen
> that breakthrough. And so I finished checking koans and moved
> into main case koans from the classic collections—each one a
> new adventure, though always referring back to the key insight.
> A few years later Oda Roshi called for a little ceremony with the

monks on which occasion he gave me my name "Chofu" or "Listen, Wind" and a *rakusu,* an abbreviated Buddhist robe, with an inscription on the back in calligraphy. This naming, and ceremony, usually delayed a few years to see if the student stays with it, is a traditional way for the teacher to acknowledge that the student has had a *kensho,* "seeing into true nature" — another name for satori. I have to laugh that such a wilderness lover as I should have had his first powerful Zen experience in the dim depths of a library! Rather appropriate, really. Zen study actually just begins and continues through hundreds of koans, but the passing of koans is not the real point. Zen practice should lead to a full ripening of insight and character and capacity of communication, and it never ends.[37]

THE LIBRARY IN THE FOREST AT KITKITDIZZE

Ideal Paradise Heaven

A mountain range, glaciers,
snowfields, meadows, talus, benches,
— wind and sleet sometimes blow —
    and every few hundred yards
    a door
that leads into a vast Library
    within with reading rooms
        &
coffee.
    — Gary Snyder (27 April 1988 GSJ)

When he returned to live in Northern California in December 1968, Snyder migrated with family and friends to the San Juan Ridge in Nevada County and began to build his homestead, Kitkitdizze. In an essay that describes the initial work of organizing his life on the Ridge — the land was ritually "opened" 19 June 1969 — Snyder notes the fundamental import of his library: "I set up my library and wrote poems and essays by lantern light, then went out periodically, lecturing and teaching around the country. I thought of my home as a well-concealed base camp from which I raided university treasuries. We named our place Kitkitdizze, after the aromatic little shrub" (APIS 255).[38] For Snyder, libraries are basic because, for moderns, books often perform a role played by elders in traditional societies:

> The original context of teaching must have been narratives told by elders to young people gathered around the fire. Our fascination with TV may just be nostalgia for that flickering light. My grandparents didn't tell stories around the campfire before we went to sleep — their house had an oil furnace instead, and a small collection of books. I got into their little library to entertain myself. In this huge old occidental culture, our teaching elders are books. For many of us, books are our grandparents! In the library there are useful, demanding, and friendly elders available to us. I like to think of people like Bartolomé de las Casas, who passionately defended the Indians of New Spain, or Baruch Spinoza, who defied the traditions of Amsterdam to be a philosopher. (And in my days as an itinerant forest worker I made especially good use of libraries: they were warm and stayed open late at night). (APIS 201; see also PW 61–62)

It is not insignificant that Snyder describes his base camp and the library it houses as "well-concealed." Intellectual life, the production of culture, and a rhetoric (if not the reality) of solitude are commonly associated in a variety of places and times. In his preface to the *Selected Poems* of Lew Welch (1926–1971?), Snyder captures these associations: "Lew really achieved the meeting of an ancient Asian sage-tradition, the 'shack simple' post-frontier back country out-of-work workingman's style, and the rebel modernism of art."[39] The poet or philosopher-sage is typically imagined as a hutted back woodsman cut off from ordinary ties. Think, for example, of Heraclitus (fl. c. 500 BCE), Lao-Tzu (fl. c. 500 BCE), Jerome (c. 347–420), Han Shan (627–650), Saigyō (1118–1190), Bashō (1644–1694), Thoreau (1817–1862), and Nanao (1923–2008).[40]

Snyder's library in the forest is indeed remote — "off the grid" — and the poet-scholar relishes his solitude. As with any supposed isolate, his efforts are in fact supported by innumerable social interactions and networks

ranging from family and immediate neighbors to activists, artists, and pro-
ducers of culture and diverse sorts of knowledge worldwide. It is paradoxi-
cally fitting that Snyder's notoriety makes possible his uninterrupted time
alone.[41]

Snyder started building his personal library at age nineteen, and the
Kitkitdizze library began in a corner of his house where his earliest acqui-
sitions still adorn a wall.[42] In 1982, when the new Ring of Bone Zendo was
finished and the local Zen group moved out of Snyder's "barn-dō," Snyder
converted the barn into a den (see frontispiece). In addition to the large area
that is his study proper, there is a room with a built-in bed (his son Kai's for-
mer room) where mountaineering equipment is now stored. This room is
on the left as one enters the library through the sliding glass door at the end
of a path between the barn and house. At the bedroom door one may turn
right, walk between stacks with Californiana on the left and Asian litera-
ture on the right, and step into an addition that was Carole Koda's study.

If one does not turn right but walks straight ahead, the first item of note
is an altar on the left just before entering the main room. The image in this
small homemade altar is that of the Dharma-protector, Fudō-myōō.[43] The
altar sits on a table with a vajra, feathers, pinecones, stones, incense, and lists
of names of those ailing and deceased.[44] Leaning next to the altar against the
wall is Alan Watts's *shakujō* (monk's walking staff).[45]

With another step, one enters the main workspace. To the left is a small
rolling table with Snyder's laptop, and a modest desk sits just beyond that.
Along the outside wall on the left one finds a work table with file cabi-
nets and bins for correspondence. A sliding glass door that opens onto a
deck — where one may pick up the path that ends on the opposite side — is
straight ahead. In the corner on the right is a comfortable chair with a read-
ing lamp beside a wood-burning stove. The setup is tidy and efficient.[46]

In addition to the opportunity to peruse books, decipher marginalia,
and sort through reading notes, my fieldwork was motivated by curiosity
about whether the shelf order of books would somehow represent Snyder's
approach to ordering the various domains of knowledge. Might the physical
layout of this library provide a map of Snyder's mind? The answer is by no
means obvious, and I dare not venture too far in this direction. However, it
is, I think, telling that poetry is shelved either on bottommost shelves or in

a dark room behind the poet's desk. Perhaps this arrangement is consistent with Snyder's notion that poetry rises up from the unconscious to reveal the mysterious and wild backcountry territory of Mind.

NOTES

1. Ezra Pound, *ABC of Reading* (New York: New Directions, 1960 [1934]), 81.

2. Gary Snyder, *The Real Work: Interviews & Talks, 1964–1979*, ed. Wm. Scott McLean (New York: New Directions, 1980).

3. Franz Boas (1858–1942) traveled to to British Columbia in 1886 and began field-work with the Kwakiutl that engaged him for a period of fifty years. See *A Franz Boas Reader: The Shaping of American Anthropology, 1883-1911*, ed. George Stocking, Jr. (Chicago: University of Chicago Press, 1974).

4. Mark Gonnerman, "'On the Path, Off the Trail': Gary Snyder's Education and the Makings of American Zen" (PhD dissertation, Stanford University, 2004).

5. Robert Sattelmeyer, *Thoreau's Reading: A Study in Intellectual History with Bibliographical Catalogue* (Princeton: Princeton University Press, 1988). Sattelmeyer's book contains a catalogue of 1,478 entries, plus two indices and bibliography. Snyder's Kitkitdizze library — intact from the time he started collecting around the age of nineteen — contains approximately five thousand volumes.

6. Snyder gives the 1905 clearcut date in Nicholas O'Connell, "Gary Snyder," in *At the Field's End: Interviews with Twenty Pacific Northwest Writers* (Seattle: Madrona Publishers, 1987), 309. Barbara Novak begins her discussion of axe-and-stump icons in American art with the following observation: "While Thoreau meditates on his use of the axe to make himself a dwelling place in nature, he also mourns lost trees, which he misses like human beings. National identity is both constructed and threatened by the double-edged symbol of progress, that axe that destroys and builds, builds and destroys. The paradoxes of this relationship to nature are sharply revealed in the 'civilizing' of the land. Progress toward America's future literally undercut its past" (*Nature and Culture: American Landscape and Painting, 1825–1875* [New York: Oxford University Press, 1980], 157).

7. Gary Snyder, "The Education of the Poet," Lecture at the Guggenheim Museum, New York City, 6 May 1986 (cassette tape recording). In a conversation on 12 July 1998, Snyder elaborated on this story: "After the accident there was nothing for me to do except read. We didn't have a radio or anything, so I started reading books recommended by the children's librarian. After a few weeks or maybe a month the activity of reading became transparent in an instant and it was as if I was taking off in a fleeing spaceship in hyperdrive. The processors kicked in and I found myself reading at the speed of speaking. My mother still remembers that I called her and exclaimed, 'I can read!' I quickly moved on to reading adult books like *Mutiny on*

the Bounty (not the children's edition). We never bought books, for that seemed like a luxury. I used the public library until college, though in high school I owned my own bird and tree books."

8. A certificate from the Seattle Public Library hung on the wall of Snyder's office at the University of California, Davis: "This is to certify that Gary Snyder has satisfactorily fulfilled all requirements of the vacation reading club for the summer of 1938. [Signed,] Ann Wilson, Children's Librarian." The following books are listed in pencil on back: "Hawes, *Dark Frigate*; Hawes, *Mutineers*; Malory, *Boys King Arthur*; Kipling, *Jungle Book*; Hawk, *Gold Trail*; Tonsey, *Chinkey the Banker Pony*; Murray, *Shoes for Sandy*; Drummond, *Monkey that Would Not Kill*." And this from John P. O'Grady: "I was an extensive reader as a kid.... It was a standard Saturday trip to the university branch of the public library to pick up a new round of books for me. I took out ten or twelve every week. I read John Muir very early on and was suitably inspired. I was inspired by how light he went.... I read the biography *John of the Mountains* [Linnie Marsh Wolfe, 1938] when it came out. I also read a number of lesser-known people: Steward Edward White's novels about the Pacific Northwest and the West. Gad, I read everything. H. L. Davis, *The Winds of Morning*, a great novel about eastern Oregon. It catches the flavor of twenties and thirties eastern Oregon sheep and ranch culture really nicely.... Now get this (laughs): The Tugboat Annie series of stories, which were based on Puget Sound and which I read as a kid living in Puget Sound, came out serially in the *Saturday Evening Post*. (Laughs.) I also read some of the standard fare of western writers, including Zane Grey. Oh, and Oliver La Farge — the novel *Laughing Boy* [1929], which was a very important novel to a lot of people and was quite a success in its own time. I'm sure it inspired D. H. Lawrence and a whole bunch of American Southwest lovers of that era, and brought a very sympathetic eye to Native Americans of the Southwest. It also has, as I recall, maybe the first account of a peyote vision, a peyote trip, in mainstream American literature — that's way back there. I was doing this a year or two before I discovered D. H. Lawrence and Robinson Jeffers, prior to reading standard literary fare, but it's more like what a kid reads when he browses around" ("Living Landscape: An Interview with Gary Snyder," *Western American Literature* 33/3 [1998]: 279–80).

9. Snyder quoted by Bert Almon, *Gary Snyder* (Boise, Idaho: Boise State University, 1979), 6–7, from a 1975 interview with Snyder by Rolan Husson, "Amerique, Ile Tortue," *Entretiens* 34 (1975), 225–32.

10. James McKenzie, "Moving the World a Millionth of an Inch: Gary Snyder," in *The Beat Vision: A Primary Sourcebook,* ed. Arthur and Kit Knight (New York: Paragon House, 1987), 16. In this same interview, Snyder also mentions his "great respect for the possibilities of libraries, for the storing and transmission of lore" and says he would like to write an essay where he will "put in a 40,000 year anthropological

perspective what universities are. They're like giant kivas that people descend into for four years to receive the transmission of the lore" (p. 15).

11. O'Connell, *At the Field's End*, 319. One thinks here of Max Weber's observation that the scholar as "craftsman still owns his own tools (in essence, a library), just as in the past the artisan in industry did." This observation is embedded in Weber's worry that bureaucratization and state-sponsored scholarship will eventuate in "the same development [that] . . . takes place in all capitalist concerns: the 'separation of the worker from his means of production.'" Weber senses a shift in the spirit of scholarship from vocation to profession, a development that, he says as he delivers this lecture at the University of Munich in 1918, "is now fully under way" (Max Weber, "Science as a Vocation," in *Max Weber's 'Science as a Vocation',* ed. Peter Lassman and Irving Velody [London: Unwin Hyman, 1989 (1919)], 5).

12. "11 June 1951–17 August 1951. Timber Scaler for U.S. Indian Service. Cecil Atkeson and Nick Welder, Warm Springs, Oregon 1.25 hr" (GS LIBRARY/ Poetry/ Criticism/ GS Notes: "Work Record," Card 5.12). "The Warm Springs Reservation lies east of the summit of the Cascade Mountains in north central Oregon. It is roughly thirty miles square, with an area of 563,800 acres. The eastern slopes of the Cascades, which are included in the reservation, are covered with fir and yellow pine forests. The timber is sold by the Indians, under a sustained-yield program, to two private logging companies. Both of these companies operate mills on the reservation and provide some wage work for Indians" (Kathrine French and David French, "The Warm Springs Indian Community: Will it Be Destroyed?" *The American Indian* VII/2 [1955]: 4).

13. Stith Thompson, *Motif-Index of Folk-Literature* (Helsinki: Suomalainen Tiedeakatemia Academia Scientiarum Fennica, 1932–1936). While defining his undergraduate thesis topic ("The Dimensions of a Haida Myth" [1951], published by Grey Fox Press as *He Who Hunted Birds in His Father's Village* in 1979), Snyder became aware of Thompson's encyclopaedic reference in world folklore. It was not available in the Reed College Library, so he wrote to Indiana University in Bloomington where Stith Thompson was teaching to ask if the *Index* was still in print. Time passed, and six paperback volumes appeared in Snyder's mail, a gift of this great reference work from Thompson along with an encouraging letter. By that time it had been decided that Snyder would be heading to Indiana for graduate school in linguistics and anthropology in the fall of 1951. Unfortunately, Thompson was on leave the year Snyder arrived in Indiana.

14. Gary Snyder, "On the Road with D. T. Suzuki," in *A Zen Life: D. T. Suzuki Remembered,* ed. Masao Abe (New York: Weatherhill, 1986), 207. See APIS 153 for another story from this hitchhike to Indiana.

15. D. T. Suzuki, *Essays in Zen Buddhism: First Series* (New York: Grove Press, 1961

[1949]), 13. This introduction is a 1911 lecture entitled "Zen Buddhism as the Purifier and Liberator of Life," first published in *The Eastern Buddhist*, the journal Suzuki founded in 1921.

16. Suzuki, *Essays in Zen Buddhism*, 18.

17. Dell Hymes, "A Coyote Who Can Sing," in *Gary Snyder: Dimensions of a Life*, ed. Jon Halper (San Francisco: Sierra Club Books, 1991), 393.

18. "Sept. 20, 1951 to November first 1951. Graduate Assistant, Indiana University, U.S. Army Airforce Language Program, teaching Turkish" (GS LIBRARY/ Poetry/ Criticism/ GS Notes: "Work Record," Card 5.13); Hymes, "A Coyote Who Can Sing," 393.

19. On Voegelin's Boasian program for Amerindian language studies, see Charles Voegelin, "Training in Anthropological Linguistics," *American Anthropologist* 54 (1952): 322–27.

20. Bidney's papers have been collected as David Bidney, *Theoretical Anthropology* (New York: Schocken Books, 1967 [1953]).

21. "Plato misses Tathata concept; hence fails to see extension of appearance into self contained ideal (suchness) form, not removed but an integral part of, the sunyata reality.-->difference between Platonic & Brahmanic (also Mahayana) idealism. --how does Plato make his metaphysical reality have anything to do with people (all imitations). Myths used as allegory by Plato to illustrate metaphysical truth.--> practical philosopher. K'ung uses parables (cf pancantantra) but not myths" (GS LIBRARY/Subjects/Philosophy: Bidney lecture [1952]).

22. Snyder, "Kenneth Rexroth," *Kyoto Review* 15 (Fall 1982): 2, cited in Katsunori Yamazato, "Seeking a Fulcrum: Gary Snyder and Japan (1956-1975)," (PhD diss., University of California, Davis, 1987), 36n12. Snyder was moved by Rexroth's *The Signature of All Things* (New York: New Directions, 1950), which, on its final page, contains the poem "Further Advantages of Learning": "One day in the Library, / Puzzled and distracted, / Leafing through a dull book, / I came on a picture / Of the vase containing Buddha's relics. A chill / Passed over me. I was // Haunted by the touch of / A calm I cannot know, / The opening into that / Busy place of a better world."

23. See John Suitor, *Poets on the Peaks: Gary Snyder, Philip Whalen & Jack Kerouac in the North Cascades* (Washington, DC: Counterpoint, 2002).

24. Gary Snyder, "Anyone with *Yama-Bushi* Tendencies," *Zen Notes* I/11 (1954): 3. My thanks to Tim Hogan for finding and mailing this to me from out of the blue. Snyder lists the following "lookout books" in his 16 August 1952 journal: "tao te ching / myths & symbols in indian art [Zimmer] / meeting of east and west [Northrop] / white goddess [Graves] / golden bough [Frazer] / 1000 faces [Campbell] /. essays in zen [Suzuki]/." There is no list from the 1953 lookout period, though in the

journal one finds: "Now I am reading *Walden* which is a novelty & a delight" (17 July 1953 GSJ).

25. Following the work of Munro Edmonson, *Lore: An Introduction to the Science of Folklore and Literature* (New York: Holt, Rinehart and Winston, 1971), Walter Ong writes: "Our literate world of visually processed sounds has been totally unfamiliar to most human beings, who always belonged, and often belong to this oral world. Homo sapiens has been around for some 30,000 years, to take a conservative figure. The oldest script, Mesopotamian cuneiform, is less than 6,000 years old (the alphabet less than 4,000). Of all the tens of thousands of languages spoken in the course of human history only a tiny fraction — Edmonson (1971: 323) calculates about 106 — have ever been committed to writing to a degree sufficient to have produced a literature, and most have never been written at all. Of the 4,000 or so languages spoken today, only around 78 have a literature (Edmonson 1971: 332). . . . Those who think of the text as the paradigm of all discourse need to face the fact that only the tiniest fraction of languages have ever been written or ever will be. Most have disappeared or are fast disappearing, untouched by textuality. Hard-core textualism is snobbery, often hardly disguised" ("Writing Is a Technology That Restructures Thought," in *The Linguistics of Literacy*, ed. Pamela Downing, Susan D. Lima and Michael Noonan [Philadelphia: John Benjamins Publishing Company, 1992], 296).

26. See Isabel Stirling, *Zen Pioneer: The Life & Works of Ruth Fuller Sasaki* (Emeryville, CA: Shoemaker & Hoard, 2006).

27. Philip Yampolsky remembers that while "Gary was a devoted Zen student, taking part in the monastery *sesshins* and studying directly under a Zen Master, he allowed ample time to devote to his writing and to indulge in the diversions Kyoto had to offer: drinks at a jazz coffee shop, the Belami, which played the records of Chet Baker; visits to tiny drinking establishments that served quantities of sake, including the delicious unrefined white milky version known as *doburoku*, which was splendidly inexpensive" ("Kyoto, Zen, Snyder," in *Gary Snyder: Dimensions of a Life,* ed. Jon Halper [San Francisco: Sierra Club Books, 1991], 64–65). In a statement read at Philip Yampolsky's memorial service in the fall of 1996, Snyder writes: "I saw Phil when I first arrived in Kyoto in 1956, my Japanese in pitiful condition, imagining myself to be in some ways knowledgeable about the Far East from reading books. . . . He worked part-time for Mrs. Sasaki, but he was really in Japan to do his Columbia University dissertation on Hui Neng, the Sixth Patriarch of early Ch'an. I learned more of Philip's background as time went on, and was charmed to discover the Franz Boas connection. Philip was fully in tune with the Boas heritage, what with his dedication to rational clarity, social compassion, and a political conscience" ("Remembering Philip Yampolsky," 11 November 1998 email from Gary Snyder).

28. Ruth Fuller Sasaki, *Rinzai Zen Study for Foreigners in Japan* (Kyoto: First Zen Institute of America in Japan, 1960), 5–6.

29. "The hermeneutical consciousness culminates not in methodological sureness of itself, but in the same readiness for experience that distinguishes the experienced man from the man captivated by dogma" (Hans-Georg Gadamer, *Truth and Method*, trans. Joel Weinsheimer and Donald G. Marshall (New York: Crossroad, 1992 [1960], 362)).

30. Rinzai and Sōtō Zen are typically distinguished by the idea that Rinzai emphasizes kōan practice and Sōtō does not: "One reason for the demise of *kōan* commentary in Sōtō Zen was the success of a late eighteenth- and nineteenth-century reform movement that sought, in the interests of unification, to standardize procedures of formal dharma transmission and eliminate the transmission of esoteric lore (including *kōan*) that had previously distinguished various branches of the Sōtō school. In their zeal to create a new identity for the Sōtō school as a whole, reformers began to celebrate the teachings of the 'founding patriarch' Dōgen (1200–1253), which they cast in a way that emphasized the differences between Sōtō and Rinzai Zen. Perhaps because influential Rinzai reformers such as Hakuin Ekaku (1685–1768) were stressing the importance of contemplating phrases in their own tradition, the Sōtō Side sought to distance itself from *kōan* as much as possible, characterizing Dōgen's approach to Zen practice as one of 'just sitting' (J. *shikantaza*). The irony is that *Dōgen's Treasury of the Eye of the True Dharma (Shōbōgenzō)*, the work that modern Soto Zen reveres as its bible, is in good measure a collection of comments on the Chinese *kung-an*, although the comments were delivered in the vernacular for the benefit of Japanese disciples" (T. Griffith Foulk, "The Form and Function of Koan Literature: A Historical Overview," in *The Kōan: Texts and Contexts in Zen Buddhism*, ed. Steven Heine and Dale S. Wright [Oxford: Oxford University Press, 2000], 25).

31. G. Victor Sōgen Hori, "*Kōan* and *Kenshō* in the Rinzai Zen Curriculum," in *The Kōan: Texts and Contexts in Zen Buddhism*, ed. Steven Heine and Dale S. Wright (Oxford: Oxford University Press, 2000), 284. See also the discussion of *kenshō* in Ruth Fuller Sasaki and Isshû Miura, *Zen Dust: The History of the Kōan and Kōan Study in Rinzai (Lin-Chi) Zen* (New York: Harcourt, Brace & World, 1966), 228–30.

32. G. Victor Sōgen Hori, "Teaching and Learning in the Rinzai Zen Monastery," *Journal of Japanese Studies* 20/1 (1994): 6n.1.

33. Michel Mohr, "Emerging from Nonduality: Kōan Practice in the Rinzai Tradition since Hakuin," in *The Kōan: Texts and Contexts in Zen Buddhism*, ed. Steven Heine and Dale S. Wright (Oxford: Oxford University Press, 2000), 248. Morinaga tells of his own experience: "One night I sat, in the middle of the night, a lump of fatigue sitting on a zazen cushion, both head and consciousness were in a haze, and I could not have roused the desire for satori if I had to when, suddenly, the fog cleared and a world of lucidity opened itself. Clearly seeing, clearly hearing, it was yet a world

in which there was no 'me'! I cannot fully explain that time. To venture an explana-
tion would be to err somewhere. The one thing I am sure of is that in this instant,
the functioning of the heart with which I was born came into play in its purest form.
I could not keep still in my uncomfortable joy. Without waiting for the morning
wake-up bell, I made an unprecedented call on the roshi. . . . When I arrived, Roshi
was still in bed. I crawled right up to his pillow and said very simply, 'I finally saw.'
Roshi sprang from his bed, examined me for a time, as if with a glare, and said, 'it's
from now on. From now on. Sit strongly.' This is all he said to me. From then on for
the next sixteen years, until my fortieth year and Zuigan Roshi's death at age eighty-
seven, whether in the monastery or back in the temple, I continued koan practice"
(*Novice to Master: An Ongoing Lesson in the Extent of My Own Stupidity*, trans.
Belenda Attaway Yamakawa [Boston: Wisdom Publications, 2002], 106–07).

34. Victor Hori, *Zen Sand: The Book of Capping Phrases for Kōan Practice* (Honolulu:
University of Hawai'i Press, 2003), 22–23.

35. Hori, *Zen Sand*, 7.

36. Snyder dedicated *Earth House Hold* (1969) to his teacher, "For Oda Sessō Rōshi
(1901–1966) / "the mysterious further higher peak." Irmgard Schlögel writes, "Sessō
Rōshi was a man of few words, and relied on teaching by personal example. He never
taught or talked abstract theories, but he embodied and lived them" ("A Zen Mas-
ter [Oda Sessō Rōshi]," *Studies in Comparative Religion* 1/4 [1967]: 181–83).

37. Snyder to Katsunori Yamazato (27 July 1987) in "Seeking a Fulcrum," 89–90. The
"checking koans" (*sassho*) Snyder refers to are a way for the rōshi "to confirm that
the insight is actually the monk's own and not something he is repeating at second
hand" (Hori, *Zen Sand*, 18). Snyder mentions this library experience in PW 151–52.

38. Snyder's 1969–71 journals indicate at least one such raiding trip a year: November
4–December 7, 1969: to River Falls, Northfield, St. Paul, Collegeville, Madison, Ste-
vens Point & New York, New Jersey, Buffalo; April 3–25, 1970: to Chicago, Long
Island, Bloomington, Fort Collins, Denver; November 4–23, 1971: to Montreal,
Portland, Orono, Colby, Wellesly, Boston, Walden, Denison, Bowling Green.

39. Gary Snyder, "Preface," in *Lew Welch: Selected Poems*, ed. Donald Allen (Bolinas,
CA: Grey Fox Press, 1976), n.p.

40. The recluse scholar-poet is a pervasive image in Chinese art, inspired in large part
by Lao Tzu, who, according to legend, was himself a librarian. Around 500 BCE,
he advised anyone who would withdraw from society to imagine themselves in a
region where "the next place might be so near at hand that one could hear the cocks
crowing in it, the dogs barking; but the people would grow old and die without ever
having been there" (*Tao Te Ching*, chapter 80, trans. Arthur Waley). Commenting
on this image, Ann Cline writes: "What began after Lao Tzu as a trickle of gen-
tleman recluses had, a thousand years later, turned into a steady stream. Educated

cosmopolites retired to the mountains and there recorded their lives in verse and in painting. The latter formed a major genre that illustrates the recluse poet's world: most typically a tiny hut set in some particularly interesting aspect of a vast mountain terrain crisscrossed by narrow paths, along which one or two human figures amble, gazing out at the vista. This recluse living apart from the world, aware of it (and later, it aware of him) but participating only in his immediate world, would eventually extend his influence not only back to the cities he abandoned, but to distant shores — Japanese and European" (*A Hut of One's Own: Life Outside the Circle of Architecture* [Cambridge, MA: MIT Press, 1997], 4). Cline traces Lao Tzu's influence on European conceptions of the solitary scholar to the seventeenth-century importation of porcelain, a technical advance in ceramics much admired in Europe and Japan: "Many porcelain imports had small snippets of poetry painted on them, which the Japanese could translate, but the Europeans generally could not. Instead, the Europeans more readily understood the images of huts and mountain landscapes that also frequently decorated these treasures" (*A Hut of One's Own*, 11–12).

These decorations seemed readily decipherable because there was already a Western tradition joining solitude and insight. In the Bible, Moses is on his own on the top of Mount Sinai, John the Baptist cries alone in the wilderness, and Saint Paul goes solo (but for his donkey) on the road from Jerusalem to Damascus. In the Middle Ages, it was thought a life of separation from society was most authentically Christian, so the monastery, the hermitage, and the reclusorium were major medieval sites for the production of religious knowledge. *Monk*, from the Greek *monus*, means "alone."

With the creation of the private study, the college, the laboratory, and the observatory in the Rennaisance, the relative isolation of the scholar strengthened the notion that "enforced solitariness" (a phrase used by Robert Burton in *The Anatomy of Melancholy* [1628]) was a necessary correlate of great learning. At the dawn of the modern period in the seventeenth century, Descartes cogitated "alone in a stove-heated room," and Newton was famous for autodidactically dwelling in his Trinity College rooms (see Steven Shapin, "'The Mind Is Its Own Place': Science and Solitude in Seventeenth-Century England," *Science in Context* 4/1 [1990]: 191–218).

In New England, Emerson taught that "greatness is the fruit of solitary effort" (in Maurice Gonnaud, *An Uneasy Solitude*, trans. Laurence Rosenwald [Princeton: Princeton University Press, 1987 [1964], 193). Thoreau devoted a chapter of *Walden* to "Solitude" (though he was seldom very much alone), and when John Muir — who crossed from Edinburgh to Wisconsin at age eleven in 1849 — sauntered to California in 1868, he was wandering on his own. In 1901, William James — who crossed back over the Atlantic to Edinburgh for his Gifford Lectures — defined religion as "the feelings, acts, and experiences of individual men *in their solitude*, so far as they apprehend themselves to stand in relation to whatever they may consider the divine"

(*The Varieties of Religious Experience* [Cambridge, MA: Harvard University Press, 1985 [1902], 34, emphasis mine).

To come full circle, there is a hut ("Ditch Hut") at Kitkitdizze where Snyder retreats so that even his neighbors might not find him. While standing in his library in 1998, Snyder told me he sometimes thinks of himself as the kind of "outlaw-poet-scholar" one encounters in Chinese folktales.

41. I was once reminded of this while at a bookstore in San Francisco's Japantown. Two photographs of Snyder at a 1993 book signing with the following caption were visible though the store's front windows: "Gary Snyder makes a rare public appearance to read and sign copies of his popular titles at Kinokuniya bookstore." Snyder has long had a claim to fame as a Buddhist and literary celebrity, but his public appearances are not all that rare. The notion that he seldom appears in public indicates the Snyder of myth, for that Gary Snyder confirms the public's hope that there are in fact individuals who exemplify mythic ideals.

42. Scott McLean remembers, "And when the library was in the main house and one borrowed books, they all smelled like smoke and talk and songs and jokes, and this lent a rather special frame to the reading" ("'Thirty Miles of Dust': There is no Other Life," in Jon Halper, ed. *Gary Snyder: Dimensions of a Life* [San Francisco: Sierra Club Books, 1991], 130).

43. Snyder writes about Fudō in exhibition notes accompanying his contributions to the Ring of Bone Zendo Dharma Art Exhibit in September 1987: "The Yamabushi [monks who sleep in the mountains] have their own lore and practice of Fudō. For the other Buddhist followers, he is seen as a Dharma-protector, a grim but compassionate tough guy, punk or street-Buddha, no bullshit, the noose is said to be a lasso and save some folks from hell whether they want it or not, or said to be for binding up destructive passions. Actually the noose stands for The Precepts. The sword is the same sword as Manjushri yields, cutting through delusion and foolishness. Such a figure appropriate to this worst of centuries, a Buddha of enlightened determination who will not back off, who is not averse to confronting the mass murder of Ukrainians, of Jews, of Cambodians, and the threat of nuclear holocaust. Who can sit down with the generals and dictators and talk even tougher than they. And then laugh about it, and convert and forgive. Or so I like to imagine" (Stanford University, Allen Ginsberg Papers, Series 1, B295, F3).

44. From Snyder's Sunday, 28 July 1996 journal: "Did an early morning okyo [chanting service] for Mark Kirihara, Hisao Kanaseki, Paul Shepard (& Yuiko Yampolsky called to tell me--yesterday--that Phil would soon be dead) — so, Philip Yampolsky. & 'all those killed during the wars' — Banrei Eko Daihishin Dharani 5 times."

45. There is a note on this *shakujō* by Snyder for the September 1987 Ring of Bone Zendo Dharma Art Exhibit: "The staff leaning in the corner, with rings on the top,

is an old Asia-wide Buddhist pilgrims' staff also called (in Skt) Khakkhara. It can be seen in 5th century paintings in the caves at Tun Huang. The jangling of the sistrum-like rings on top were to warn animals and insects to slip away and not get accidentally stepped on. It was often used in early times for begging, a mendicant would shake the rings in front of the door of a house. In the hands of the Yamabushi it is useful as one of the ritual objects employed in exorcising demonic forces. This Shakujo used to belong to Alan Watts" (Stanford University Archives, Allen Ginsberg Papers, Series 1, B295, F3).

46. With its bedroom, altar and stacks, the layout is akin to the famous library of Michel de Montaigne, established in Bordeaux in 1571: "The library is first and foremost a place of solitude. In fact, it is part of a whole complex of solitary dwelling, which consists of the tower's three stories. This solitary complex includes a chapel on the first (ground) floor, a bedroom ("where I often lie down to be alone") on the second floor, and the library, with a study and wardrobe adjoining it on the third" (Adi Opher, "A Place of Knowledge Re-Created: The Library of Michel de Montaigne," *Science in Context* 4/1 [1990]: 169). Significantly, Snyder's library sits right on the ground.

BIBLIOGRAPHY OF REFERENCES
CITED IN TEXT AND NOTES

Almon, Bert. *Gary Snyder*. Boise, ID: Boise State University, 1979.

Austin, J. L. *How to Do Things With Words*. Cambridge, MA: Harvard University Press, 1962.

Bahk, Jane. "Vonnegut Bemoans 'Creeping Illiteracy.'" *Campus Report* [Stanford University] (19 May 1993): n.p.

Bashō. *Back Roads to Far Towns*. Trans. Cid Corman and Kamaike Susumu. New York: Grossman Publishers, 1968.

Basso, Keith R. *Wisdom Sits in Places: Landscape and Language Among the Western Apache*. Albuquerque: University of New Mexico Press, 1996.

Bersani, Leo, and Ulysse Dutoit. *Caravaggio's Secrets*. Cambridge, MA: MIT Press, 1998.

Beyer, Stephen. *The Cult of Tara: Magic and Ritual in Tibet*. Berkeley: University of California Press, 1973.

Bidney, David. *Theoretical Anthropology*. New York: Schocken Books, 1967 [1953].

Bielefeldt, Carl. "Dogen's 'The Mountains and Rivers Sutra.'" MA Thesis, University of California, Berkeley, 1972.

Boas, Franz. *A Franz Boas Reader: The Shaping of American Anthropology, 1883–1911*, Ed. George Stocking Jr. Chicago: University of Chicago Press, 1974.

Boulding, Kenneth. *The Image*. Ann Arbor: University of Michigan Press, 1961 [1956].

Bush, Susan. "Yet Again 'Streams and Mountains Without End.'" *Artibus Asiae* XLVIII (1987): 197–223.

Butler, Judith. *Excitable Speech: A Politics of the Performative*. New York: Routledge, 1997.

Calinescu, Matei. *Rereading*. New Haven: Yale University Press, 1993.

Castro, Michael. *Interpreting the Indian: Twentieth-Century Poets and the Native American*. Albuquerque: University of New Mexico Press, 1983.

Chang, Garma C. C. *The Buddhist Teaching of Totality: The Philosophy of Hua Yen Buddhism*. University Park: Pennsylvania State University Press, 1971.

Cleary, Thomas. *Entry Into the Inconceivable: An Introduction to Hua-yen Buddhism*. Honolulu: University of Hawaii Press, 1983.

_____, trans. *Entry into the Realm of Reality, the Guide: A Commentary on the Gandavyuha by Li Tongxuan*. Boston: Shambhala, 1989.

_____, trans. *Entry into the Realm of Reality, the Text: The Gandavyuha, the final book of the Avataṃsaka Sutra*. Boston: Shambhala, 1989.

_____, trans. *The Flower Ornament Scripture.* 3 vols. Boston: Shambhala, 1983–86.

Cline, Ann. *A Hut of One's Own: Life Outside the Circle of Architecture.* Cambridge: MIT Press, 1997.

Cook, Francis H. *Hua-yen Buddhism: The Jewel Net of Indra.* University Park: Pennsylvania State University Press, 1977.

Daily Tasks in the Zen Woods. Nevada City, CA: Ring of Bone Zendo, n.d.

Davis, Matthew and Michael Farrell Scott. *Opening the Mountain: Circumambulating Mount Tamalpais: A Ritual Walk.* Emeryville, CA: Shoemaker & Hoard, 2006.

Dean, Tim. *Gary Snyder and the American Unconscious: Inhabiting the Ground.* London: Macmillan, 1991.

_____. "T. S. Eliot, Famous Clairvoyante." In *T. S. Eliot: Essays on Gender, Sexuality, Desire.* Ed. Cassandra Laity and Nancy N. Gish, 43–65. Cambridge: Cambridge University Press, 2000.

di Prima, Diane. "Rant" (1985). In *Poems for the Millennium, Vol. II: From Postwar to Millennium.* Ed. Jerome Rothenberg and Pierre Joris, 449–50. Berkeley: University of California Press, 1995.

Dōgen. "Mountains and Waters Sūtra" [*Sansui-kyō*]. In *Moon in a Dewdrop: Writings of Zen Master Dōgen.* Trans. Kazuaki Tanahashi, 97–107. San Francisco: North Point Press, 1985.

_____. "The Sounds of the Valley Streams, the Forms of the Mountains" [*Keisei Sanshoku*]. In *How to Raise an Ox.* Trans. Francis Cook, 97–107. Los Angeles: Zen Center of Los Angeles, 1978.

Duncan, Robert. "The Truth and Life of Myth" (1968). In *Fictive Certainties: Essays,* 1–59. New York: New Directions, 1985.

Eliade, Mircea. *Shamanism: Archaic Techniques of Ecstasy.* Trans. Willard R. Trask. New York: Bollingen, 1964.

Eliot, T. S. "Tradition and the Individual Talent" (1919). In *Selected Prose of T. S. Eliot.* Ed. Frank Kermode, 37–44. New York: Harcourt Brace Jovanovich, 1988.

_____. *The Waste Land* (1922). In *Collected Poems, 1909–1962,* 37–55. New York: Harcourt, Brace & World, 1971.

Emerson, Ralph Waldo. "The Poet." In *Essays and Lectures.* Ed. Joel Porte, 445–68. New York: Library of America, 1983 [1844].

Fenollosa, Ernest. "The Chinese Written Character as a Medium for Poetry." In *Instigations of Ezra Pound, Together with an Essay on the Chinese Written Character by Ernest Fenollosa,* 357–88. New York: Boni and Liveright, 1920 [c. 1902].

Foulk, T. Griffith. "The Form and Function of Kōan Literature: A Historical Overview."

In *The Kōan: Texts and Contexts in Zen Buddhism*. Ed. Steven Heine and Dale S. Wright, 15–45. Oxford: Oxford University Press, 2000.

French, Kathrine and David French. "The Warm Springs Indian Community: Will it Be Destroyed?" *The American Indian* VII/2 (1955): 3–17.

Gadamer, Hans-Georg. *Truth and Method*. 2nd, revised ed. Trans. Joel Weinsheimer and Donald G. Marshall. New York: Crossroad, 1992 [1960].

Ginsberg, Allen. *"Howl" and Other Poems*. San Francisco: City Lights Books, 1956.

_____. *"Kaddish" and Other Poems: 1958-1960*. San Francisco: City Lights Books, 1961.

_____. Stanford University. Papers. Green Library, Department of Special Collections. Collection No. M733.

Gonnerman, Mark. "'On the Path, Off the Trail': Gary Snyder's Education and the Makings of American Zen." PhD Dissertation, Department of Religious Studies, Stanford University, 2004.

Gregory, Peter. "What Happened to the 'Perfect Teaching'? Another Look at Hua-yen Buddhist Hermeneutics." In *Buddhist Hermeneutics*. Ed. Jr. Donald S. Lopez, 207–30. Honolulu: University of Hawaii Press, 1988.

Griffiths, Paul. *Religious Reading: The Place of Reading in the Practice of Religion*. New York: Oxford University Press, 1999.

Gross, Rita. *Buddhism After Patriarchy: A Feminist History, Analysis, and Reconstruction of Buddhism*. Albany: State University of New York Press, 1993.

Grossman, Allen. "My Caedmon: Thinking about Poetic Vocation." In *The Long Schoolroom: Lessons in the Bitter Logic of the Poetic Principle*, 1–17. Ann Arbor: University of Michigan Press, 1997.

Guillory, John. *Cultural Capital: The Problem of Literary Canon Formation*. Chicago: University of Chicago Press, 1993.

Hardin, Garret, "The Tragedy of the Commons." *Science* (December 1968): 1243–48.

Hare, Thomas. *Zeami's Style: The Noh Plays of Zeami Motokiyo*. Stanford: Stanford University Press, 1986.

Hass, Robert, ed. *The Essential Haiku: Versions of Bashō, Buson, & Issa*. Hopewell, NJ: Ecco Press, 1994.

Heffernan, James. *Museum of Words: The Poetics of Ekphrasis from Homer to Ashbery*. Chicago: University of Chicago Press, 1993.

Henigan, Tom. "Shamans, Tribes, and the Sorcerer's Apprentices: Notes on the Discovery of the Primitive in Modern Poetry." *Dalhousie Review* 59: 4 (1980): 605–20.

Hobson, Geary. "The Rise of White Shamanism as a New Version of Cultural Imperialism." In *The Remembered Earth: An Anthology of Contemporary Native American*

Literature. Ed. Geary Hobson, 100–08. Albuquerque: University of New Mexico Press, 1981.

Hori, G. Victor Sōgen. "Kōan and *Kenshō* in the Rinzai Zen Curriculum." In *The Kōan: Texts and Contexts in Zen Buddhism.* Ed. Steven Heine and Dale S. Wright, 280–315. Oxford: Oxford University Press, 2000.

_____. "Teaching and Learning in the Rinzai Zen Monastery." *Journal of Japanese Studies* 20/1 (1994): 5–35.

_____. *Zen Sand: The Book of Capping Phrases for Kōan Practice.* Honolulu: University of Hawai'i Press, 2003.

Howard, Richard. "Gary Snyder." In *Alone with America: Essays on the Art of Poetry in the United States Since 1950*, 485–98. New York: Atheneum, 1969.

Hunt, Anthony. *Genesis, Structure, and Meaning in Gary Snyder's* Mountains and Rivers Without End. Reno: University of Nevada Press, 2004.

_____. "Singing the Dyads: The Chinese Landscape Scroll and Gary Snyder's Mountains and Rivers Without End." *Journal of Modern Literature* XXIII/1 (1999): 7–34.

Hymes, Dell. "A Coyote Who Can Sing." In *Gary Snyder: Dimensions of a Life.* Ed. Jon Halper, 392–402. San Francisco: Sierra Club Books, 1991.

James, William. *The Varieties of Religious Experience: A Study in Human Nature.* Cambridge, MA: Harvard University Press, 1985 [1902].

Kaza, Stephanie and Kenneth Kraft, eds. *Dharma Rain: Sources of Buddhist Environmentalism.* Boston: Shambhala, 2000.

Kerouac, Jack. *The Dharma Bums.* New York: Penguin Books, 1986 [1958].

Koda, Carole. *Homegrown: Thirteen Brothers and Sisters, a Century in America.* Santa Barbara, CA: Companion Press, 1996.

Kojiki [Records of Ancient Matters]. Trans. by Donald L. Philippi. Tokyo: University of Tokyo Press, 1968.

Koyama, Hiroshi, ed. *Nō kansho annai* [A Guide to Nō]. Tokyo: Iwanami Shoten, 1989.

Kraft, Kenneth. "Nuclear Ecology and Engaged Buddhism." In *Buddhism and Ecology: The Interconnection of Dharma and Deeds.* Ed. Mary Evelyn Tucker and Duncan Ryūken Williams, 269–90. Cambridge, MA: Harvard University Press, 1998.

Langer, Susanne K. *Philosophy in a New Key: A Study in the Symbolism of Reason, Rite, and Art.* Cambridge: Harvard University Press, 1957 [1942].

Leclercq, Jean. *The Love of Learning and the Desire for God.* 2nd ed. Trans. Catherine Misrahi. New York: Fordham University Press, 1974.

Lee, David Jinsoo. "American Nō: Gary Snyder's *Mountains and Rivers Without End.*" Honors Thesis, Department of English, University of California, Berkeley, 1997.

Lee, Sherman E. and Wen Fong. *Streams and Mountains Without End: A Northern Sung*

Handscroll and Its Significance in the History of Early Chinese Painting. 2nd, revised ed. Ascona: Artibus Asiae, 1967 [1955].

Lévi-Strauss, Claude. "The Effectiveness of Symbols." In *Structural Anthropology*. Vol. 1. Trans. Claire Jacobson and Brooke Grundfest Schoepf, 185–205. New York: Basic Books, 1963.

Loy, David. "The Religion of the Market." *Journal of the American Academy of Religion* 65/2 (1997): 275–90.

Lukas, Anthony J. *Big Trouble: A Murder in a Small Western Town Sets Off a Struggle for the Soul of America*. New York: Simon & Schuster, 1997.

McClean, Scott. "'Thirty Miles of Dust: There is No Other Life.'" In *Gary Snyder: Dimensions of a Life*. Ed. Jon Halper, 127–38. San Francisco: Sierra Club Books, 1991.

McNeil, Katherine. *Gary Snyder: A Bibliography*. New York: The Phoenix Bookshop, 1983.

Martin, Julia and Gary Snyder. *Nobody Home: Writing, Buddhism, and Living in Places, Gary Snyder in Conversation with Julia Martin*. San Antonio, TX: Trinity University Press, 2014.

Miller, James E. *The American Quest for a Supreme Fiction: Whitman's Legacy in the Personal Epic*. Chicago: University of Chicago Press, 1979.

Milton, John. *Paradise Lost* (1667). Ed. Scott Elledge. Norton Critical Editions. New York: Norton, 1975.

Mohr, Michel. "Emerging from Nonduality: Kōan Practice in the Rinzai Tradition since Hakuin." In *The Kōan: Texts and Contexts in Zen Buddhism*. Ed. Steven Heine and Dale S. Wright, 244–79. Oxford: Oxford University Press, 2000.

Morinaga, Sōkō. *Novice to Master: An Ongoing Lesson in the Extent of My Own Stupidity*. Trans. Belenda Attaway Yamakawa. Boston: Wisdom Publications, 2002.

Murphy, Patrick. "Gary Snyder: An International Perspective." *Studies in the Humanities* 26/1-2 (1999): 1–136.

Nishitani, Keiji. *Religion and Nothingness*. Berkeley: University of California Press, 1982 [1961].

Nogami, Toyoichiro. "Nōkyoku no kosei" [The Structure of Nō]. *Nōgakuzensho* [A Complete Book of Nō]. Vol. III. Ed. Toyoichiro Nogami, 1–40. Tokyo: Sogensha, 1980.

Novak, Barbara. *Nature and Culture: American Landscape and Painting, 1825–1875*. New York: Oxford University Press, 1980.

Obata, Chiura. In *Obata's Yosemite: The Art and Life of Chiura Obata from his Trip to the High Sierra of 1937*. Ed. Janice T. Dreisbach and Susan Landauer. Yosemite National Park, California: Yosemite Association, 1993.

_____. In *Topaz Moon: Chiura Obata's Art of Internment*. Ed. Kimi Kodani Hill, Timothy Anglin Burgard, and Ruth Asawa. Berkeley: Heyday Books, 2000.

O'Connell, Nicholas. "Gary Snyder [Interview]." In *At the Field's End: Interviews with Twenty Pacific Northwest Writers*, 307–22. Seattle: Madrona Publishers, 1987.

O'Grady, John P. "Living Landscape: An Interview with Gary Snyder." *Western American Literature* 33/3 (1998): 275–91.

Ong, Walter. "Writing Is a Technology That Restructures Thought." In *The Linguistics of Literacy*, ed. Pamela Downing, Susan D. Lima, and Michael Noonan, 293–319. Philadelphia: John Benjamins Publishing Company, 1992.

Opher, Adi. "A Place of Knowledge Re-Created: The Library of Michel de Montaigne." *Science in Context* 4/1 (1990): 191–218.

Orr, David W. *Earth in Mind: On Education, Environment, and the Human Prospect*. Washington, DC: Island Press, 1994.

Pallis, Marco. *Peaks and Lamas*. New York: Alfred A. Knopf, 1949 [1939].

Paul, Sherman. "Ethnopoetics: An 'Other' Tradition." *North Dakota Quarterly* 53/2 (1985): 37–44.

Paz, Octavio. *The Other Voice: Essays on Modern Poetry*. Trans. Helen Lane. New York: Harcourt Brace Jovanovich, 1991.

Pine, Red. *The Heart Sutra: The Womb of Buddhas*. Washington, DC: Shoemaker & Hoard, 2004.

Robbins, Jill. *Altered Reading: Levinas and Literature*. Chicago: University of Chicago Press, 1999.

Robertson, David. "The Circumambulation of Mt. Tamalpais." *Western American Literature* XXX/1 (1995): 3–28.

_____. *Real Matter*. Salt Lake City: University of Utah Press, 1997.

Said, Edward. *Orientalism*. New York: Random House, 1978.

Sakaki, Nanao. *How to Live on the Planet Earth: Collected Poems*. Nobleboro, ME: Blackberry Books, 2013.

Sasaki, Ruth Fuller. *Rinzai Zen Study for Foreigners in Japan*. Kyoto: The First Zen Institute of America in Japan, 1960.

Sattelmeyer, Robert. *Thoreau's Reading: A Study in Intellectual History with Bibliographical Catalogue*. Princeton: Princeton University Press, 1988.

Scarry, Elaine. *The Body in Pain: The Making and Unmaking of the World*. New York: Oxford University Press, 1985.

Schloegl, Irmgard. "A Zen Master [Oda Sessō Rōshi]." *Studies in Comparative Religion* 1/4 (1967): 181–83.

Schwenk, Theodor. *Sensitive Chaos: The Creation of Flowing Forms in Water and Air*. New York: Schocken Books, 1976 [1965].

Scott, Joan W. "The Evidence of Experience." In *Questions of Evidence: Proof, Practice, and Persuasion across the Disciplines.* Ed. James Chandler, Arnold I. Davidson, and Harry Harootunian, 363–87. Chicago: University of Chicago Press, 1994.

Shapin, Steven. "'The Mind Is Its Own Place': Science and Solitude in Seventeenth-Century England." *Science in Context* 4/1 (1990): 191–218.

Silko, Leslie Marmon. "An Old-Time Indian Attack Conducted in Two Parts." In *The Remembered Earth: An Anthology of Contemporary Native American Literature.* Ed. Geary Hobson, 212–16. Albuquerque: University of New Mexico Press, 1981.

Smith, Eric Todd. *Reading Gary Snyder's* Mountains and Rivers Without End. Boise, ID: Boise State University, 2000.

Smith, Wilfred Cantwell. "Objectivity and the Humane Sciences: A New Proposal." In *Religious Diversity.* Ed. Willard G. Oxtby, 158–80. New York: Crossroad, 1982 [1975].

Snyder, Gary. "Amazing Grace" (1982). In *A Place in Space: Ethics, Aesthetics, and Watersheds,* 94–98. Washington, DC: Counterpoint, 1995.

———. "Anyone with *Yama-Bushi* Tendencies." *Zen Notes* i/11 (1954): 3.

———. *Earth House Hold: Technical Notes & Queries To Fellow Dharma Revolutionaries.* New York: New Directions, 1969.

———. "Ecology, Literature, and the New World Disorder" (2003). In *Back on the Fire,* 21–35. Emeryville, CA: Shoemaker & Hoard, 2007.

———. "The Education of the Poet." Guggenheim Museum Lecture, New York City, 6 May 1986 [cassette tape recording].

———. "Entering the Fiftieth Millennium" (1996). In *The Gary Snyder Reader: Prose, Poetry and Translations, 1952–1998,* 390–94. Washington, DC: Counterpoint Press, 1999.

———. "Exhortations for Baby Tigers" (1991). In *A Place in Space: Ethics, Aesthetics, and Watersheds,* 205–13. Washington, DC: Counterpoint, 1995.

———. File Card Notes. Kitkitdizze Library, 1949– .

———. "Foreword." In *A Zen Forest: Sayings of the Masters,* Ed. Sōiku Shigematsu, vii–xii. New York: Weatherhill, 1981.

———. "Goddess of Mountains and Rivers" (1980) in *A Place in Space,* 85–90. Washington, DC: Counterpoint Press, 1995.

———. *He Who Hunted Birds in His Father's Village: The Dimensions of a Haida Myth.* Bolinas: Grey Fox Press, 1979 [1951].

———. *Hory a řeky bez konce* [Mountains and Rivers Without End]. Trans. Lubos Snizek. Prague: Mata, 2007.

———. "Is Nature Real?" (1996). In *The Gary Snyder Reader: Prose, Poetry and Translations, 1952–1998,* 387–389. Washington, DC: Counterpoint Press, 1999.

_____. "Japan First Time Around" (1956). In *Earth House Hold*, 31–43. New York: New Directions, 1969.

_____. "Ladakh" (1992). In *The Gary Snyder Reader: Prose, Poetry and Translations, 1952–1998*, 353–59. Washington, DC: Counterpoint Press, 1999.

_____. Letters to Philip Whalen. Reed College Library, Portland, Oregon.

_____. *Luputtomat vuoret ja joet* [Mountains and Rivers Without End]. Trans. Jyrki Ihalainen. Tempere, Finland: Palladium Kirjat, 2010.

_____. *Montagnes et rivières sans fin* [Mountains and Rivers Without End]. Trans. Olivier Delbard. Monaco: Rocher, 2002.

_____. *Mountains and Rivers Without End*. Washington, DC: Counterpoint, 1996.

_____. *Myths & Texts*. New York: New Directions, 1978 [1960].

_____. "The Old Masters and the Old Women" (1981). In *A Place in Space: Ethics, Aesthetics, and Watersheds*, 99–108. Washington, DC: Counterpoint, 1995.

_____. "On the Road with D. T. Suzuki." In *A Zen Life: D. T. Suzuki Remembered*. Ed. Masao Abe, 207–09. New York: Weatherhill, 1986.

_____. *Owari naki sanka* [Mountains and Rivers Without End]. Trans. Katsunori Yamazato and Shigeyoshi Hara. Tokyo: Shichōsha, 2002.

_____. "Poetry and the Primitive: Notes on Poetry as an Ecological Survival Technique." In *Earth House Hold*, 117–30. New York: New Directions, 1969.

_____. "The Politics of Ethnopoetics" (1975). In *The Old Ways*, 15–43. San Francisco: City Lights, 1977 [1975].

_____. *The Practice of the Wild*. San Francisco: North Point Press, 1990.

_____. "Preface." In *Lew Welch: Selected Poems*. Ed. Donald Allen, n.p. Bolinas, CA: Grey Fox Press, 1976.

_____. *The Real Work: Interviews & Talks, 1964–1979*. Ed. Scott McClean. New York: New Directions, 1980.

_____. *Regarding Wave*. New York: New Directions, 1970.

_____. *Riprap and Cold Mountain Poems*. San Francisco: North Point Press, 1990 [1965].

_____. *Six Sections from* Mountains and Rivers Without End. San Francisco: Four Seasons Foundation, 1965.

_____. *Six Sections from* Mountains and Rivers Without End, *Plus One*. San Francisco: Four Seasons Foundation, 1970.

_____. "Suwa-no-se Island and the Banyan Ashram" (1967). In *Earth House Hold: Technical Notes & Queries To Fellow Dharma Revolutionaries*, 135–43. New York: New Directions, 1969.

_____. *Turtle Island*. New York: New Directions, 1974.

_____. Unpublished manuscript journals. Kitkitdizze Library, 1947– .

_____. "A Village Council of All Beings: Community, Place, and the Awakening of Compassion" (1992). In *A Place in Space: Ethics, Aesthetics, and Watersheds*, 74-81. Washington, DC: Counterpoint, 1995.

_____. "Walked Into Existence" (1987). In *A Place in Space: Ethics, Aesthetics, and Watersheds*, 121–25. Washington, DC: Counterpoint, 1995.

_____. "Walking the Great Ridge Omine on the Womb-Diamond Trail" (1993). In *The Gary Snyder Reader*, 371–82. Washington, DC: Counterpoint, 1999.

Snyder, Gary, and Doug Flaherty (interviewer). "Road Apple Interview with Gary Snyder" (1969/70). In *The Real Work: Interviews & Talks, 1964–1979*. Ed. Scott McClean, 15–22. New York: New Directions, 1980.

Snyder, Gary, and Gutetsu Kanetsuki, eds. *The Wooden Fish: Basic Sutras & Gathas of Rinzai Zen*. Kyoto: The First Zen Institute of America in Japan, 1961.

Snyder, Gary, and James McKenzie (interviewer). "Moving the World a Millionth of an Inch: Gary Snyder," In *The Beat Vision: A Primary* Sourcebook. Eds. Arthur and Kit Knight, 1–27. New York: Paragon House, 1987.

Snyder, Gary, with Ludi Hinrichs and Daniel Flanigan. *Gary Snyder:* Mountains and Rivers Without End *in a Musical Collaboration*. Tokyo: Yamakei Publishers, 2003. [Audio CD of 5 July 2002 Performance at Sogetsu Hall, Tokyo.]

Snyder, Gary, and Paul Geneson (interviewer). "The Real Work" (1976). In *The Real Work: Interviews & Talks, 1964–1979*. Ed. Scott McClean, 55–82. New York: New Directions, 1980.

Stevens, Wallace. *The Collected Poems of Wallace Stevens*. New York: Alfred A. Knopf, 1995 [1954].

Stewart, Susan. "Lyric Possession." *Critical Inquiry* 22: 1 (1995): 34–63.

Stirling, Isabel. *Zen Pioneer: The Life & Works of Ruth Fuller Sasaki*. Emeryville, CA: Shoemaker & Hoard, 2006.

Suitor, John. *Poets on the Peaks: Gary Snyder, Philip Whalen & Jack Kerouac in the North Cascades*. Washington, DC: Counterpoint, 2002.

Suzuki, D. T. *Essays in Zen Buddhism: First Series*. New York: Grove Press, 1961 [1949].

_____. "The Gandavyuha, the Bodhisattva-Ideal, and the Buddha." In *Essays in Zen Buddhism (Third Series)*, 75–102. London: Rider and Company, 1953 [1934].

_____. *Manual of Zen Buddhism*. New York: Grove Press, 1960 [1934].

_____. *Training of the Zen Buddhist Monk*. New York: University Books, 1959 [1934].

_____. *Zen and Japanese Culture*. Princeton: Princeton University Press, 1959 [1938].

Tanahashi, Kazuaki, ed. *Moon in a Dewdrop: Writings of Zen Master Dōgen*. San Francisco: North Point Press, 1985.

Taussig, Michael. *Shamanism, Colonialism, and the Wild Man: A Study in Terror and Healing*. Chicago: University of Chicago Press, 1987.

Thompson, Stith. *Motif-Index of Folk-Literature*. 6 vols. Helsinki: Suomalainen Tiedeakatemia Academia Scientiarum Fennica, 1932.

Thoreau, Henry D. *Walden*. Princeton: Princeton University Press, 1971 [1854].

Torgovnick, Marianna. *Gone Primitive: Savage Intellects, Modern Lives*. Chicago: University of Chicago Press, 1990.

Tsurumi, Shunsuke. *Ame-no-uzume-den* [Legends of Ame-no-uzume]. Tokyo: Heibonsha, 1991.

Ueda, Makoto. *Literary and Art Theories of Japan*. Cleveland, Ohio: Western Reserve University, 1967.

Voegelin, Charles. "Training in Anthropological Linguistics." *American Anthropologist* 54 (1952): 322–27.

Watts, Alan. *Beat Zen, Square Zen, and Zen*. San Francisco: City Lights Books, 1959.

Weber, Max. "Science as a Vocation" (1919). In *Max Weber's 'Science as a Vocation.'* Ed. Peter Lassman and Irving Velody, 3–31. London: Unwin Hyman, 1989.

Welch, Lew. *I Remain: The Letters of Lew Welch & The Correspondence of His Friends, Volume I: 1949–1960*. Bolinas, CA: Grey Fox Press, 1980.

Whitehead, Alfred North. *Science and the Modern World*. New York: Macmillan, 1939 [1925].

Whitman, Walt. "Song of Myself" (1855). In *Complete Poetry and Collected Prose*, ed. Justin Kaplan, 27–88. New York: Library of America, 1982.

_____. "Out of the Cradle Endlessly Rocking" (1859). In *Complete Poetry and Collected Prose*, ed. Justin Kaplan, 388–94. New York: Library of America, 1982.

Wigglesworth, Chad, ed. *Distant Neighbors: The Selected Letters of Wendell Berry and Gary Snyder*. Berkeley: Counterpoint Press, 2014.

Wright, Dale. *Philosophical Meditations on Zen Buddhism*. Cambridge: Cambridge University Press, 1998.

Yamazato, Katsunori. "Seeking a Fulcrum: Gary Snyder and Japan (1956–1975)." PhD Dissertation. Department of English, University of California, Davis, 1987.

_____. "Snyder, Sakaki, and the Tribe." In *Gary Snyder: Dimensions of a Life*. Ed. Jon Halper, 93–106. San Francisco: Sierra Club Books, 1991.

Yampolsky, Philip. "Kyoto, Zen, Snyder." In *Gary Snyder: Dimensions of a Life*. Ed. Jon Halper, 60–69. San Francisco: Sierra Club Books, 1991.

Yeats, William Butler. "A General Introduction for My Work." In *Essays and Introductions,* 509–26. New York: Macmillan, 1961 [1937].

_____. *Selected Poems and Two Plays.* Ed. M. L. Rosenthal. New York: Collier Books, 1966.

Zeami, Motokiyo. *Kadensho.* Trans. Chuichi Sakurai, et al. Kyoto: Sumiya-Shinobe Publishing Institute, 1968.

_____. *Nōsakusho* [The Book of Nō Composition]. In *Zeami Jurokubushu Hyoshaku,* Vol. I. Ed. Asaji Nose. Tokyo: Iwanami Shoten, 1940.

_____. "Yamamba." In *Japanese Noh Drama,* 161–78. Vol. II. Tokyo: The Nippon Gakujutsu Shinkokai, 1960.

_____. "Yamamba" [The Mountain Crone]. In *Japanese No Dramas.* Ed. and trans. Royall Tyler, 309–28. New York: Penguin Books, 1992.

CONTRIBUTORS

DAVID ABRAM, cultural ecologist and philosopher, is the author of *Becoming Animal: An Earthly Cosmology* (2010) and *The Spell of the Sensuous: Perception and Language in a More-than-Human World* (1997). His work has helped catalyze the emergence of several new disciplines, including the burgeoning field of ecopsychology. A recipient of the Lannan Literary Award, he held the Arne Naess Chair in Global Justice and the Environment at the University of Oslo in 2014. Director of the Alliance for Wild Ethics (AWE), he lives with his family in the foothills of the southern Rockies.

WENDELL BERRY, a former Stegner Fellow at Stanford University, is the author of over fifty books of poetry, fiction, and essays. His correspondence with Gary Snyder from 1973 to 2013 has been published by Counterpoint Press as *Distant Neighbors* (2014). For over forty years, he has lived and farmed with his wife, Tanya, in Kentucky.

CARL BIELEFELDT is the Evans-Wentz Professor Emeritus of Buddhist Studies at Stanford University. He is the author of *Dōgen's Manuals of Zen Meditation* (1988) and other works on Zen Buddhist history and thought. He serves as co-editor and translator for the Sōtō Zen Text Project, which provides materials for the international study and practice of Sōtō Zen. He is the founder and co-director of the Ho Center for Buddhist Studies at Stanford, formerly the Stanford Center for Buddhist Studies.

TIM DEAN, Professor of English at the State University of New York at Buffalo, earned his bachelor's degree in American Studies at the University of East Anglia and his PhD at The Johns Hopkins University. His undergraduate thesis is published as *Gary Snyder and the American Unconscious* (1991). As a 1997–98 Humanities Center Fellow at Stanford, Dean explored the idea of poetic impersonality in the work of Snyder and other American poets. His books include *Beyond Sexuality* (2000), and, as editor, *A Time for the Humanities: Futurity and the Limits of Autonomy* (2008).

JIM DODGE holds an MFA from the University of Iowa and is Emeritus Professor at Humboldt State University where he directed the Writing Practices Program for fifteen years. He has authored three novels, *Fup* (1983), *Not Fade Away* (1990), and *Stone Junction* (1990), and a collection of poetry and prose, *Rain on the River* (2002).

MARK GONNERMAN completed his PhD in religious studies at Stanford University with a dissertation entitled "'On the Path, Off the Trail': Gary Snyder's Education and the Makings of American Zen" (2004). In 2003, he founded the Aurora Forum at Stanford University, a public conversation series with people who turn vision into action for positive social change. He is currently a professor and director of the William James Center for Consciousness Studies at Sofia University in Palo Alto. He and his wife, Meri Mitsuyoshi, live in San José, California. Visit www.futureprimitives.info.

ROBERT HASS earned his doctorate in English at Stanford University and is a Distinguished Professor of Poetry and Poetics at the University of California, Berkeley. He has published many volumes of poetry and criticism, including *What Light Can Do* (2012), *The Apple Trees at Olema* (2010), and *Time and Materials* (2008). He has co-translated several volumes of poetry with Nobel Laureate Czesław Miłosz and one book of translations of classic poets in the haiku tradition, *The Essential Haiku: Versions of Bashō, Buson, and Issa* (1994). A MacArthur Fellow and a Guggenheim Fellow, he was twice a recipient of the National Book Critics Circle Award, once in poetry and once in criticism. He served as Poet Laureate of the United States from 1995 to 1997.

ANTHONY HUNT earned his PhD at the University of New Mexico and was for thirty years a professor of modern and American literature at the University of Puerto Rico, Mayagüez before retiring in 2002. He is the author of *Genesis, Structure, and Meaning in Gary Snyder's* Mountains and Rivers Without End (2004).

STEPHANIE KAZA is Professor of Environmental Studies at the University of Vermont and Director of the Environmental Program. Her books include *Mindfully Green* (2008); *Hooked! Buddhist Writings on Greed, Desire, and the Urge to Consume* (2005); *Dharma Rain: Sources for Buddhist*

Environmentalism (2000, co-edited with Kenneth Kraft); and *The Attentive Heart: Conversations with Trees* (1993).

JULIA MARTIN teaches English at the University of the Western Cape near Cape Town, South Africa. She is the author, with Gary Snyder, of *Nobody Home: Writing, Buddhism, and Living in Places* (2014).

MICHAEL MCCLURE is a poet, playwright, novelist, and documentary filmmaker. He has lived in the San Francisco Bay Area since 1954 and first read his poetry at the Six Gallery Reading in October 1955. He is the author of numerous collections of poetry, including *Of Indigo and Saffron* (2011), *Mysteriosos and Other Poems* (2010); *Touching the Edge: Dharma Devotions from the Hummingbird Sangha* (1999); and several essay collections, including *Scratching the Beat Surface: Essays on New Vision from Blake to Kerouac* (1994). His honors include a fellowship from the Guggenheim Foundation, a grant from the National Endowment for the Arts, and an Obie Award for Best Play.

NANAO SAKAKI (1923–2008) is famous for his life as a wandering poet-storyteller in the tradition of Saigyō, Bashō, and Ikkyū. Gary Snyder writes that Nanao "is one of the first truly cosmopolitan poets to emerge from Japan, but the sources of his thought and inspiration are older than east or west. . . . His spirit, craft, knowledge of history, make him — whether he likes it or not — an exemplar of the lineage that goes back to the liveliest of Taoists, Chuang-tzu. His poems were not written by hand or head, but with the feet." For more on Nanao's remarkable life and work, see *Nanao or Never* (2000) and *How to Live on the Planet Earth* (2013).

JACK SHOEMAKER has made significant contributions to virtually every facet of the American book publishing industry. With William Turnbull, he founded North Point Press in Berkeley, which published 365 books over its twelve-year life span. When North Point closed in 1991, he moved to Pantheon Books and served as West Coast Editor. In 1994, he left the Bay Area for Washington, DC, where he became editor-in-chief at Counterpoint Press. After founding Shoemaker & Hoard, he returned to Counterpoint in Berkeley in 2007 as Editorial Director and Vice President. He is the 2013 recipient of the Jack D. Rittenhouse Award in recognition of his extraordinary and influential career in American arts and letters.

ERIC SMITH is the author of *Reading Gary Snyder's* Mountains and Rivers Without End (Boise State University, 1999). After completing his PhD in the literature of place at UC Davis, he turned down a tenure-track position in favor of returning to his home region in Portland, Oregon, where he serves as creative director for a communications agency. He spends his free time on family, music, and poetry.

GARY SNYDER is a poet, essayist, and erudite protector of the Wild. He has authored many books of poetry and prose, among them *Danger on Peaks* (2004); *The Gary Snyder Reader* (1999); *Mountains and Rivers Without End* (1996); *No Nature* (1993); *The Practice of the Wild* (1990); *Axe Handles* (1983); and *Turtle Island* (1974), which received the Pulitzer Prize in Poetry. He has been honored with the Wallace Stevens Award from the American Academy of Poets, the Bollingen Prize, the John Jay Award for Nature Writing, a Guggenheim Foundation Fellowship, the Masaoka Shiki International Haiku Grand Prize, and the *Bukkyo Dendo Kyokai* award for his work of furthering worldwide appreciation of Buddhist traditions. He is a professor emeritus of English at the University of California, Davis. He lives at Kitkitdizze, his homestead on the San Juan Ridge in the foothills of the Sierra Nevada.

KAZUAKI TANAHASHI is an accomplished Japanese calligrapher, Zen teacher, author, and translator of Buddhist texts from Japanese and Chinese to English. His translations of Dōgen are available in *Moon in a Dewdrop* (1995); *Enlightenment Unfolds* (2000); *Beyond Thinking* (2004); and *Treasury of the True Dharma Eye: Zen Master Dogen's* Shobo Genzo (2011).

RICHARD VINOGRAD is the Christensen Fund Professor in Asian Art in the Department of Art & Art History at Stanford University, where he has taught since 1989. He is the author, with Robert Thorpe, of *Chinese Art and Culture* (2001).

KATSUNORI YAMAZATO is President and Professor of American Literature at Meio University in Northern Okinawa. He holds a PhD in English from the University of California, Davis where he completed his 1987 dissertation: "Seeking a Fulcrum: Gary Snyder and Japan (1956–1975)." He has written on and translated Snyder's work for Japanese- and English-speaking readers. With Shigeyoshi Hara, he has translated *Mountains and Rivers Without End* into Japanese.

INDEX

168; as performance, 4, 35, 46, 285–90; poems about animals, 180–81; publication history, 149–51; as wisdom book, 204. *See also* instruction, poem as; Nō drama; travel

Mountains & Rivers Workshop (Stanford), 3, 13–18, 33, 46, 75n1, 219, 291; "Ethics & Aesthetics at the Turn of the Fiftieth Millennium" (symposium), 3, 13, 105–6, 261, 275, 278. See also Stanford University

Mountains and Waters Sūtra (*Sansui-kyō*) (Dōgen), 17, 21, 34, 137, 215–18, 220–32, 234, 241, 243, 270–72

Mountain Spirit, 6, 21, 58, 60–61, 95, 119–22, 141, 154, 195, 222, 254, 289

movement. *See* travel

Muir, John, 146, 242, 250

Murphy, Patrick, 23n6

Muse, 33, 49, 263

Museum of Fine Arts, Boston, 291

museums. *See* Cleveland Museum of Art; Field Museum of Natural History; Museum of Fine Arts, Boston.

"Myth, Poetry, Landscape" (Snyder), 119

Myths & Texts (M&T) (Snyder), 16, 71, 148–49, 151, 153, 173, 177, 184, 185, 187–89, 291

Nalanda, 98

Nanao. *See* Sakaki, Nanao

narratives, 157, 216, 304; and ideologies, 157; and myths, 4, 12, 15, 20, 59, 71, 74–75, 86, 117–18, 135, 144–49, 156, 165–66; 181; 187; 195, 197, 198, 200, 216, 230–32, 314n41. *See also* oral (non-writing) cultures

Narrow Road to the Deep North (Bashō), 161–64, 224

Native North Americans: 43, 114, 123; and the American unconscious, 46–47; borrowing from, 34, 55, 66, 69–74, 236; Haida, 12; Hopi, 286; Koyukon, 97, 287; medicine bundles, 204;

mythologies, 173, 178, 286; Navajo, 66, 99; recovery of cultural properties, 78n25; Salish, 189, 286; Warm Springs Indian Reservation, 295; Western Apache, 100–101, 119; Wovoka, 95, 233, 290. *See also* Turtle Island

national parks, 184; Yellowstone, 146; Yosemite, 146

nature, 203, 270–73; and city, 226, 274; and culture, 219–20, 226, 228; definitions of, 219–20; not a virgin, 272. See also ethics; more-than-human world; nonhuman nature; the Wild

net-network, 8, 12. *See also* interdependence

Nevada City, CA, 151

New York City, 251

Nietzsche, Friedrich, 156

nihilist, 158, 239, 247

1980s, 38, 150, 151, 155, 158, 178, 216

1950s, 71, 120, 150, 151, 158, 183, 184, 205–06, 217, 224, 299

1990s, 151, 155, 158, 160, 183, 199

1970s, 38, 70, 72, 150, 151, 158, 216, 261, 270,

1960s, 109, 150, 151, 155, 158, 159, 182, 217, 277

1930s: 275

Nishitani, Keiji, 26n24

Nō drama, 14, 15, 24n10, 34, 76n4, 111–14, 124n2, 174, 269–70, 285; Buddhist elements in, 269; in North America, 112, 119–22; *jo-ha-kyū* structure, 112–14, 122; *kusemai* (song-dance), 112, 119; *michiyuki* (journey going song), 113, 115, 269; and *Mountains and Rivers Without End*, 113–14, 153–54, 269–70; musicality of, 270; *nanori* (self-introduction of character), 113; *shidai* (entrance song), 113, 120; and Yeats, 270.

nonhuman nature, xi, 22, 46, 47, 53, 56–57, 65–67, 73. *See also*, ethics; more-than-human world; the Wild

Sappa Creek (ship), 263

Sattlemeyer, Robert, 292; *Thoreau's Read-ing*, 292

Schwenk, Theodor, 27n25

Schafer, Ed, 33

Science and the Modern World (White-head), 10, 28n26

Seattle 187, 204, 207, 249, 292; art museum, 39; public library, 293, 306n7, 307n8

Sebeok, Thomas, 295

selves, 263; and no-self, 263–64; 266, 279

Sesshu Tōyō, 203, 207

Seton, Earnest Thompson, 293

Shakespeare, William, 125, 267

shamans, 14, 49–75 *passim*, 83, 153, 157, 182, 201, 262; white, 70–72, 236, 267

shape-shifting, 9, 93, 95, 211, 247, 251

Shasta, Mount, 194, 247

Shelley, Percy Bysshe, 287; "The Cloud," 287

Shiva, 286

Shivananda, Swami, 277

Shōbōgenzō (Treasury of the Eye of the True Dharma) (Dōgen), 5, 217, 231

Shoemaker, Jack, 13, 35

Shōkoku-ji, 299

Silko, Leslie Marmon, 71–73, 236

Smith, Eric Todd, 17, 23n6, 291

Smith, Wilfred Cantwell, 10

"Smoke Hole, The" (Snyder), 196

Smokey the Bear. *See* Fudō-myōō

"Smokey the Bear Sutra" (Snyder), 27n30

"Snow Man, The" (Stevens), 158

Snyder, Gary: as American pragmatist, 275–76, 277; and anthropology, 149, 291–92, 295–96; and appreciation of landscapes, 38–39; and authenticity, 236; and book learning, 291–306; and the *Buzoku* (Tribe), 109; and Circum-ambulation of Mt. Tamalpais, 116; as inhabitant, 237; and Dōgen, 17, 34,

216, 270–72; and Ezra Pound, 145–47, 185; at Indiana University, 111, 295–96; and Japan, 93–94, 111–12, 154, 217, 274, 275, 299–300; and John Ashbery, 157; and John Milton, 136–37, 139; *kensho*, 302–3; Kitkitdizze library, 292, 303–6; in Kyoto, 10, 111, 115, 116, 120, 131, 154, 223, 299–300, 300–302; in Leh, 22; and language study, 295; life peri-ods, 151; as mountain lookout, 297; and Mountains & Rivers Workshop, 3–4, 13, 291; and myth studies, 12, 86, 114, 156–58, 182, 191, 236, 270, 296; and Native North Americans, 232–33, 236; as nonjudgmental, 234; Numata Foun-dation award, 274–75; as poet and phi-losopher of place, 1, 97–99, 101, 231–32, 237, 278–80; and posthumanism, 123; as proletariat, 235, 298; Pulitzer Prize, 151; and quest for a new humanity, 114; at Reed College, 12, 111; religio-ecolog-ical convictions, 121, 217; and renewal of oral culture, 103, 298; as scholar, 139–40; Suwa-no-Se Island, 125; and T. S. Eliot, 145–46; at University of Cali-fornia, Berkeley, 111, 299; and vocation as poet, 296–97, 299; youth, 292–93, 306–7nn7–8; as Zen student, 70–71, 206, 258, 277–78, 297, 302–3, 310n27; Zen name (Chōfū), 115, 121, 303

Snyder, Gary: works of: "Anyone with *Yama-Bushi* Tendencies," 297; *A Place in Space* (APIS), 22, 39, 246, 247; "A Village Council of All Beings," 22, 45; *Axe Handles*, 37, 41; "Blue Moun-tains Constantly Walking," 222, 229, 271; *Earth House Hold* (EHH), 112, 120, 131n1, 291, 312n36; "Ecology, Litera-ture, and the New World Disorder," xi; *Eight Songs of Clouds and Water*, 40; "Four Changes" (Snyder), 242; *Gary Snyder Journals* (GSJ), 20, 23n5, 24n11,

NOTE OF APPRECIATION

The Mountains & Rivers Workshop was made possible by the work of many people, a fraction of whom I acknowledge and appreciate here. In addition to funding provided by the Andrew W. Mellon Foundation through the Stanford Humanities Center, our research workshop was supported by the following Stanford University departments and programs: The Center for Buddhist Studies, Center for East Asian Studies, Department of Art, Department of Asian Languages, Department of Comparative Literature, Department of English, Department of Religious Studies, Humanities Special Programs, Institute for International Studies, Office of the Dean of Humanities and Sciences, Office of the Vice Provost for Undergraduate Education, the Stanford Channel, and the Office of the Dean of Continuing Studies.

Of course not all workshop presenters and participants are published in this volume. The following contributors — in addition to those whose work appears here — come readily to mind for their extraordinary interest in this effort: Mark Berkson, Raoul Birnbaum, Ari Borrell, Sandy Costa, Matthew Davis, Susan Dunn, Zoketsu Norman Fischer, John Frankfurt (for leaving a ladder and not locking the door), David Freyberg, Albert Gelpi, Douglas Kerr, Richard Kollmar, Michele Gill, Tom Hare, Linda Hess, Kimi Kodani Hill, Katie Rose Hillegass, Charles Junkerman, T. C. (Jack) Kline III (for guerrilla theater operations), Susan Matisoff, Ray McKee, David Robertson, Theodore Roszak, Ramón Saldívar, Haun Saussy, Yūdō Kenneth Schnell, Susan Sebard, Alexander Stewart (for guerrilla theater action plans), Davis TeSelle, John Wallace, and Carleen Wayne.

Special thanks to Professor Carl Bielefeldt, who fully supported this endeavor from the outset. Carl is an extarodinary person of great learning and compassion for *bombu* such as myself.

Gary Snyder's generosity is legendary, and it has been my great pleasure and good fortune to experience it firsthand. Gary, Carole Koda, Daniel Flanigan, and other members of the community on the San Juan Ridge broadened my awareness in ways that defy any hope of repaying the debts I incurred.

With regard to the production of this book, I am grateful to Judy Gilbert for cheerfully and reliably transcribing workshop talks from cassette tape recordings; to Tim Hogan for reading and readily responding with his perspicacious heart-mind; and to Jack Shoemaker, a master of blunt communication and discerning advice. Thanks also to Counterpoint Press's Irene Barnard, Valerie Brewster, Matthew Hoover, Denise Silva, Kelly Winton, and Charlie Winton, who keeps it all going.

And I am deeply appreciative of the support I and this project have received from Susan Pennypacker, Gregory Kaplan, and Meri Mitsuyoshi. Without them (thanks to Meri, especially), the Mountains & Rivers Workshop and this volume would still be just a very good idea.

.